A COLONIAL WILLIAMSBURG LOVE AFFAIR

....

TALES, TAKES, AND TIPS FROM A LIFETIME OF VISITS

DEBRA BAILEY

Intropak Publications
Durham, NC

Intropak Publications
PO Box 80246, 1 Floretta PL Rm 208, Raleigh NC 27676-9803

Book Layout ©2015 BookDesignTemplates.com

Ordering Information:
Quantity sales. Special discounts are available on quantity purchases by corporations, associations, and others. For details, contact the "Special Sales Department" at the address above.

Library of Congress Control Number: 2017918252

A Colonial Williamsburg Love Affair / Debra Bailey. -- 1st ed.
Print: 978-0-9995722-0-7
eBook: 978-0-9995722-1-4

Publisher's Cataloging-In-Publication Data
(Prepared by The Donohue Group, Inc.)

Names: Bailey, Debra (Debra A.)
Title: A Colonial Williamsburg love affair : tales, takes, and tips from a lifetime of visits / Debra Bailey.
Description: 1st ed. | Durham, NC : Intropak Publications, [2017]
Identifiers: ISBN 9780999572207 (print) | ISBN 9780999572214 (ebook)
Subjects: LCSH: Colonial Williamsburg (Williamsburg, Va.)--Description and travel. | Bailey, Debra (Debra A.)--Travel--Virginia--Williamsburg. | Colonial Williamsburg (Williamsburg, Va.)--Miscellanea.
Classification: LCC F234.W7 B35 2017 (print) | LCC F234.W7 B35 (ebook) | DDC 917.55425204--dc23

This book is dedicated to the many who made it possible:

The wonderful staff at CW,

My parents, who first brought us there,

My sisters, who share my love of it,

My family and friends, who have understood yet another trip there,

Terry Doyle, the best teacher I ever had,
and the reason I dare to write,

I love you all.

Most especially,

to Matt, the Light of our lives, and photographer extraordinaire,

And to Ed—my partner, soulmate, support, and love—

you always insisted that I was precious,
and kept saying it until I believed it.

I love you both and will, forever.

CONTENTS

ACKNOWLEDGEMENTS

This book would never have happened without those dedicated and wonderful people at CW who give so much to make the place what it is. To the memory of John Ross Hamant—aka, Benjamin Franklin, FDR, and that wonderfully alive voice on all the bus recordings, thank you. I appreciated your generosity during our interview, and I send my deepest condolences to your family. RIP. Also to Katrinah Lewis, and the other historical interpreters who dare to give voice and life to those many silent, enslaved individuals, thank you. All of you show true courage every day in how you assume those roles, and bravely stand before strangers to try and change the world. I honor all of you.

To become a physical reality, this book benefited from the help of several professionals. Thanks to Don Weisse, for the compassionate and solid editing advice. That very early, confused draft needed your fresh eyes and structural advice. Also, a large thank you goes to Carl Graves at Extended Imagery whose cover art was perfect the first time out. Finally, to Tracy Atkins and the staff at The Book Makers, who packaged and helped me launch this book! Thank you all.

On a personal note, I am grateful for all of the people and gifts in my life—a richness I never expected and never take for granted. While many of you will remain anonymous, know that I remember each and every one of you and carry you all in my heart.

Some special mentions are important. First, for childhood companions—"the kids," and our "Wiffle ball" group on Donahue

Street (you both know who you are), and the Vaskos, for great times at Cape Cod, your pool, fireworks, and in the garden—my deepest thanks and love. Those memories have sustained me for a lifetime.

To Terry Doyle—passionate, devoted teacher for forty years—.thank you and much love. Your role-modeling fired and sustained me, and still does. From that magical moment in freshman English when you strode to the front of the room and *took command*, you changed my life. Your words in my journal so many years ago—"You are quite a writer with a great imagination"—surprised me, and made all the difference.

Also many thanks and love to the following: Barbara Vosk, you are a true blessing. Your excellent guidance, compassion, and affirmation have been a lifesaver, and a gift. No doubt, you have been that same lifesaving gift to so many others. The same appreciation goes to Rabbis Lucy Dinner, Ari Margolis, and Leah Citrin-Nelson, and all of my friends at Temple Beth Or in Raleigh. You have supported me as I sought the answer to my own "forty years of wandering in the desert," and you welcomed me to the tribe. At long last, I am home.

To my parents—thank you for those childhood vacations. From Cape Cod to Canada, Edison's lab, the rock quarry, and CW, you instilled in me a passion for learning. And to Bernice and Terry, my co-sojourners in life, thank you for your support and sharing your memories for this book. Bernice, I will always cherish that day we explored CW and discovered those cookies! Your life has been a journey of trials and triumphs and I honor and respect all you have accomplished. You are amazing. Terry, while you couldn't join us that day in CW, over the years you have captured the soul of that place, family get-togethers, and all of your travels, with your gifted photography. Your ability to capture sensitive moments is superb, as is your ability to create them—case in point, that last apple-pie-making session with Dad. Pure heart and genius. I love you all and thank you.

A very special thank you to all of the children in our family. You have shared our joy, both of CW and of our family, even as you've had to endure, again and again, your moms and I going on about our stay at the Orlando Jones house many years ago. I appreciate the specialness in each one of you and the gifts you bring to our lives. I love you all deeply.

To Matt, our precious son, the best gift life ever gave us! How did we get so lucky? I thank God that He...or She, chose us to be your parents. You've taught me so much, and I would have been so much the poorer in spirit without you. I love watching your journey and hearing your thoughts. Thank you for your courage and honor; your devotion to your Dad and I; for Sunday morning breakfasts; and especially, for not hating CW! By the way, that day there many years ago with all the cameras—your photos were the better compositions. Know that I will love you forever.

Most especially, to Ed, the love of my life. There are not enough thanks and hugs to cover all you have given me, and all you are to me. With regards to this book, you read it over and over and over... and over, at great personal effort. And you risked telling me when something wasn't right. In life, you have walked with me every day, through every kind of adventure or trial. For you, who restored my soul and taught me to love; for you, who risked hearing my truth and fighting for my heart; for you, who gave more gifts than I can ever list here, you have my heart *totally*, and forever. Every day with you is a treasure, and *you* are precious. As it is inscribed on my wedding band: All my love.

There is one last thank you, and it is to that divine power in the Universe that has continued to bless and guide me. I never expected to have so many gifts, people, and joy in my life. In thanks, I say: *Baruch Atah Adonai, Eloheinu Melech Ha'Olam,*

Sh'hecheyanu, V'Kiyemanu, V'Higianu LaZman HaZeh—Praised are You, the Eternal One, our God, Ruler of the Cosmos, who has kept us alive, sustained us, and enabled us to reach this moment.

Amen.

PROLOGUE

....

Imagine crossing the street and entering 1775. Left behind, as much as you choose, are the stresses and annoyances of the 21st century. Around you are hundreds of historically accurate, restored or reconstructed, furnished buildings, circa the 18th century. The streets are alive with people dressed in the garb of the mid-1700s. Their speech carries more formality, with a "Good Day" replacing the more modern "Hello." Down the mile-long central road in the town, horses *clip-clop* along as they pull fancy carriages. Everywhere you look, something is happening—a blacksmith works a forge then pounds out nails to be used for repairs on a nearby house; a shopkeeper expounds to a patron on the variety of scented candles displayed in a bin; and a wig-clad man rides his horse down the street greeting all he meets and engaging them in conversation about the latest British indignities. In the town's center, an open-air market offers everything from fresh vegetables and seeds, to woven blankets, toys, and a visit by sheep from a nearby pasture. And across the street, hungry visitors crowd around the posted bill of fare to decide what they will eat at one of the four operating taverns in the town.

Is this all a dream? A mirage? Not at all. This is 21st-century Colonial Williamsburg—CW for short—doing what it does best every day—being one of the largest living history museums in the United States! It is a life-sized, ongoing colonial town replicating a particular place and time—the 18th-century capital of the

Virginia colony. As the seat of power during the Revolution, it was host to famous participants like George Washington, Patrick Henry, and Thomas Jefferson. It was home to events that led to the Revolution and eventually, to a new nation. And it was home to a large population of enslaved and free blacks and American Indians who played no small role in the events of the day.

The site is over 300 acres in size with the core of the town— referred to as the "Historic Area"—composed of colonial homes, pastures, gardens, functioning stores, taverns, and trade shops— most of which can be toured by visitors. The main street—Duke of Gloucester Street—runs a mile from the Capitol building at the east end, to the Wren building at the College of William and Mary at the west end. In the middle of the Historic Area is the Magazine—where locals stored their arms and gunpowder—and the elaborate Governor's Palace with its many support buildings. Two other streets run parallel to Duke of Gloucester Street, one on either side of it, and that entire area forms the hub of the restored colonial capital of Virginia.

CW also offers amenities such as several onsite hotels, four tavern restaurants, two art museums, three golf courses, a spa, and historic as well as modern shops and restaurants. To go to CW is to step back to another time, without giving up modern-day conveniences such as air-conditioning and heat, lighting, indoor plumbing, and electricity.

Over the years, friends who were considering a visit to CW would ask me about it, knowing I'd been there and loved it. I'd go on about CW for as long as they'd let me, recounting the 10,000-plus different things I loved and wanted to do again. I am the sort of person who, if you ask me for a book on a topic, I'll bring you ten...or more. As I spoke, I could see them wilt under the weight of the information I was dropping on them. So, to save them from that, I decided to write a book.

Who am I? Well, for starters, I am a fortunate woman. Among the many blessings in my life, I can include having a place to visit that I absolutely love and which has nurtured my soul through good times and bad, for over fifty years now. Even better, both my husband and son fell in love with CW, too. So, there was never of question of not returning. Given all this, I like to think of myself as a Colonial Williamsburg-phile, CW-phile for short.

I originally started writing this book as if composing a long letter to a friend to share travel tips. By the end, though, I had created something much different. Instead of a travelogue, what I created was a story of soul—mine and CW's—as I sought an answer to the question: Why do we fall in love with the places we do?

To find an answer to that question, as well as provide those travel tips, I've set this book up in two parts. Part I is the "Tales and Takes" section. Each chapter starts with a short story or "Tale"—which is a memory or vignette of a particular moment from my various trips over the years. The rest of each chapter in Part I is the "Takes" section. These offer reflections on what those various experiences meant to me. Combined, they can give you a taste of the magic that is a CW visit.

Part II shifts gears and provides those tips my friends were looking for on how to have a good visit there. It is not a compilation of the latest prices and dates, but a collection of subtle things I've picked up from many trips.

So now, I invite you to join me on my quest for answers. Enjoy the trip!

PART I

....

TALES
AND
TAKES

CHAPTER ONE

....

TEN YEARS OLD, $4,
AND FREEDOM

Summer, 1965

It was a golden moment in the life of a ten-year-old—we, my nine-year-old sister and I, were allowed to stay in CW for the day and explore...on our own! No parents in tow! It was our family's first visit to CW and we had done some touring of the historic town the day before. But today my parents wanted to do other things. Specifically, they wanted to visit the Williamsburg Pottery Factory—an acres-sized area with a series of buildings located a few miles from Colonial Williamsburg. There they sell everything from clay planters made locally, to onyx chess sets from Mexico.

In keeping with the atmosphere of rebellion fostered by CW, my sisters and I rebelled against being dragged to the Pottery Factory. The idea of being forced to waste a day looking at endless shelves of knick-knacks, dishes, planters, and God knows what else, was too much to bear. Knowing we could instead be wandering the streets of a colonial town, stepping on the creaky original floorboards of an honest-to-goodness 18th-century house, or standing where the Declaration of Independence was read almost two centuries earlier, we were consumed with despair. We viewed the Pottery Factory as nothing short of hell. We were greatly relieved and eternally grateful therefore, when, for whatever reason, my parents felt we—my younger sister and I—could be left to our own devices in CW. After all, my sister and I had our maps, knew how to get around, and had about four dollars between us. What else could we need? My youngest sister was not so lucky, however. Being four years younger than me, she was forced to accompany them that day...and has never let us forget it. Not wanting to give my parents a chance to reconsider their decision, my other sister and I wasted no time. We ran down the Visitor Center stairs, caught the gray shuttle bus, and headed out.

There were many places we wanted to see—everything, actually—but we decided to start with the Governor's Palace at the first bus stop. As soon as the doors opened, we bolted ahead of everyone else and raced toward the Palace entrance. I never actually gave a thought to there being an actual "palace" in Williamsburg. I just took it for granted that of course the governor there would live in one. In fact, the place looked like royalty lived there. For example, while standing in line to enter the Palace area, I happened to glance up. Atop the elaborate wrought-iron gate that formed the entrance, was a crown. And on either side of the gate were two brick pillars. At the peak of one was a sculpture of a fierce lion wearing a crown and bearing a shield that also had a crown. The top of the other pillar bore a unicorn sculpture with the animal grasping the same crown-topped coat of arms. Given the abundance of crowns on that portal, it's no wonder everyone considered it a palace.

The historical interpreter in colonial garb—a full, ankle-length, blue skirt, with a delicate, white, flowered blouse, and a straw bonnet to shield her from the sun—stood off to the side. She was assembling a group of visitors for a tour of the main building and waved us over. However, we wanted to explore the grounds first, or as one of the visitors said, the "compound." I never knew any place referred to in that manner before but I took his word for it, given the size of the place.

We stopped first at a larger structure that had meeting rooms and offices—where most of the governing work seemed to take place. Uninterested in meeting rooms, we ran into the nearby kitchen. It was fascinating to watch the woman at work there. She wore a simple gray-striped shift, and white apron, with a ruffled white cap on her head. Her movements were measured and slow, and she kept wiping her brow onto her sleeve. Reaching for one of the large metal spoons hanging on the side of the fireplace she ladled freshly cooked peas into a ceramic bowl. The room smelled of sweet, sautéed onions, which were browning in a skillet. The large wooden prep table held some of the other preparations for that day's dinner. These included a steaming bowl of green pole beans, loaves of something she called "Sally Lunn" bread, a platter of slender asparagus tips, and an apple pie, cooling. Small clear cups of candied walnuts and dried apricots surrounded a pine-apple neatly arranged on a delicate crystal serving plate. On the floor was a basket of freshly picked parsnips, carrots, and radishes. A whiff of something slightly fishy wafted past us and I turned to see a man in dark breeches and a gray apron carry in a bushel basket of fresh oysters to be shucked. In spite of the heat I could have stood there all day watching them work. But we had to keep moving.

Nearby there were several other small brick outbuildings crowded together in a brick-paved area. There was a scullery for washing dishes; a laundry; a privy—bathroom—which boggled my mind when I thought about having to run outside all the time for that. It also struck me that they had to have separate buildings for all the jobs we did in our small apartment at home. Next to those places stood other outbuildings such as a wellhouse, a salthouse, and a smokehouse, where the scent-soaked walls gave off hints of bacon and smoked ham. These buildings were all pretty much the same—square, with white-siding, and round-edged, wooden roof shingles. Given the thin tar-like roof shingles we had on our house at home, I was surprised to see wooden ones here. But an even bigger surprise sat in one corner of this area. It was a small, brick, hexagonal building with a wooden door and some holes in the brick walls, apparently to let in either light or air. I heard one of the interpreters call it a "bagnio," which meant "bathhouse." It was apparently considered a real rarity in Virginia at that time. She described it as a place where over-heated high officials could cool off from the summer temperatures while discussing the latest political issues of the day. I thought it was kind of strange that, for starters, a place to take a bath was rare. It also seemed odd that a group of people would sit around in a large bathtub to discuss affairs of state. But I chalked it up to different times.

On the other side of the Palace was a spotless, leather-scented stable. It's dark, wood-paneled walls were adorned with various harnesses, reins, and related gear. Next to it was a large building that housed the governor's carriages. A large, enclosed elaborate box with the seats sat there supported by four large wheels. A man in breeches wearing a rough, cloth apron kneeled by one of the wheels as he examined the spokes. The wheel was almost as high as the man's chest. He called himself a wheelwright and said that his work was to build these wheels. On the walls around him were various sizes of hand saws, as well as chisels, files, and rasps. Standing up from his squatting position, he brushed off his hands and went back to smoothing the wooden spokes that would become a new wheel.

Scattered around the rest of the grounds were more privies—obviously important—as well as brick guardhouses, a potting shed, and a tool shed. My favorite spot, though, was the cellar under the Palace. We descended the steep, narrow, brick stairs and ducked under the doorframe to avoid hitting our heads. The moment we reached the bottom it was like stepping into a secure, snuggly world of our own. First, it was dark, lit only by dim electric candles—authentic-looking with flame-shaped lightbulbs versus actual fire and no doubt safer. It was a soothing reprieve from the bright sunlight we'd been running around in. Comprised of several small, vault-like rooms with arched brick ceilings and walls, these chambers were cool and comfortable, unlike the heat and humidity outside. In this temperate environment, wine bottles and jars labeled as pickled vegetables lined the shelves. Even though it was cool in the basement, I thought it was odd that they would be able to store the vegetables without refrigerators and not have them go bad. In other rooms, casks of ale and barrels of food were kept at the ready for whatever the governor might need. Closing my eyes, I imagined the basement filled to the brim with all kinds of supplies for the governor's parties. I wondered what they actually ate back then and if it was different from what we had now. My sister headed for the stairs so it was time to go. However, between the coolness, the dim light, and the quiet, I hated to leave.

Eventually, we lined up for our turn to tour the Palace itself. When we were finally admitted, we were led into an impressive foyer that characterized the military nature of the Governor's position. It was a large circular area with dark, wood-paneled walls all around us and a white fireplace off to one side. The floor was white and black tiles, a striking change from the usual wood floors of most buildings. But what had everyone craning their necks and turning around this way and that was what was on the walls. All about us were precisely arranged groupings of flintlock pistols, swords, muskets, and rifles hanging on the walls. Everywhere you looked, there were arms on display. The way they were positioned on the walls was as if they were in their own type of military formation. I wondered who had the job of climbing up there to get them down should you need them.

Off to one side of this chamber was a butler's room from which visitors might be offered refreshments. Shelves stretched almost to the ceiling, lined with glass bottles and goblets. A couple of business ledgers sat on the butler's desk.

Moving from the tiled entry room, we stepped onto the regular wood floors that led down the hall to the large staircase. The wood-paneled walls extended down this hall, wrapped around the corner, and continued on up the stairs. The staircase itself was all wood, with hand-carved mahogany railings extending up to the next level. And of course, these walls were adorned with more sabers and muskets. On the second level, we stopped in the governor's study...a kind of private office. I imagined this as a place of action, the center of it all. The table, books, quill pens, ledgers, and inkstands gave quiet witness to the important moments that took place there. I could imagine a cluster of magistrates and burgesses hunched over the desk, arguing the pros and cons of their strategies.

We entered various bedchambers where the guide went on about the type of wallpaper, tapestries, bedding, or the number of layers of clothes a woman had to wear. Most of this part of the tour did not appeal to me, though I did love the floral-patterned drapes that surrounded the beds. It just seemed like a very snuggly idea to be able to pull them shut around you once you were in bed, as if you were in your own protected cave. You could sit up all night reading and no one would know the difference. I also liked that each room had its own fireplace. The other interesting thing was that none of the rooms had closets the way I understood them. They either had closets the size of a room, or they had free-standing cabinets to hold their clothes. I was used to small closets—little recesses set into the wall of a room that

I had to share with my sisters—not something that was another room in itself.

We continued back down the wide staircase and entered the main ballroom. It was a fairly large and open room with huge portraits on either side of the doorway and an elaborate chandelier hanging down from the ceiling. Closing my eyes, I envisioned fancily-dressed guests surrounding banquet tables overflowing with trays of freshly-hunted roast fowls, smoked hams, and samplings of the food stocks from the cellar. And, of course, all were accompanied by a string quartet and harpsichord. The tour guide mentioned that now they sometimes hold candlelit concerts there in the evenings for visitors. Looking at the harpsichord, I thought it sounded kind of interesting to be here at night listening to music. I remember making a mental note to do that someday when I was older. On the side of the room was an ornate, cast-iron metal stove—their only way to heat the place. I hadn't thought about the fact that there were no thermostats, and this room also lacked the fireplaces that were in the rest of the house.

Our tour ended at the back door of the ballroom. At that point, we stepped outside, and into a world of color that awed me. It was the most beautiful garden I had ever seen, and huge! Beautifully trimmed hedges in intricate geometric patterns spread out from the back of the Palace. Blooms of reds, yellows, purples, and oranges surrounded and accented them. Floral scents filled my nose, accompanied by the subtle hum of dozens of honeybees flitting in and out of the flowers.

We walked down the main pathway turning our heads this way and that to take it all in. It seemed endless. It was at that moment we both spotted it—a full-sized maze! I was used to the kinds of mazes that you traversed on a book page using a pencil, but never one you could actually *walk* through. The hedges that lined its paths seemed three-stories high. My sister and I raced up and down the narrow dirt paths, seeking the middle. We didn't know what was there, nor did we care. We just took on the challenge of finding it. Giggles and yells from other kids in the maze told us we were not alone. Turning a corner, we dead-ended into a wall of boxwoods. Backtracking, we zipped up and down, in and out of turns, until finally we emerged into the center of it all—a small enclosed garden patio with wooden benches. A number of adults were there, relaxing, but we had no time for relaxation. We had conquered the challenge! It was time to move on.

We dashed toward the ivy-covered, arched arbors off to the left and just beyond those, we discovered a large still pool...the governor's canal. Benches lined the walkway above the pool and beds of flowers cascaded down the hill to the water's edge. I imagined a warm, dusky evening, where the beautifully attired guests sat sipping their wine after a hearty feast, watching the setting sun's glow spread across the water.

Speaking of the sun's movements, we realized the day was passing, so it was time to move on. From the Palace, we ran down the street and stopped at the George Wythe House. We were unaware of his stature as a learned law professor, or as Thomas Jefferson's tutor. Instead, I remember being amazed that someone would have a small farm right in the middle of town. Wythe had extensive flower and vegetable gardens behind the house, and the usual assortment of buildings for that time, such as a privy, a well, a separate kitchen, and a smokehouse. Apparently, they kept the kitchens separate because they sometimes caught on fire. There was also a lumber house, a poultry house, and a stable. Most impressive to me, though, was something I'd never seen before—a dovecote, which is a house for wild doves. The tall wooden structure with the small entry holes fascinated me. I couldn't believe that people actually made a home for pigeons, as I thought of them, much less that they used their eggs, and sometimes the doves themselves, for their meals. Given that I was used to seeing pigeons on the streets back home eating whatever was in the gutter, I cringed a little considering them as "food."

Needing a bit of a rest, we caught another one of the classic gray CW buses and rode for a while. Finally, ready to resume, we exited at the stop for the Capitol building and the Gaol (the English spelling for "jail"). While the Capitol was important for its place in the government, we headed to the Gaol first.

The world gaol is an interesting word in itself. The CW website describes it as evolving from a word that means "cage." And cage, it is. At the time, I recall that I thought of it as a place full of excitement and mystery, where captured pirates plotted their inevitable escapes to return to yet another exotic sea-faring adventure. Looking back, I realize that, yes, there were pirates, but escape was rarely their end, and many of the people who ended up in those straw-covered rooms suffered terribly from the conditions and treatment. In fact, my impression of the gaol that day quickly changed. The rough wood floors were covered with straw and the room itself was dim. Heavy chain links that secured prisoners to the wall were strewn across the floor. There was little for bedding or blankets, and the toilet was disturbing. It was a large box with wooden stairs and at the top was a seat with a hole. It was right next to a barred, open-air window. There didn't appear to be any way to heat the place in the winter, and the summer—well given how warm we were that day, I couldn't begin to imagine how bad it was to be locked in a room that also contained your outhouse. The tour guide told us that the cells were usually overcrowded and the prisoners often caught something called "Gaol fever." He mentioned that the place wasn't designed for long-term stays. I hoped not. He also added that the prisoners mostly ran the gamut from debtors, runaway slaves, and sometimes a mentally ill person. During the Revolution, there might also be spies, captured military prisoners, or traitors. Frankly, just looking at the heavily -bolted, iron-reinforced doors to the dark cells, I couldn't wait to leave. Glancing out the window, I noticed an equally disturbing view—gallows. Outside, people were laughing and having their pictures taken while standing in the stocks. We decided to pass on that.

Back in the sunshine, we shook off the gloom of the Gaol and headed for the Capitol. Standing in a line that followed the brick wall around the building, we waited to be admitted for the next tour. The two-story building was made entirely of brick. The right and left ends were round structures, with a rectangular "arcade," as the tour guide called it, connecting them. That part had offices upstairs and arched doorways on the main level. I tried to imagine being a Burgess rushing through them to an important meeting that would decide the fate of the colony.

That feeling intensified when we were ushered inside and led to one of the legislative chambers. It was a somewhat empty and austere place, with off-white walls interrupted by deep circular wells that held large windows. A huge dark-wood seat—almost throne-like—sat at the front of the chamber directly in front of one of the windows. Wooden benches with green cushions lined the walls of the chamber. This was the House of Burgesses, where all the elected, upper-class men of the colony gathered to manage the business of governing. All of our group walked around with an appropriate sense of decorum. Even though this building was a reconstruction of the original Capitol—which had burned down twice before—we still spoke in hushed tones trying to show appropriate respect for the sorts of things that happened here. I envisioned the likes of Patrick Henry, George Washington, or Thomas Jefferson debating what to do about King George III's unfair taxes. And the tour guide shared how in one session Patrick Henry likened George III to Caesar, noting that if things like the

Stamp Act continued, George III might meet the same fate as did Caesar at Brutus' hand.

However, a ten-year-old can only handle so much seriousness. After exiting the Capitol, we hopped back onto the bus at the nearby stop and just rode around for a while. I loved the ability to get on and off the bus whenever we felt like it, and the ease with which we could be quickly delivered anywhere in the Historic Area. There was something so grown-up and liberating about it.

Properly invigorated we decided to make the Magazine our next stop. The metal plaque on the building told us this octagonal-shaped brick structure was original, not a reconstruction. Located in the center of the Historic Area, it housed the weapons, powder, and ammunition for the local merchants as well as for the colony's army and navy. You could tour the building, upstairs and down. We climbed a very narrow spiral staircase to the upper room where racks of military supplies—blankets, cartridge cases, muskets, and rifles—adorned the walls. The canteens surprised me—they were to hold water but were made of wood. I wondered if they ever leaked.

A man in a black wide-brimmed hat, long white pants and a green vest sat on a wooden powder keg and explained how the place functioned. He also answered the myriad questions about all of the equipment there. The lower level was the storage area for the wooden barrels that held gunpowder in the 1700s. The parade ground outside of the building was used for drilling by the militia.

We were getting into early afternoon by this point and still had so much ground to cover. There were trade shops to explore and not a moment to waste. A quick strategy session with my sister resulted in the decision to visit the Post Office, the Printer, Anderson's Blacksmith Shop, and a silversmith.

The Post Office was a history-book geek's heaven, with all kinds of 18th-century-looking booklets, pamphlets, and writing supplies for sale. All of the booklets had been printed onsite in the Printer's shop downstairs. I didn't necessarily know what all of the various booklets were about, but I knew enough history to know they were special and important and that was all that mattered. The print shop was located on the ground level of that building, so we raced out the front door and hopped down the shady stairs next to the building to visit it. Excited that there was no line, I gripped the door handle and pushed, but it wouldn't budge. The Printer apparently was not open that afternoon, much to our dismay. I pressed my face against the window in the door and peered inside. Attached to the back wall of white bricks were shelves with stacks of blank paper. Off to the right side a string held freshly printed pages, kind of like a clothesline except for newspaper pages. Right near the door on the left, was a tray with many sections. Each pocket held large numbers of metal strips. We knew they had to do with printing the words onto the paper, but weren't sure how they worked. But the main attraction—the printing press itself—stood right in front of us in the center of the room. It was a strange-looking wooden contraption. One end was tall like a bookcase, with a long metal arm that stuck out away from it. The middle was like a flat desk with a metal plate on it, and the left was a large open frame attached to the flat desk by a hinge. It looked like it went up and down onto the metal plate.

Disappointed that we couldn't get in, we headed off for the next stop, the silversmith. I vividly recall staring longingly at pewter mugs on the shelf. I so wanted one. We heard that people could buy historic-looking ones at the Craft House, but I knew there was no hope of getting one. That was an expensive store, I didn't have the money, and I knew my parents wouldn't buy it. So, I just stood there and admired them. To me they represented everything colonial. I could just imagine sitting by the fireplace in a candlelit tavern, eating my meal with pistol-grip tableware, and drinking my ginger-ale out of a real pewter mug.

Even though we weren't into shooting firearms, we stopped at the gunsmith's shop. It was fascinating to watch his process, which combined the talents of a woodworker, engraver, and metal worker. He showed us blocks of wood that were eventually shaped, then polished, to create shiny and sometimes ornate stocks for the rifles and muskets. We learned that the more-wealthy clients often asked for images or their initials to be engraved on decorative strips of metal attached to the stock. To craft the intricate parts for the gun's mechanisms as well as the barrel, he used a small metalworking shop in the back room. He explained how the barrel was made from a flat piece of metal that was heated in a forge and molded around a rod. They then welded the seam shut and filed the barrel into an octagonal shape, again, by hand. Pointing to a back workroom, he described his pride and joy—a hand-run machine to bore and rifle the barrels. He shared how he recently used all that equipment to make an entirely hand-made rifle! I looked at the equipment and wondered how you could do that, all without electricity!

His mention of heating the metal in a forge reminded us that we hadn't yet found the Blacksmith Shop. Though we were starting to tire, my sister and I headed out to look for it, and along the way, we encountered something called an apothecary. Stepping into the room, I was struck by what a quiet, orderly place it was. I was immediately entranced with the array of jars on the counter filled with dried plants. These, we learned, were the 1700s equivalent of medicines. Even more alluring to me were the cabinets behind the counter. They contained row upon row of neatly arranged drawers with small labels on them. Each held exotic things like foxglove, cinchona, and gum arabic. I didn't know what any of those things were, but I just *loved* the labeled cabinets. I so wished I could have a set of them in my room at home. I am not even sure what I would have put in them, but I just loved how they looked. There was something about the calm of the place, and the aura of "secret medical knowledge" that appealed to me. Maybe that was nature's way of suggesting my future career in the medical field. At the time though, I just wanted those cabinets. The back room was less to my liking when I saw the metal tools and blades used for bloodletting. I could handle the jar of leeches. But those blades, coupled with the sets of pliers to yank teeth, were enough to propel us out the door.

Now, in spite of how much fun we were having and how energetic we were at the start, our energy was almost gone. Even though we had ridden the shuttle bus numerous times, we had just as often run up and down the mile-long Duke of Gloucester Street in our quest to see everything. My feet hurt. My sister complained about being hungry. Frankly, my own stomach had started growling too. It was clear we were going to need food.

I looked around but there weren't any snack stands to buy a cookie or root beer. But we weren't concerned. We remembered there were a couple of taverns open. Deciding to postpone our hunt for the Blacksmith Shop, we climbed on the bus and rode until we came to the stop near Chowning's Tavern. Running up to the menu board outside the building, we scanned the offerings. The idea of savoring a plate of food like the colonials would have had, seemed like just the thing for our tired bodies. We salivated over descriptions of thick ham slices over chunks of fresh bread accompanied by a slab of cheddar cheese. Our stomachs growled. Then we looked at the price. Nothing on the menu matched our wallets. Suddenly the economic reality of our four dollars started to come clear. We moved on. I felt a little panicky. What if all of the places were more expensive than we could afford?

Trudging up Duke of Gloucester Street, the King's Arms Tavern sign came into view on the right side of the street, it's bright sign declaring that it had the finest food. We were both pretty tired by this point and as we approached the outside menu board, I wasn't hopeful. I had a hunch my sister wasn't either, given her silence. In looking over the menu we realized, probably just like many a poor early-1700s traveler before us, that this was a place we couldn't afford. It was more expensive than Chowning's Tavern. Neither of us said a word, but inside I was feeling tired and angry. It would still be a while before we met up with our parents...and their wallets. What were we going to do? Then we spotted a sign of hope.

Across the street, people emerged from an alleyway on the side of the Raleigh Tavern with little brown paper bags in their hands. Some of them were pulling out what looked like pastries and cookies. So, we crossed over to investigate. The tavern itself was not one that served food—it offered tours, concerts, and other programs. But obviously, there was a source of food somewhere nearby given the number of people with little bags of goodies. Pastries...maybe four dollars could get us a pastry to split?

We turned the corner and discovered a small, white building with black shutters tucked behind the main tavern. The Raleigh Tavern Bakeshop! Inside the brick-floored building with working colonial ovens in the back that smelled of burning wood, was a feast fit for a king: Sally Lunn bread, Queen's cake, apple turnovers, and gingerbread cookies—a soft, crumbly creation about the size of a slice of cake. Best of all, we could afford *any* of them.

We didn't waste our money on ginger ale, since there was a water fountain down the street. We just bought all the gingerbread cookies we could afford and then headed outside. Sitting in the shade of a tree, we ripped open the crinkly bag and tore into the warm mounds of flour-coated delight. Waves of sharp, sweet, ginger-spiced sensations spread across my tongue. Neither of us said a word. We just kept eating until they were gone.

Needless to say, we survived our "near starvation experience" and the cookies sustained us long enough for our parents to arrive and get us a big dinner. We never did get to find the Blacksmith Shop but that was okay. Finding that bakeshop was the best moment in the entire day!

I don't know if it was the hunger, the adventure, the exhaustion, or the cookies themselves, but those cookies are seared into my memory forever. No matter how many times I visit CW now, I never fail to stop at the Raleigh Bake Shop. Maybe the cookies taste the same as then, maybe nothing will ever match the sensory delight of that day. But it doesn't matter. I bite into a gingerbread cookie and my tongue still remembers that spicy moment from so many years ago and a day of freedom, excitement, and adventure. Simply said, the gingerbread cookies aren't just cookies. They are that day, that sense of exhilaration, and that whole first trip to CW, all held in a little brown bag.

Of course, some things have changed over the past fifty years. For one, there are more trades and more places to tour. And now there are programs to participate in and more interpreters than ever to engage with. I will share more about those changes in later chapters.

Also, frankly, I am still surprised my parents let my sister and me explore there alone. I can't imagine that happening in today's world. But back then it didn't seem so strange. And even though at that point CW seemed endless, much bigger than it appears to me today, it was that day spent free to explore that huge world that gave to us both the sense that we could tackle impossible tasks and succeed. For sure it gave birth to my lifelong love affair with CW.

Whatever the reason, I am simply grateful that my parents released us from a bland, lackluster day, and instead gifted us with an adventure in independence. As an adult, I will allow that the Pottery Factory is actually a cool and unusual place. But for me it will *never* match the heart of CW. That adventure spawned more in me than they will ever know.

As an aside, needless to say I was correct that my parents wouldn't buy a mug. Frankly, I understand—it was too expensive. They offered to try and find a similar one at the Pottery Factory. But I so wanted to go into the Craft House and get one of the authentic, historically-accurate pewter mug reproductions. It's funny but I mentioned this to my sister, who after all these years, confessed to feeling the same thing. As adults, we have since indulged that desire and I have a few "real, authentic, CW-sold" pewter pieces sitting on my shelf at home—symbols of a day that set the course for a lifetime. In an equally interesting twist though, the adult me eventually also learned to appreciate the Pottery Factory, including those onyx chess sets. When my father died, I decided to keep the one he and my Mother had purchased that day so long ago. In its own way it, too, captured the memory of that special day and what it triggered.

CHAPTER TWO

....

A TASTE FOR TAVERNS

Summer, 1968

Even though we had evening dinner reservations, it was still somewhat light outside. The crowds of the day hadn't eased much. Given that it was the height of tourist season, many were staying late in the Historic Area. Outside of the various taverns, clusters of people waited their turn to enter and enjoy a sumptuous feast, colonial-style. Ahead of us on the right side of Duke of Gloucester Street was our target—the King's Arms Tavern. A white post with an ornate sign bearing the unicorn and lion coat of arms—symbols of the British empire—stood near the roadway. At the top of the panel was painted "King's Arms" and at the bottom were the words "Good Eating." A smaller board below that one declared this was the King's Arms Tavern and had the words, "The Best Foods," painted in cursive lettering.

The tavern was a long building—two buildings actually—comprised of the main building and the Alexander Purdie House on the left. The Purdie wing was painted a light brown, while the main tavern had a white exterior, dark shutters, and a covered porch centered on its front face. Each side of the porch had a set of stone steps leading up to the front door, giving the building a symmetrical appearance. People lined up on either side of the porch, eagerly anticipating the moment when the hostess would consult her clipboard, call their name, and beckon them to follow her inside. I alternated between staring at the door, and pacing on the brick sidewalk, as if either would make the time go faster. After what seemed an eternity, the door opened and a woman in a light tan gown stepped out. She *slowly* perused the clipboard, looked our way, looked at the clipboard, then wrote something on her clipboard. I held my breath until I thought I would burst. As if in slow motion, she looked up, opened her mouth, and *finally* called *our* name.

I ran up the stairs two-at-a-time and was the first one inside. The entry hall had well-worn, wide, wood-plank flooring. To the right was a curved staircase ascending to the second floor. Stained wood edging ran along the right-side wall. The left side of the staircase was edged with a polished dark wood bannister supported by blue-painted balusters, and a curved metal handrail. Whitewashed walls extended upward and out of sight. Above us hung a brass-rimmed, glass-paneled chandelier that gave off the proper glow of candlelight even as the flames were electric bulbs. In front of us were a number of parchment sheets pinned to the wall. The tour guide said they included things like a license, a menu, and a price list. Though there were many people in the building already, the noise level was a low hum. The aura of refinement the place gave off seemed to inspire an awed hush in all even as waiters and waitresses swept between the tables to deliver dinners and clean off plates. This was, after all, the tavern where only the best came to eat. So, I guess everyone behaved in a manner befitting such an establishment.

Our hostess stood off to the side, quietly speaking to another who wore a long apron over her dress. They huddled over the seating plan and I could see from the number of tables drawn on it, that the interior was much larger than I thought it would be.

Finally, she turned to us, gathered up the menus and asked us to follow her.

We were led down a long hallway, walking on aged wooden floorboards that creaked beneath our feet. As we passed different dining rooms I could see that the decor in each varied. Some rooms had rugs while others were bare wood floors. Patterned wallpaper contrasted nicely with tan chair rails and baseboards in one room. In another, a dark-wood-framed mirror hung on the wall between two windows. The wavy old glass in the windows gave everything outside a distorted, "wobbly" kind of look. Black-and-white prints of colonial maps adorned the other walls.

The place felt endless, like a world all its own. Awareness of anything outside quickly drifted away, replaced instead with a dream-like reality that seemed to take us further back in time the deeper into the building we went.

The hostess finally turned into a room with dark, wood-paneled walls. In one corner a server stood behind a bar pouring out drafts of ale or glasses of wine. We were seated near a large fireplace that had wood paneling all around it and a large black-and-white 1700s map of the New England colonies on the wall above the hearth. Given the summer season, the fireplace was not lit, but I could dream. Pewter plates stood on the mantel leaning back against the wall.

She seated each of us one at a time, enacting her well-practiced routine of placing our menus on the table in front of us and properly settling us in. The chairs too, had an elegance—nothing wobbly or unfinished about them. They had finely curved, open, dark wood backs. Our table did not have the rough-hewn plank surface one might find in a more modest establishment. Instead, the polished, smooth, reddish wood surface almost gleamed in the subdued light. In the middle of the table a tall, tan, tapered beeswax candle stood in a brass holder enclosed in a hurricane glass to protect the flame from drafts as the staff rushed by. Its candlelight cast a soft bronze glow on the walls, creating a warm pleasant feeling in the room, and the colonial pistol-grip tableware seemed authentically "old" to me. A pewter salt cellar, sugar bowl, and pepper shaker stood at one end of the table, and colonial-patterned cups and plates completed the table setting. Surrounded by such an abundance of pewter, I felt a visceral joy. It was as if I had lived before in colonial times, and now in this moment was somehow re-experiencing that earlier life with a fond recognition.

I picked up my menu to check out the selections and noticed the words, "where all the best people resorted." That's just what this felt like. The menu was actually an old-style printed parchment card with the words *The Evening's Bill of Fare* across the top. *Fare.* The word itself was lovely to hear. How elegant I felt, as if we were some wealthy family of a local plantation owner being treated to a meal fit for the governor himself.

The dinner descriptions, while foreign to my McDonald's-based palate, were out of this world. Perusing the offerings, I came first to peanut soup. I never knew peanuts were good for anything other than Fluffer-Nutter sandwiches. Who knew you could make soup out of peanuts? Given that it was a locally-grown crop and it was on the menu . . . excuse me, the Bill of Fare, it must have been true. I had to have it.

A colonial game pie was in the list of entrees. Colonial game. That had such a historic sound to it. The description read: Tender venison, rabbit, and duck braised in a fine port wine sauce with mushrooms, aromatic vegetables, and bacon lardons put forth under a flaky pastry crust. I'd never had any of these things before, and had no idea what a bacon lardon was. But slipping into my daydream of the colonial past, visions of breech-clad men astride horses hunting my dinner in the forest outside of town, played in my head. Who ate like this? Certainly, not anyone in my life. So yes, colonial game pie was also a "must have."

Coming by to take our order, the waitress in her gown and white cap smiled when I pronounced my choices. She gathered up the menus and left us to await our feast. Music that was true to the time period wafted through the rooms, growing louder as the strolling musicians approached. One man played a mandolin, the other a violin. I couldn't take my eyes off of them as we were serenaded. Did I know if they played strains of Vivaldi, Corelli, or Telemann? No, at least not by name. But I *knew* in my soul the music was from that time, and again I had that gut feeling of familiarity with my surroundings. If nothing else proved we had stepped back in time, *this* moment did.

I spent my time while waiting to eat, soaking in the sensual delight of the place oblivious to anything being said around me. For me, there was only the subdued light from flickering candles, the low hum of voices, and the abundance of aromas from all the various dishes people indulged in around us. After what seemed an eternity, my peanut soup arrived. It was brown and thick, the consistency of liquid peanut butter. I was a little apprehensive as I lifted the spoon to my mouth. But as the buttery-flavored mixture coated my tongue and throat in warmth I just smiled. It not only looked like liquid peanut butter, it also tasted that way too ... except better. The soup came with something called "sippets," or little toast points. They were handy for soaking up every last drop of soup.

While I was immersed in this task, my dinner arrived. Holding the white china plate with a towel, the waitress set it down before me. A lightly-browned crust topped the entire pie, garnished with generous dollops of red currant jelly. The waitress warned me not to touch any of the plates. As is always the case, I immediately did that anyway, just to see how hot it was. I was not disappointed.

Colonial Game Pie, garnished with jam and
accompanied by root vegetables.

Piercing the top, I pulled open the flaky crust with my three-pronged fork. Steam poured out. I peered into the bowl and was met with a wave of wine-soaked spicy smells. Small onions and chunks of mushrooms bubbled in the thick, dark-brown gravy.

The bacon strips—lardons—were mixed in with the various meats. I couldn't identify which was rabbit, or duck, or venison, but it didn't matter. All the meats melted in my mouth, softened to perfection by the sauce. The blend of spices and herbs provided tantalizing sensations of flavor. The lardons had a smoky flavor, which blended in nicely with the thick sauce that reminded me of Boston baked beans. I didn't know what they used, but it was "dinner heaven." The pie disappeared without a struggle.

If I was disappointed that the game pie was gone, that emotion was softened by the fact that we still had dessert to go. Exotic names were sprinkled across the bill of fare. Syllabub. What was a syllabub? And for that matter, how did one even pronounce it? The description itself was finely crafted artistry: Wine-laced cream whipped to froth seasoned with lemon zest and garnished with seasonal berries. Whatever "froth" and "lemon zest" were, I wanted them. And the seasonal berries, too. Maybe seasonal berries were no different than anything we might have bought at the A&P back home. But when you put it on a Bill of Fare in fancy calligraphy in a colonial tavern lit by candles and accompanied by chamber music, it simply had to be different. I would have the syllabub, too.

It arrived, looking almost too good to eat. Almost. It was beautiful—dollops of heavy cream whipped to perfection, folded into a parfait glass on a plate, and adorned with mixed berries and a sprig of mint. There is something about a dish—it could be a peanut-butter sandwich—that when artfully presented and delivered on fine pattered china just seems to make it a divine experience. To say it was delicious, is an understatement. Sugar-laced waves of lemon with a hint of sherry spread over my palate, each flavor subtly vying for my attention in its turn. It would have disappeared instantaneously except that I wanted to draw out the sensual joy of every single mouthful.

But eventually, even the syllabub was gone, and the dinner drew to a close. The dream woven in the tavern that night was complete. It was more than I could have hoped for, and nothing like I could have imagined on that day two years earlier, when exploring CW with my sister. All I can say, is that it was worth waiting for, and returning to...which I have, many times. But the memory of that very first dinner will always burn brightest in my memory.

Now, aside from that glorious first experience and the subsequent enjoyable dinners at the various CW taverns, I sense something deeper operating here for me. These places hold *such* a draw for me. In fact, I am currently writing a historical fiction set during the Revolution and I set a major scene in a Williamsburg tavern. What is that all about?

Certainly, part of it is me. There's memories of past trips and a fondness for all the times spent there with family. Also, being a person who spends a lot of time in my imagination, I can think of no better place to let my mind roam free to dream. Even deeper, there is an emotional connection. These are places that provided sustenance, shelter, and safety to weary travelers. The hearty food they served was designed to fill you up and fuel you for whatever lay ahead. Perhaps on this point, it connects to my own Eastern European background. My grandparents came from "the Old Country," as they referred to Slovakia, and I grew up eating the barley soup my grandmother made. They survived the Great Depression and to them the best welcome they could give any visitor was a hot meal. Then there's shelter and safety. Just as I appreciate a good hotel room after a long journey, any traveler in the 18th century who'd slept on the hard ground in the cold, might have felt relieved to be inside a warm tavern, out of the elements. Certainly, the actual comfort experienced by overnight guests in 18th-century taverns, even in the best ones, was a far cry from our modern hotels. In fact, the word "comfort" was probably a relative term. Certainly, if you were wealthy and could pay for your own room in a place like the King's Arms Tavern, your stay would be quite nice. However, for anyone else, you not only didn't get your own room, or your own bed, you were lucky to even share a bed with one or two other men. On especially busy nights, you might have only gotten a corner of a room on the floor! But still, you weren't on the side of the road in the rain.

Also, the taverns abound with the sensory details I revel in. Table settings give the appearance and textural sense of the time. The decor further enhances the experience. Then, there are the menus—those beautiful "Bills of Fare"—and the foods listed on them that just totally cement the illusion. Printed on parchment-colored card-stock with colonial-style printed and cursive text, the menus are a work of art. Add to their appearance, the food descriptions, which are artful, suggestive, and historic. Sprinkled with words such as savouries, pasties, fowl, and rasher, just reading them takes you back in time.

Speaking of back in time, another thread that hooks me is all the history in them. History of the Revolution. History of the people caught up in something much bigger than themselves. History of the taverns themselves. History of the food they serve. Historically, taverns were places of action and intrigue, the nexus for important moments during the Revolution. Everyone from traveling merchants to spies, simple farmers to statesmen and soldiers crossed paths there. While the idea that the Revolution's origins were often conceived in a dark tavern corner seems at best, irreverent, and at worst, impossible, yet, these are the places that hold the DNA of our American past. They bore and gave nurturance to those early hopes for all willing to strive for that precious dream of freedom. So, perhaps these places as ground-zero for conflict and rebellion, is part of the allure that colonial taverns have for me.

As to the history of the taverns, I love to go into each one at CW and read the story of that particular place, which is printed on the menu. Each tavern had a different evolution and cast of characters. The history of the taverns is like a history of Williamsburg itself, in miniature. The food is a source of information about the colonial past. Even though the dishes are prepared in modern kitchens with current-day ingredients, all of the recipes originated in the 18th century. They are simply adapted for today's foods, methods, and tastes. Also, the menus at each tavern give a glimpse into the social structure of 1700s Williamsburg. The lofty ingredients (and prices) of the King's Arms spoke to the high social status of its patrons. In contrast, the hearty portions and more common foods served at Chowning's convey a working man's environment— inexpensive food and lots of it.

Lastly, there is story. As a writer, I can just *feel* the echoes of dramatic events. This has been a great help as I work on my own story, a mid-grade historical fiction entitled *The Reluctant Hero*. Set in Williamsburg during the Revolution, it is the story of a young man caught between his drive to protect his family against the upheaval of the times, and his desire for his Patriot father's approval. Caleb just can't fathom why his father would be willing to throw away their family's security for an ideal. Caleb is not an idealist, he just wants a roof over their head, food on the table, and everyone safe. Yet events beyond his control will eventually force him to make his choices on the big questions of the time, as evidenced in the following scene:

The Raleigh Tavern, Summer, 1775

The hour was late. Raucous, wine-soaked patrons filled the tavern, sweaty faces alternately yellow then bronze in the flickering candlelight. The smell of spilled ale mixed with that of burnt wood and unwashed bodies. Clouds of pipe smoke ringed the clusters of arguing men.

Standing in the doorway, Caleb scanned the room. His left hand clenched and unclenched. The fisted right hand hid the carefully folded parchment. Peering deep through the smoke, he spotted his quarry. In the back corner, two men sat hunched over a small table, heads so close they nearly touched. He could see lips moving but heard nothing. It was a wise move, he thought, using the noise and shadows to shield their conversation. Their probable treason was well hidden in plain sight.

Caleb bounced lightly on his toes, legs tensed like a reined-in horse ready to bolt. He glanced at his right hand. The parchment. This was the line in the sand he had vowed never to cross. He was not his father. His father and brother had been adventurous fools. What did it get them, or their family?

He turned away, then stopped. Drawing in a deep breath, he glanced again toward the men in the corner. His mouth felt like cotton. He could barely swallow. Closing his eyes for a moment, he struggled to ignore the voice in his head reminding him that once set in motion, this deed could not be undone. There would be no return from this moment. Opening his eyes, he turned back and headed across the room.

Suddenly, the two men in back stood up. Had something alerted them? Did interested ears draw too close for comfort? One of the men glanced at a pocket watch. The other took a last swallow of brandy. Both disappeared into the blackness of the back hallway. Across the room, a man moved to follow them, his cloak drawn closely about his face.

Caleb's heart pounded. Something seemed amiss. He should take his leave now, while there was still time to pull back from this foolishness. His breaths came fast and shallow. Perspiration spread across his forehead. He couldn't make up his mind, but his feet kept moving toward the hall, as if possessed by their own will.

Inching forward through the darkness, he strained to hear any sounds, but the hall was silent. His fingers slid along the wood paneling as he rounded a corner. Suddenly Caleb gasped and nearly fell backwards. The dark-caped shape stood right before him. Standing this close, Caleb couldn't miss the glint of steel in the man's right hand. He turned to run, but two dark shapes had slipped behind him, blocking his path. They were the two men from the back table.

One man chuckled. The other, the man with the pocket watch, spoke. "So, young master, have you made your choice?"

From *The Reluctant Hero*, by D. A. Bailey

Now, should you visit any of CWs taverns, I can't promise you the suspense and intrigue that Caleb experienced. But in Part II of this book, I *will* give a review of the kinds of things to enjoy at each of the various taverns. Bon appetit!

CHAPTER THREE

....

FOR THE LOVE OF DETAILS

Summer, 1968

It was a soft, bleating sound followed by the tinkle of a bell. Though barely audible, it was just enough to wake all three of us.

Curious, my sisters and I climbed up and peeked out the window over my bed. There on the street below, a young boy was guiding an entire herd of sheep east, toward the Capitol. With the sun just a reddish glint on the horizon, the sheep had a pink glow in the diffuse light. He called quietly to them as he urged them forward. A few strayed onto the sidewalk but he deftly flanked them—as if anticipating that move—and continued to nudge them up the street. It was like watching a bunch of fluffy ping-pong balls bobbing in a current of water.

Part of me wanted run downstairs right then and run my fingers through their soft, wooly coats. The other part of me was glued to the window, mesmerized by the sight, and afraid to break the magic of the moment. Pulling my blanket closer, I flattened my face against the window, and strained to watch them stumble up Duke of Gloucester Street and out of sight. Dropping back down onto my bed, I tried to sleep, but it was no use. After all that excitement, I was just ready to start the day.

We were staying in one of the historic houses in CW right on Duke of Gloucester Street, one that had belonged to a man named Orlando Jones. As to who Orlando Jones was, I didn't know or care. All I knew was that we were in *one of the old colonial houses* in the Historic Area, and we had just watched a real shepherd guide his sheep up the street! Yes, he worked for CW, but for a brief moment, it just felt like the 1700s.

Our whole visit was such an exotic experience. First, we had to park our car behind the house, in what felt like a secret parking lot. To get there, we had to drive around the outskirts of the Historic Area, because cars were not allowed to drive in the center. So right off the bat just approaching the house had a feeling of mystery to it. Then we had to walk through the back-garden area to get to the house. Imagine, a *back garden*...and not just some vegetable garden, but a flower-filled *pleasure* garden. Definitely a touch of luxury. My sisters and I shared a room upstairs, just down the hall from the bathroom. We didn't have a TV in our room but that was okay, because we were busy having an adventure. Besides, for those couple of days it felt like we had stepped back in time, so a TV would have felt out of place.

It is now over fifty years later and I still feel joy at that memory. Someday I may grow old and forget who I am, but I suspect I will always remember the Orlando Jones House. Every time we go to CW, I bore my husband and son with the same, "*Look!* There's the place I stayed in when I was a kid!" During extended family reunions, usually held in CW, my husband and son also have to listen to my sisters and mother go on about that as well. The rest of the family just rolls their eyes. They're all used to it by now, and put up with it. But for my sisters, my mother, and I, that one visit was a permanently magical experience—a few days out of a lifetime—that still burns in our hearts. What is that intensity all about? While I can't speak for anyone else, I know what it is for me. Details.

I am a detail freak. It's simply who I am. To encounter a situation where there is an abundance of details, is for me, an endorphin-laced ecstasy. And when I create something, I am just as detailed in how I do it. One of my hobbies is oil painting—landscapes, seascapes, undersea scenes—and my painting style, for better or worse, is very detailed. If I include a fish, I hunt down image after image of it, observing the raw umber line along its back, the soft Naples yellow spots on its fins, or how in a particular light, the back is a mottled blend of raw and burnt siennas. In the end, I want you to know it is not just a fish, but a southern flounder. I want to deliver a precise image of nature, not just an implied one.

Also, I love to learn. Details are tremendous teachers. Anytime I spot anything unusual—an odd adornment on a wall, a subtle detail in a backyard—it immediately triggers a question, which leads to an answer, which triggers more questions. And on and on and on. For me I can never get enough of details. They are an all-you-can-absorb buffet of information.

Another thing that fosters my love for things others miss, is that I am shy. At social functions, for example, I am delighted to remain in the background. Why endure small talk when there are carved door-frame moldings to examine, or art on the walls to inspect? As an introvert, I revel in befriending an overlooked wall pattern or noting the sensations and smells of a room. In case this strikes an extrovert as "sad," know that I live for these moments. Our world is often too loud and too fast, so any excuse to slow down and observe the overlooked is for me, like having an extra dessert at dinner.

Lastly, even if I weren't naturally predisposed to loving details, I'd appreciate them anyway. It is a remnant of my past—an occupational hazard of decades in the medical field. In jobs where there is no acceptable margin of error, you learn to pay attention to the small things because they can mean the difference between life and death. So, after a while, it becomes second nature.

But however my love of them came about, I am also not satisfied with just any old, half-baked details. Just as my work in the medical field had to be precise, details that attract me must be done well. Otherwise it feels like betrayal. Or a cop-out. I want honest-to-goodness truth-in-execution, a solid effort, not just some half-hearted attempt.

In a well-executed detail, I can feel the love someone put into their creation. And I respond to that love. Because I can feel truth and integrity behind that object, I trust the work. That trust creates great appreciation for the effort, and by extension, for the people there and the place itself. In today's world, effort like that is often missing because people just don't have the time. And details are an added expense to produce. So to encounter that level of quality is refreshing, comforting, and deeply emotional.

Emotions. Yes, I respond with great emotion to these touches, just as another person might be emotional over an artistic masterpiece in a museum. Why do we respond so intensely to moments like that? Enter the brain. Those particular experiences are stored through an interaction of two brain structures, the amygdala, and the hippocampus. I happened on a 2004 research article in the journal, *Current Opinion in Neurobiology*, which summed it up best. When those two brain systems get together "...the memories for emotional events have a persistence and vividness that other memories seem to lack." So, when I encounter some carefully crafted item I feel a level of excitement and joy that really sticks with me. And there are a lot of those moments in CW.

For example, before they make any historic reproductions—whether pottery, dishes, wall hangings, paint, or fabrics—everything is researched to document and match the original processes and materials used as much as is possible. Consider the clay bricks they use in their buildings. They are made and fired onsite using the techniques from 200 years ago. Then there's the nails pounded out in their own onsite forge. Even the "wooden roof shingles"—which are now made of more durable material for sustainability reasons—are still made to the best level of authenticity they can create. The goal has been to meet the highest quality answer to "how *exactly* was this done or what did it look like in the 1700s?"

Also, if they found that they did something wrong, they actually fixed it. A good example of this is the Peyton Randolph house on Nicholson Street across the green from the Courthouse. For so many years it matched the common perception of colonial houses—whiteboard exteriors, black shutters. Somewhere along the line, however, they discovered, by analyzing paint layers on the house, that for the period they were representing, the Peyton Randolph house should have been *red*. They had it wrong. So, they made it right. How often does someone repaint an *entire house*, just to get the details right?

Even in small touches, that caring is evident. What do you say about someone who takes the time to put up a sign—and not just some flimsy temporary thing, mind you, but a durable and attractive one—to not only ask you to respect the carpenter bees, but to tell you a little something about what they are doing? I mean, look at this sign. It isn't cheaply made and it's not just tacked up on a wall. It has a solid post and its design matches the decor of its surroundings. Someone cared enough about the bees to protect them. Someone cared enough about the visitors to educate them. And someone cared enough about the sign itself to make it its own durable work of art.

This effort extends even to something as low-key as infrastructure repairs. When they were recently redoing some of the brick walkways in the Historic Area, they generated a beautiful and informative sign so visitors would understand what was happening and why.

CARPENTER BEES
at WORK

*Females of this solitary-nesting species are non-aggressive
and serve as valuable pollinators. Males hover near nests
and do not have a stinger. Thank you for giving them
space during their active season.*

*This handsomely executed sign about the carpenter bees
is an example of the quality work done by the CW staff.*

So maybe one of the reasons I love going to CW is that my
"detail-freak" nature gets to revel in an amazing array of experiences, all of which honor traditions of love, truth, and care. It
feeds my soul. CW is a place whose staff cares as much about
what they do and create, as the people I used to work with in the
hospital cared about their patients.

In some of the coming chapters, this theme of details will show
up again and again. Things like—How do they do something?
How do they know something is fact? What did CW look like in
the 1700s? Who were the people that filled that landscape? Most
of all, who are some of the people there now who demonstrate
such care, integrity, and love for the truth in all they do, and
why do they do it? I suspect that the some of the answers to my

questions: "Why visit CW?" and "Why do I keep going back?" will be found in those stories.

Speaking of details, earlier I asked the question—who *was* Orlando Jones? I now have an answer. Orlando, the owner of that house, was the son of the very first rector of Bruton Parish Church, Rowland Jones. Orlando apparently was wealthy as he also owned land in York and King William counties. In addition, he served in the House of Burgesses many times. But maybe he is most famous by association. He just happened to be the grandfather of Martha Custis, a woman who would go on to marry an up-and-coming military and political leader by the name of George Washington!

If you're interested, a Google search of "Orlando Jones House" will yield a few images of the interior and exterior. Enjoy!

CHAPTER FOUR

....

THE RIDE OF ROYALTY

Spring, 2016

Sitting on the bench outside of the Lumber House across from the Palace Green, we savored gentle breezes in the shade of a large old oak. We were there to take my eighty-five-year-old mother for a carriage ride, something she hadn't done in years. I heard a distant *clop-clop-clop* on a nearby street and soon spotted the carriage approaching. The horses pulling it just ambled along... except when they reached the corner of Duke of Gloucester and Palace Streets. That seemed to be the horses' one moment of "rebellion" as they picked up the pace to a trot for several seconds. I wondered if that was them letting off a little steam for having to move so slowly and steadily over most of their route, or if the driver directed them to speed up to make the ride around the corner a little smoother?

I watched as the carriage pulled up to the hitching post and the driver helped the riders down. He was a quiet sort of man, which pleased me because I was not in a mood to chat. I simply wanted to experience the ride. He stopped to inquire if we were his next group, then headed into the Lumber House for a moment. The horses pawed at the ground and pushed against the other. They seemed to act like a couple of six-year-old boys who were told to stand still and instead they tried to annoy each other. When the horses stopped fidgeting, I slowly went over, looked one in the eye, and greeted him. He eyed me, unmoving, with a look that seemed a mix of "I hope she's not going to bug me" and "Humph, another tourist!"

Very patient horses indulging "yet another tourist!"

The driver returned and introduced us to our horse team—Duke and Dan. We then set about helping my mother up into the carriage. She is pretty spry but my heart pounded a bit when I saw the horizontal steps collapse as she stepped on them. It was like watching someone try to climb the sheer face of a cliff while it turned to sand under their feet. I had visions of broken hips, but she just climbed right up.

It was an open carriage. On the plus side, that meant 360-degree visibility and being open to the elements—light, temperature, sounds, and smells. It would be a total sensory experience, something we lose touch with in our modern world driving in our enclosed cars. The downside to being in an open carriage was the same thing—being open to the elements. I had worried about the cool weather and possible rain, so I had brought an umbrella. I had even regretted not asking for an enclosed carriage. But the almost blinding sun dispelled those worries. If anything, I regretted not having a ball cap to shade my eyes. As for the cold breeze that the cut through my flannel shirt, well, Mom was wrapped in my down vest so she was fine. Besides, she was too engaged in looking all around to even notice the wind.

We settled back on the leather-cushioned seats as the driver climbed up and took the reins. Sand ground loudly under the metal-rimmed wheels as the horses began to back the carriage away from the hitching post. They seemed to know exactly what to do almost without the driver telling them. Doing this so often, the horses probably even knew the precise number of steps to take backwards.

As the team pulled away, the carriage lurched forward and turned east up Duke of Gloucester Street. The leather harnesses on the horses creaked in time with the suspension of the carriage. It wasn't the kind of creak that made you worry something was loose or going to fall apart, but more the kind of sound you'd expect from a heavy, solidly-built vehicle beginning to pick up the pace. To say that we sped up is a relative expression. That brings up thoughts of cars accelerating on a highway entrance ramp. In terms of our carriage-ride, it meant we were moving ahead more than we were standing still. Carriage rides are a "majestic" process; a journey in slowing down to savor a variety of sensations, moment-by-moment. They aren't rushed, and that's how it should be.

The *clop-clop-clopping* of their metal horseshoes against asphalt pavement was the dominant sound now as we moved up the street. Surprisingly, the ride was incredibly smooth, jerking a bit more only as we entered a turn. At that point, the methodical *clop-clop-clop* on the straightaway transitioned to more of a *clip-clop, clip-clop* then became a staccato rhythm of beats: *de-da, de-da, de-da,* kind of like the Morse code bursts my father would send out on his ham radio set. A second later the beat seemed to develop an arrhythmia, becoming a series of rapid *clip-clip-clips*. Just as quickly, the horses slowed down and returned to those steady *clop-clop-clops* as we finished the turn and resumed ambling up the road.

The open breezes carried the smells of the day. Being spring it was the aroma of fresh cut grass, punctuated by fresh manure, a more pleasant mix than it might sound. In the summer, it is the smell of blossomed gardens and ripe harvests and during the fall, the smells of sweet rot joins the mix as things settle into the earth before winter. But through it all, no matter the season, is the manure.

We sat there enjoying my mother's reaction almost more than the ride itself. She turned back and forth in her seat as she tried to take in all the views. She couldn't seem to get enough of all the scenery. As we approached the Orlando Jones house I pointed it out to her but did not need to remind her of our stay there many years ago. Her eyes were glued to the house with a distant look, as if she was suddenly back fifty years remembering another time, and no doubt my dad, who had died a few years ago.

Continuing on, I wished the ride would never end. It was a piece of heaven that day. Between the weather, the sensations, smells, sounds, and my mother's happiness, it could have gone on forever as far as I was concerned.

The shifting of the *clop-clop-clops*, to the more staccato beats and arrhythmic lurches of the carriage told me we were close to another turn and the return to our starting point. The horses, knowing their work, slowed down, and step-by-step moved into place at the post, then halted. Another group of tourists was waiting for their turn.

Getting down was a little more daunting than climbing up and I was deeply aware of my mother's fragile bones. But again, she just went with the flow, slid down the steps, and touched the ground still upright, no worse for the wear. I actually regretted at that point not having signed us up for a longer tour, but she said this was just perfect. She tires easily, so it might have been too much of a good thing to ride any longer. So instead, we slowly made our way down the street, heading for an early lunch at the DoG Street Pub. We stopped at a number of benches along the way to rest. Mom was tired and spoke little as she rested, but her smile said it all.

We have taken carriage rides numerous times over the years. They were always a big hit when our son was young. And now my husband and I will occasionally do one ourselves just to relax, soak in the colonial atmosphere, and enjoy yet another visit to CW. It is a main activity for families and first-time visitors, and no matter the weather—extreme heat or bad storms being the exceptions—it is one of the most common sights to see people riding around town in one of CW's horse-drawn carriages. Some of the vehicles seat just four adults, others hold several. Some are open-air, others are enclosed. And it is not just the average visitor who has enjoyed these jaunts. This activity is a favorite of "royalty" of all kinds, ranging from presidents to actual royalty. Queen Elizabeth II of England has actually visited CW twice during her reign and rode in a special carriage reserved for such visitors, both times. Heads of state from all over the world have also enjoyed this opportunity as well as celebrities, including John Wayne, PBS' Mr. Rogers, and even Lassie.

Speaking of royalty, one thing to remember when you enjoy a carriage ride is that you are having an experience the average Williamsburg resident of the past did not have. These carriages were used by the elite landowners, the aristocrats of that society. The local populace could never have afforded such a vehicle. So, it really was a ride of royalty.

In an effort to be more aware of my experience this time, I tried to pay more attention to things the driver shared. Also, I had done a bit of reading on the "Making History Now" blog http://makinghistorynow.com/. They had a number of good articles about the drivers, the horses, and their care. For example, regarding the horses, each one is an individual with their own unique personality. They all have names that are even on a plaque in their stalls back at the stable. There's Chief, Toby, Gunner, Lancer, Isabella, Captain, Duke, Dan, and Ranger, just to name a few of the current group. And the names change over time as new horses arrive and others move on to a gentle retirement.

The driver can tell you about the particular horses leading your carriage because driver and horses are a close team on their daily rounds. The drivers are keenly attuned to their charges. They pay close attention to their behavior and needs, and know which horses are best to team together. The drivers also pick up on the subtle nuances most of us miss, looking for signs that indicate if a particular horse is not feeling well, needs a rest, a drink of water, or is overheated. For example, one driver explained that even though that April morning was cool for me, the horses were just fine. "They really like the winter time," he said. I noticed some of the horses were shaved close to the skin in areas where the harness was against their body. The driver explained that some of the horses prefer that because otherwise the harness will rub against their coat and irritate their skin. It also allows them to cool down better in the warmer temperatures, when the harness could be too warm for them. If the carriage driver feels it's important to the horse, the driver will even change plans and take the steed back to the stable to see to its needs. They also see to it the horses get their farrier and veterinarian visits to keep them in good shape. As to the horses' temperaments, our driver noted that though the horses know the rules and maintain a slow and steady pace, given the choice, they would enjoy trotting and running a bit.

In addition to being aware of the condition of the horses, the driver also pays close attention to the carriage itself. Ours was built in 1810 in London, and was restored at CW in 1928. Maintenance is a priority, and in 2016, several of the carriages had just returned from a trip to a shop in Poland. There they had been torn down, rebuilt, given new springs, upholstery, metalwork and in some cases, even new bodies. Given the heavy use these carriages get, there are constantly things to replace, such as worn out metal wheel rims, carriage steps, wheel bearings, and such. CW has different types of carriages. Enclosed ones are for use especially in the later fall and colder weather. Open ones see a lot of use in the spring and summer. Some are used strictly for visits by royalty while others are for daily use. They even have special ones for weddings.

As distinctive as all of the horses and carriages are, the drivers themselves are very special, too. They are a wonderful mix of tour guide, host, and multi-tasker, juggling many roles as they guide their four-legged charges through the town. In fact, in the 1940s, carriage drivers and coachmen were the first character interpreters CW had, not to mention that many were African American and thus broke ground as the first African American interpreters as well.

They come prepared and well trained. First, they have to know all the little details of CW to answer questions. They must enjoy working with the public and need to handle anything from routine tours to visits from celebrities. Some of the drivers are quiet and say little unless asked, preferring not to intrude on the riders' experiences. But they are happy to answer any questions. One in particular who was featured in an article on CW's blog, a man named Adam, is full of life and eager to share all he's learned. Adam is one of those staff members who has been "part of the family" at CW. He started working there as a child, and even earlier than that he was always running all over the grounds. His mother worked there and so have some of his siblings and cousins. He looks happy directing his charges as he calls out to interpreters along his route and animatedly shares stories with his carriage guests.

There's a lot of training involved to be a carriage driver—safety, handing emergencies, and of course, "driver's ed." They are evaluated and have a course of study to get through. Most have had some experience with horses, though rarely do any have driving experience. As they go through their training, they start with small vehicles. As their skills improve, they move to larger and larger carriages. It can take about two years for drivers to be well trained, and even after that, most of them will tell you they are constantly being taught every day by the horses they work with.

Once the training is completed they must pass an exam and a road test. Aside from knowing how to assess the health of their horses as well as the status of their carriages, drivers have to be well skilled in managing the vehicle, the horses, and the combination of the two.

I recently learned that CW is now also offering oxen-drawn cart rides, the more usual mode of transportation for the average person back then. That one is on my wish list to check out, and if it is workable, I may have to bring Mom back for that one.

It's funny what goes through your mind as you move slowly around the Historic Area in the carriage. Of course, I'd like to say there were deep epiphanies and lofty thoughts, and perhaps there were one or two. But the overwhelming question running through my mind during the last ride was, "Who cleans up after the horses, and when?" Yes, ever the practical mind. I had noticed that just the evening before, that the horses had left many "gifts" on the roads. But this morning there was barely a trace of them, like someone swept the street clean. Did people actually come in here at night and sweep the streets?

Doing a little digging I discovered the answer: It's the early morning "poopmobile" that cleans the streets as well as nearby pastures. It is a golf cart with a bright blue machine on its back powered by a red Honda motor. A large hose is attached to it for "vacuuming." It is an Australian-made Maxi Vac manufactured by a company called Greystone and it makes a tough job a lot easier. One staff member drives the cart while the other hops out and essentially vacuums-up the poop. And this vac can handle wet or dry. They make the rounds of the streets leaving the roads clean to start the day and safer to stroll on. They also vacuum a number of the pastures, which has the benefit of improving animal health. By removing the manure there, it reduces the flies and the parasites that are normally drawn to it, thus reducing the diseases they might cause.

The gathered manure—with each load holding about five-six wheelbarrows full—is dumped in a central area where it is then composted. It is a great mulch for the gardens around CW because it has a high grass and hay content. Not only does the garden staff make use of the precious mulch, but gardeners in the greater Williamsburg area seek it out as well. As the staff note, there is plenty to go around and there's always more on the way! So now having my question about the disappearing street piles answered, I can sleep at night. Time for another ride soon to contemplate some equally deep question.

CHAPTER FIVE

....

REVQUEST: PURE GENIUS

Summer, 2014

The music was like something out of a Jason Bourne movie. The man in the red jacket hustled down the narrow hallway. Surreal shadows splayed on the dark wall as he moved past the single wall sconce. His voice was low but urgent as he turned to you. "The cause for America is in the greatest danger, and your help is needed to secure our freedoms!"

In spite of your fear you listened, uncertain of what you were getting into. He halted in a darkened room at the end of the passage. The only light was from the fireplace. As your eyes adjusted, you suddenly recognized Benjamin Franklin seated at the table. He got right to the point. "I have a most urgent mission for you to undertake." Your immediate thought was regret at getting involved, but you continued to listen.

"We have come to *such* a condition that we no longer have a choice." Your heart pounded and you wondered what was coming. Franklin leaned forward, peered deep into your eyes, and suddenly almost bellowed in defiance: "We *must* declare independence from Great Britain!"

With that dramatic delivery, the video ended and the TV went black. My husband and I stood up and smiled. It was time to begin the mission. We were staying at the Williamsburg Lodge for a week, celebrating our 25th wedding anniversary, and we were eager to participate their newest "RevQuest-Save the Revolution" program. The new one was called "The Old Enemy." You started by viewing the video at the Lodge, then armed with that information, you collected your materials from the front desk and began. I couldn't wait to get started.

Every year from 2011 through 2015, from April through the fall, CW offered a new RevQuest adventure for their guests to take part in. In RevQuest, guests were tasked with a particular problem to solve so as to protect and preserve the Revolution. You had to acquire information, decode messages, and figure out a number of puzzles to achieve this.

Today, we were to be secret agents for the Committee for Secret Correspondence, tasked by Benjamin Franklin himself to secure a much-needed secret ally from France. That person was crucial to the Colonies' success. In order to deliver on this, we needed our "packet of secret orders." So, we headed for the hotel's admissions desk.

Since we already had our annual admissions passes, the woman there told us we just needed our orders envelope. Opening a drawer, she pulled out a six-by-nine-inch tan envelope with the word "secret" stamped across the front in large, red, block letters. She also handed us each a purple "RevQuest" scarf. That was the signal to anyone we were to rendezvous with, that we were part of this secret group. Without that, they would not respond to us.

Everything we needed to complete our mission would be located in the CW Historic Area. However, we needed to be discreet, follow the instructions, and of course, use our "special messaging devices"—our cell phones.

My husband and I stepped outside into a shady spot and huddled over the orders booklet that was in the envelope. We were

*Scarf and supplies provided to visitors participating
in CW's RevQuest Game.*

to use our messaging device to text a code and alert our contact that we were ready to meet. The contact, an agent from London, directed us to a spot behind the Robert Carter house and gave us his alias to use as a code.

Arriving there we noticed a man with a purple ribbon on his jacket. We made eye contact. He gave a quick nod then continued strolling, so we headed behind the house. A small group of other "agents" was also gathered there in back of a shed. Shortly after our arrival, the gentleman joined us. He pretended surprise at seeing us all, and began to chat about the weather. As he talked, he was checking to see that we all had the scarves. Then he turned the conversation to more pointed things—like did we know his alias. Once assured we were all legitimate, he lowered his voice and directed us to gather close. Warning us that we could not be too careful, he provided us instructions on how to use the ciphers to determine the locations of other clues. Impressing upon us the importance of this mission, he wished us safe travels and departed as quickly as he had arrived.

We spent the next few hours hunting for people, messages, and new instructions. One of the nice things about the RevQuest adventures was that they took place during the day, which meant we could pace ourselves, stop for an iced tea while we solved a riddle, and then continue. Slinking down a narrow alley between two houses on Duke of Gloucester Street, we found a small note pinned to the wall. Following our texted instructions, we located and decoded other hidden messages using the Mrs. Johnston and Pigpen ciphers we had been provided. We were slipped a note by a woman sitting outside the Post Office, then met up with the French envoy to confirm his help. Finally, we used a map to determine the best route for the Committee's leader to travel to France for a meeting. Turning this information over to the leader's representative we received a token of achievement and a hearty thank you for helping the cause.

The following year's RevQuest had an even better, and particularly poignant ending. All of the participants were to meet at a stage located behind the Palace gardens. My husband and I were there early, relaxing after our "hard" work. A sudden wind gust whipped through the trees. Looking up I noticed the blue sky had gone gray, and in the distance, threatening, black, anvil-shaped clouds barreled toward us. My husband saw them too and remarked that perhaps we should seek shelter. I hesitated, stubbornly wanting to complete our RevQuest game. Even now in my sixth decade, I can still be that ten-year-old who doesn't want to miss a moment at CW, even when threatened by a downpour. However, unlike that ten-year-old, I *don't* like sitting around in soggy clothes. Sighing, we got up and went back toward the front of the Palace.

We managed to get close to the stable in the corner of the Palace grounds when the sky basically opened. Soaked, we ran into the stable, shaking our arms to shed some of the rain. We weren't alone for very long. Fifteen to twenty other tourists as well as a man dressed in colonial farmer's garb came running in behind us. Each arrived in varying degrees of "drenched." One of the boys, seemingly oblivious to the fact that his soaked clothes stuck to him and his hair was plastered against his forehead, summed up what I was feeling: "But now we won't get to finish RevQuest!" All of us stared quietly at the almost solid sheet of rain outside the building's door. Even most of the adults registered disappointment on their faces.

At that moment, the man in colonial dress stepped forward and greeted us. He was the person who was to host the final installment of our RevQuest adventure at the back of the gardens. Glancing outside he noted that while we were rained out for getting together in the gardens, the stable was as good a place as any to hold our final meeting. No one disagreed and in fact, it was such a bonded feeling there—the camaraderie of all of us gathered there sheltered from the storm while playing our game to the end—that maybe this was the better way to end.

After we finished our adventure, I looked around the stable. All of the various groups and families huddled together over their game-quest booklets, comparing notes on how they each had solved the quest. They discussed codes they struggled with or hidden messages they had almost missed. By the time the rain stopped and the sun came out, all of us parted, a little more, friends, and a little less, strangers.

To me, the RevQuest programs were pure genius on CW's part. It is unfortunate that they discontinued them after 2015. We had gone back to CW every one of those years (except the first one as we didn't know about it), just to play the new version.

From a visitor's perspective, it was a creative way to turn what could have been the passive experience of walking by a bunch of old houses, into an active and engaging quest that had life-and-death consequences built into the story line. For parents, it was a way to teach that whole "critical-thinking" skill to their children. The educator in me *loved* that you had to *think* to do this. You didn't have to be a genius, but you did have to analyze, use logic, and solve a puzzle. You had to measure things, use maps, factor in angles, and decode things. By its very nature, you *had* to bring your brain to the problem. And as an aside, it was also a very clever way to turn people's obsession with their cellphones into a way to get them obsessed with CW. Using cell phones brilliantly engaged any child or teen who hated "dumb old history" to have a great time. They were learning history and didn't even realize it.

Even as I knew it wasn't real, I still found the child in me eagerly anticipating each new Secret Orders packet whenever we arrived. Frankly, it didn't matter how old you were. In fact, that was part of the genius of the series—it hooked everyone, whether you were six or sixty. Even better, it *bonded* everyone. Where else could you get an experience that actually *united* generations into a solid team? Imagine, teens and parents not only talking to each other but working together!

And that sense of bonding was not just within a family or group playing the game. It extended to strangers. On one RevQuest experience, I had totally missed one of the stops. Wandering around the

Blacksmith Shop's yard, I started to understand that others had a sheet of paper I was missing, and it was crucial to the next step. I reached out to a nearby family who helped get me back on track. In return, I helped them figure out the puzzle they were trying to solve involving a pencil, some string, a map, and a codebook. We ended up meeting a few more times on our quest and then again at the end. We all had a great time wrapping up our adventure, and several of us got to know each other a bit, sharing where we were from. I even invited one group from California to visit my museum in Raleigh, should they ever be back this way.

To me, there was nothing more satisfying—and hopeful in our current world—than to look around and see groups of strangers huddled together struggling, *together*, to solve the problem at hand. That, to me, was the *real* achievement CW fostered. How often do strangers ever *willingly* interact with each other like that? It takes a truly unique approach to create that kind of friendly bond. For a brief moment in time, everyone was on that quest seeking a goal that was bigger than any of us. And even though we all knew it was a game, we all still bought into it. Someone once said that the success of a good fantasy story was the reader's willing suspension of disbelief to embrace the story's reality and purpose. That is exactly what I saw on the streets of CW, with RevQuest.

Why was it so bonding? Its format is called an alternative reality game (ARG). Wikipedia describes an ARG as an interactive narrative that "uses the real world as a platform and uses transmedia storytelling [digital media] to deliver a story that may be altered by players' ideas or actions." Jane McGonigal, an author, TED-Talk speaker, and guru of video-game and alternate relative game development, wrote a book called *Reality is Broken: Why Games Make Us Better and How They Can Change the World*. In it she speaks of the positive effects of gaming. She notes that good game stories give clear goals and a sense of heroic purpose. Furthermore, the effect continues past the game, as participants are more likely to set ambitious real-life goals, believe they are up to any challenge, and become more resilient in the face of failure. Her games utilize a positive psychology approach to create real and positive impacts on emotions, relationships, engagement, and being of service to something bigger than ourselves.

Also, it was just plain fun. Call me silly, but I *loved* the *tangible* things that came with it—the RevQuest scarf and the sealed envelope of Secret Orders! I especially loved the little RevQuest pencils. During one year's quest, they didn't include a pencil in my envelope. I went all over CW to various locations hunting down one of those pencils. To me it wasn't complete without one. At the William Pitt Store, the woman behind the counter just gave me a strange look when I expressed total excitement that she had *three* pencils that had been left behind. I took them all!

Finally, the time slot helped, too. Usually these sort of mystery, or action-based games were reserved for the evening audiences and required a special admission fee. RevQuest was offered during the day and came with your admission ticket. For those who could not stay for the special evening events, it provided that same opportunity for something special.

Having heard all about the program, you may wonder why it was discontinued. A recent post on CW's Facebook page indicated that the Foundation leadership evaluated the numbers of participants and made the strategic decision to "refocus resources on new and engaging experiences for families." I can understand that resources—financial and staff-related—drove the decision. CW noted that participation for RevQuest peaked in 2013 and by 2015 dropped down to 4%. I am not sure how they determined that, because based on comments I've seen on their blog, it appears there are a number of visitors who were disappointed that RevQuest was no longer offered. However, if the numbers are true, they were spending a lot of money for materials, logistics, and the cell phone support system for fewer people playing. Further, the way the game was set up, it required a fair number of the character interpreters to be constantly available at several locations throughout the day. That can be an unsustainable drain on your personnel.

Could it be done differently today? Possibly. For one thing, I noticed that the Air & Space Museum which runs their own ARG program, TechQuest, has it sponsored by McDonald's. That is a thing that's growing in the museum world these days—corporate sponsorship. Perhaps CW could consider getting a corporate sponsor to defray the costs of running such a program. Or I have also noticed there are companies now that put on quests and scavenger hunts as part of corporate team-building exercises. They handle the whole thing. Maybe CW could consider outsourcing the quest's management? I guess it would ultimately depend on the costs, though.

Another way to help defray costs would be to make the RevQuest itself a special program. If you want to participate in their one-hour "Escape the King" experience at night, you have to buy a ticket. So why not have a small fee for those of us who would love to have their daytime quest experience back? Or just downsize the program. If a smaller number of visitors are using it but are really engaged and want it back, maybe CW could offer a smaller, shorter version that could be done without as many employees required to support it. In fact, it might be worth considering if there is newer technology now that could be used instead. A phone app instead of so many employees?

I cannot answer these questions. But CW did these programs for five years and did a superb job. And especially in this time of restructuring and refocusing on their core historic mission, this one just might be a winner. So, I just *had* to write about them.

The quests were a pure joy to participate in and reading their Facebook page and seeing the comments from visitors who want it back, I only hope they will reconsider someday, and find a way to make it available without draining their staff or their wallets. I can hope!

CHAPTER SIX

....

HOW DO THEY DO IT?
BEHIND-THE-SCENES

Summer, 2016

The early morning coolness felt delicious, especially as the bright sun hinted at the day's heat to come. A woman in a long, peach-colored dress and white apron, greeted us with a pleasant "Good Day" as we headed down Duke of Gloucester Street. We had just come from the Raleigh Tavern Bakeshop and as we strolled and munched on gingerbread cookies we spied some very strange goings-on ahead of us at the William Pitt Store.

Workmen, in "camo" shorts had erected a scaffold that held sheets of shiny black material covering both of the store's front windows. A man in 21st-century attire, complete with running shoes, was deep in conversation with an 18th-century-clad one wearing a tricorn hat. Next to them, along the side of the store, were tripods, lights, reflectors, a bin with more rolls of various-colored sheets, carts piled high with tools and extension cords, black suitcases with photographic equipment, and racks of assorted support poles. No, this was not a time warp where people from different centuries could cross paths with each other. We had just discovered the secret to how CW gets such high-quality photos for all their books, calendars, and cards!

It was clear that they go all out for these shoots given the extent of top-of-the line equipment there. Everyone moved quickly, each person seeming to know without speaking, exactly what they were to do. I asked the man in camo shorts why the building's front windows were covered and he explained that the black sheeting blocked any sunlight from streaming into the building. Instead, they would set up their own lighting, reflectors, and additional sheets inside, to give them total control of the interior appearance and light quality. We watched them work for a while longer, fascinated by it all. One of my biggest joys in life is not so much the end product, but getting to experience the behind-the-scenes story of how something gets done.

My husband and I are geeks—geeks about different sorts of things, but geeks nonetheless. And mind you, I say that with great pride, head held high. I bestow that description on another person only as an ultimate compliment! My husband is into electronics, mechanics, and how things are put together, while I am into bacteria, nature, and creative ways to get kids thrilled about science. We are both into the nuts-and-bolts facts behind history—including all the details about how things *really* were done. On a trip to Newport, Rhode Island many years ago, we toured the mansions there—the vast and ornate summer "cottages" of the early 1900s rich and famous. There were the standard tours from room to room, pointing out this architecture, that decoration, the ocean view—all of it great. They also had special events you could sign up for. One was a very lovely cocktail party with glasses of wine, tasteful hors d'oeuvres, and classical music. They also had a behind-the-scenes tour of all the hidden places never seen by the elite who lived there. Essentially our choice came down to sitting on the patio sipping drinks in the evening sun, or crawling through basement passages and back rooms to see how the place was heated in an age before modern utilities were in place. As nice as the first one was, there was no question. We opted for the latter. So, you can well imagine that when we discovered several years ago that CW offered some "Behind-the-Scenes" tours, we took them, and some, more than once just in case we missed something.

The very first one we took was the "Bits and Bridles" tour. It was a behind-the-scenes look at where CW kept all their horses, carriages, and some of their other animals. We were immediately intrigued as we couldn't imagine where CW had managed to hide this facility. As many times as I'd been all over the Historic Area, I never saw a trace of it.

Tickets in hand, we approached a sheltered bench on the corner of Nicholson and Botetourt Streets where we were told our guide would meet us. We spotted a small cluster of people—everyone from kids through grandparents—waiting there. A few moments later, a man wearing a golf shirt, khakis, and a CW volunteer badge strode up and invited us to follow him down the street. Mystified, we followed him east down Nicholson, in the direction of the gaol and the Capitol building. I couldn't imagine where he was taking us. I'd never seen a stable in this area. But before we reached the gaol, the man turned left. He led us down a narrow road tucked into the trees and hedges. I had to laugh. Talk about being oblivious to my surroundings. As many times as I'd walked Nicholson Street, I'd always ignored this subtle side road.

As we came around a curve in the path, we saw it. Amazed, is the best word I can think of to describe both my surprise at how well they hid it in plain sight, as well as the facility's appearance. I would never refer to it as a mere horse barn. Cinder-block walls were capped with a peaked ceiling made of light-colored wood beams. The atmosphere was bright and airy, even in the heat and humidity. Floor fans created a breeze in the hall and each stall had a fan over it to circulate the air. The stalls, which took up half the building, were made of metal pipes with wood-paneled sides. A gold-topped post marked each one. On the back wall of every stall was a plaque that bore the name of the horse who lived there. The concrete floors were immaculate, and the sweet smell of fresh hay, wood, and leather permeated the entire building. The structure was, in a word, beautiful. Well-maintained and spotless, the horse facility is a credit to the dedication of the people who work there.

The center of the building housed the carriages used in CW. They varied in fanciness, size, and whether they were open or enclosed. A covered entryway adjoined the carriage area. This was where the horses were hitched or unhitched from their wagons and given a thorough examination by their drivers. That spot was an interesting juxtaposition of present and past as tricorn-hatted men in waistcoats and leather riding boots discussed in 21st-century language, some aspect of the horse's care with ball-capped staff in hiking shorts and running shoes.

The far end of the building housed a farrier's shop. Nippers, hammers, rasps, and a variety of hoof knives hung on the walls. The farrier first explained that the hooves of a horse bore the tremendous strain of the horse's weight and absorbed the pounding pressure as it galloped. It was essential that the hooves were well-cared for. Since the hooves continue to grow, something like our finger- and toenails, they had to be kept trimmed and level. He used a tool called nippers, which looked like oddly-shaped bolt cutters, to cut off any easy-to-reach pieces of hoof material. Then he would then use the knives to carve out the hard-to-reach spots. Rasps were used to sand down the hooves, and then the horseshoes were attached by hammering nails into the outer wall of the hoof.

The day we toured, the room was very hot and there was no fan there. As the leather-aproned man explained about the importance of well-balanced horseshoes, and how many shoes a horse goes through in a typical season, the teenage girl next to me went from red, to pale, to "passed out." One minute she was standing, the next moment she crumpled into the arms of the farrier and her father, both of whom responded quickly. It was only momentary and nothing serious. As her father noted, just too much heat and not enough water. But she was mortified as only a teenager can be whenever they do something they feel is embarrassing. Like being noticed. So, once she had some cold water and recovered, she beat a hasty retreat. I hope she managed to enjoy the rest of her day. Lesson to all of us though—when touring the stables on a hot day, bring a water bottle.

During the tour, various staff members touched briefly on their Rare Breeds initiative—their effort to maintain animal lines that would have been found in the 1700s. We saw a few chickens there at the stable—all historic breeds. One in particular, a breed called a "Silkie," caught my eye. The hen was all black and had very fluffy feathers that gave her a puffed-up appearance, especially around her head. I couldn't even see her eyes. We learned from the guide that there was a specific "Rare Breeds" walking tour that delved deeper into the subject. So as soon as we finished at the stable, we headed for a ticket office to sign up for that one.

The "Rare Breeds" walking tour was truly unique, bringing to the forefront topics one rarely notices or thinks about. Just like all else in the colonial town, the animal breeds are as historically accurate as possible. Most are ones that would have been found in the 1700s but are no longer commercially raised. All are maintained to preserve the genetic diversity of the livestock and to prevent the loss of endangered breeds.

A combination of a talk on modern animal husbandry and rare breed survival, with a walk down various tree-lined back lanes on a sunny day, it was a lovely tour. Cooled by a soft breeze, we visited various fields around the Historic Area to view Canadian horses, Red Devon milk cows from England (no Holsteins), and

Dominique Chickens. This last breed was a black-and-white thin-striped hen whose color pattern bore somewhat of a resemblance to the striped wings of a Downy Woodpecker. We heard about Runt pigeons, which were domestic pigeons often called squab when used for food. Milking Shorthorn (Durham) oxen were in another field. They originated in England and were an average, easy-to-maintain, highly fertile breed. The guide noted that they were often out working in various fields in CW or pulling wagons for visitors' rides. A regal-looking Old English rooster, his feathers streaked with various colors, strutted around one yard, while in another field fluffy Leicester Longwool lambs nestled in the grass next to their mothers.

Why bother with maintaining non-commercial breeds besides historical accuracy or the status of having an unusual breed? The following quote from the book *Link to the Past, Bridge to the Future* by John P. Hunter, sums it up:

> "After decades of selective breeding, chemical enhancement, and stagnant environs, many present-day food animals are simply dependent on that combination to survive...There has to be import given to the fact that a breed no longer in fashionable or commercially viable vogue...is healthier...We may not know exactly how the characteristics these rare breeds possess may one day save our bacon...but, it is a bank account we cannot afford to close."

Having spent that day immersed in all kinds of background details, it was enough to whet our appetites for more. So, the next day we indulged in the "Behind-the-Scenes Tour at Bruton Heights." Bruton Heights is CW's thirty-acre research campus within walking distance of the Historic Area. It has three facilities there—the John D. Rockefeller, Jr. Research Library, the

Conservation Building, and the renovated Bruton Heights School. The last was originally built in the 1930s by the federal government, CW, the Rockefeller family, and the town of Williamsburg as a community center and educational facility for the town's African American students during segregation. Once segregation ended in 1966, it continued on as an elementary school for the town until the 1990s when it was phased out. At that point, CW acquired it and renovated it as part of the research campus.

It is used today for meetings, presentations, symposia, and also houses the sound-mixing facilities for CWs educational productions. These range from sound recordings and podcasts, to films and TV shows. There is also a museum in the renovated school building that documents the school's history. Touring the museum, it was obvious there were many success stories in the students, but the overall approach—segregation—was beyond my ability to stomach. Sorrowful. The museum itself is well worth touring. I just find the attitudes from that time, incomprehensible.

The next building we toured was the conservation facility. It housed sophisticated storage areas and state-of-the art preservation laboratories. On that particular day, we were taken through the textiles lab, a quiet area with a sense of calm that permeated the entire place. Before us lay a large 1700s-era tapestry stretched out on a table. Several staff members stood around its perimeter—sometimes remaining motionless as they studied a particular spot. One might then work carefully to attach a single colored string in a patterned section that had apparently unraveled. They honored the value of the historical object, literally in their hands, with slow, skillful, precision. Aware of the pricelessness of the tapestry before them, and aware of their responsibility for its proper restoration, they were careful not to lean on it or handle it any more than was absolutely necessary. Watching them, I was astounded by their patience, something I certainly don't have.

For them, time was an element to be used in generous doses to achieve their desired end. The restorers seemed oblivious to our presence, focused solely on the small patch of cloth before them. Looking at the finished section, you could not tell where the 1700s "original" work ended and the 21st-century repairs began. I suspect their work is the historical equivalent of brain surgery. I've only seen such meticulousness before in a documentary of a Vatican art museum's restoration lab. I would consider the CW staff as equal in their expertise.

In a coming chapter, I will share in greater detail, the tour through the research library. For now, I will remark on something that is related to the theme of "how do they do it?" It can be discovered not so much in any one particular tour, but in your own observations and it's fun to look for. There is an art form hidden right there in plain sight all throughout CW. And that art form is the way CW weaves in the infrastructure for modern conveniences and appliances without destroying the historical aura. The streets are tar, not mud, but you don't think much about it. There are electric lights mounted on those lampposts, power outlets in your hotel room to charge your cell phones, no guests need to use a chamber pot, and there's even a port on the desk for your computer. They don't shun air conditioning or central heating; in fact, environmental controls are key to preserving art works, original furniture, tapestries, artifacts, and the materials used in building the structure. Instead, they incorporate these things in such a way that they either blend into the background, are hidden in plain sight, or are "camouflaged" to appear like a well-house or some other historic structure. Even right in the center of the Historic Area where the illusion of stepping back in time is at its strongest, consider the largely ignored manhole cover in the grass to the right of the courthouse. Right where you stand feeling very "1700s" in the sunlight, that slab of metal covers one of the car tunnels that goes under the historic town. The tunnel allows you to drive from one end of the Historic Area to the other without ever being seen. While the manhole cover is there, is just blends into the soil and grass and no one seems to pay it any attention. All of these things are done ever so subtly. Perhaps it is also that the rest is done so well and they have so successfully created the "historical dream" as reality, that you "notice, but don't notice" the things that weren't there in 1775. You just overlook them.

There are a few more behind-the-scenes experiences I will talk about later in this book. If you are the type of person who is even slightly excited about the "how do they do it" question, you will love these tours. They are an orgy of trivia and a buffet of historical information that you can revel in.

CHAPTER SEVEN

···

WHAT DID IT LOOK LIKE?
THEN AND NOW

Summer, 2014

Standing under the huge old tree near the Magazine, I glanced west toward the ravine. There was no moon that night to lighten the darkness there. Instead, it was like a solid black wall—inky and impenetrable. The area carried an energy as if this was a place where "things had happened." Slowly I walked up to the tree line, shivering a little as I wondered if *something* beyond my vision was staring back, watching my every move. Face-to-face with the leaves, I peered into its depths, half expecting to see shadows stealing through the brush. I even turned my head to use my peripheral vision, which is better at seeing at night. But nothing short of night-vision goggles would pierce that darkness. Suddenly afraid, I quickly backed up, never taking my eyes off the bushes for a moment. Had one of them moved just a bit too much, I would have turned and ran.

The next day I scanned that same hilly terrain. Under blue skies and sunshine, it was a natural haven. Tucked behind the buildings on Duke of Gloucester Street, the mass of lush foliage, underbrush, and tree limbs masked the serene pastures where sheep placidly grazed. I walk down along its edge to Francis Street and headed down the road, all the while looking up at that ravine. It was so different now. I shook my head and shrugged off the previous night's terror—no doubt the result of poor lighting, and the book I was writing.

I often strolled through CW, not as a tourist, but as an author seeking out "spots with conflict potential." I looked for, or rather, felt my way to spots that seemed to possess an aura of risk, tension, or outright terror. And for sure, that ravine at night reeked of it. But looking at it in the light of day, I had to consider that my feelings were just the result of an overactive imagination.

All of this though, did get me thinking more about what this area was like in the 1700s. What was here in the ravine back then? Farms? A tavern? Nothing? Who was here? And what did *they* see at night? These days that area borders on Francis Street, which is a straight thoroughfare running the length of CW, parallel to Duke of Gloucester Street. But back then was it the same? Or was the ravine even deeper...and more ominous at night? Looking around, I noticed that there were small brooks trickling on each side of the road. They gave little hint of where they came from or where they went. Were they there three hundred years ago? Or was there a rushing torrent you didn't dare cross? If only the trees could talk.

I then started looking around CW in general. Wandering the streets, tree-lined, level, and peaceful, I wondered—was it like this three centuries ago? If you could transport a townsperson from the 1700s to present-day CW, would they even recognize this place? The more I looked, the more questions I had. For example, there was the pond behind the Governor's Palace that I'd visited since I was a kid. To me, the pond just existed in a vacuum, plopped in place right there with no beginning or end. However, as an adult, I began to wonder, where *did* all the water come from, and go to? And exactly what existed behind the Palace three hundred years ago. Today there is a fine CW border wall with modern neighborhoods and roads on the other side. But what was back there then?

And what about the number of sheltered brooks quietly bubbling along as you strolled through modern-day CW? The one behind the Post Office, for example, right next to the Printer's and the Bookbinder's shops raised a number of questions in my mind. It was located about twelve feet below road grade, down in a ravine reached by steep stairs. It was a beautifully landscaped site now, but what was it like back then? Was it even there? Who built the brick retaining wall? And did that peaceful little brook ever flood out the shops?

So, between the brooks and ravines, the road changes and mystical pond sources, I decided it was time for answers. My search started with CW itself. I figured somebody there had to have documented any changes they made. And if any of those spots had been excavated, the archaeology staff would have reports of their findings. Given the depth of their online resources, I started at my favorite spot: http://www.history.org/, and I hit the jackpot. There in their records were numerous reports documenting the evolution of CW over the years.

After hours of reading a number of the papers, I finally learned that the canal at the Palace was created by the demand of Governor Spotswood in the early 1700s. He wanted that pond and told the burgesses that if they wouldn't pay for its installation, he would. In one way, it made sense as it was a natural place for a pond. The land sloped in such a way that water from the Palace site naturally drained down into the gully there. Also, it was fed by a natural spring. The governor got his way and even ended up creating terraced gardens along the steep slopes above the gully. So, the final product was the canal and fish pond with gardens on the slopes that we see today. I couldn't find out how it emptied back then, but now the canal empties into a drain at its north end, no doubt a more modern bit of infrastructure.

While hunting down that information I also discovered a few other things about the Palace grounds that I had missed on earlier visits. Right behind the maze was a large hill with a flat top referred to as "the Mount." A set of stairs led to the top which provided a great vantage point to look down into the maze and watch all the action. On the backside of that hill, however, was another surprise— a brick-arched doorway with a tunnel entrance that descended below the Mount. It is now blocked off so you cannot enter. Given the age of the tunnel it would be too dangerous. However, I learned that the tunnel led to the remains of an ice house. Blocks of ice were cut from local rivers during the winter, hauled to the ice house, and stored down there so that the governor and his family could enjoy cold drinks in the summer. I peered down into it and imagined what it must have been like to wrestle large ice blocks up from the river to this doorway, and then drag them down into the dark hole below.

At the same time, I found out what came before all those modern neighborhoods were built behind the CW border wall. During the 1770s there was a forested area behind the Palace property. Trails were cut into the woods so the Governor and his guests could take carriage rides back there.

As to my question about whether those babbling brooks were always that way, nothing could be further from the truth. A few years ago, as I studied a 1781 Frenchman's military map of CW, I realized just how extensive the river system was that ran right through the colonial town. West of the Palace, there was a river that flowed right down through town and continued on, probably underneath Duke of Gloucester Street. In fact, that mysterious ravine to the west of the Magazine had a river running through it. And the area on Francis Street, south of that ravine, had a number of river branches crossing it.

In comparing Francis Street in the 1700s to today, for sure there was a change. I did some digging and found a clue about some of those changes, in an article on the http://history.org/ website:

"One ravine, in particular, was so wide and formidable that Francis Street originally only went as far as the western edge of Market Square until about the turn of this century. The ravine was then partially filled so that Francis Street could link up with France Street to the west, which ran in front of the Public Hospital. These two streets finally became the modern Francis Street of today, now extending the full length of the original town."

Reading on, I learned about the challenges CW faced in restoring the Historic Area. Waterways had to be diverted and they had to deal with severe ravine slopes. Today's level, paved, easily-walked mile of Duke of Gloucester Street gives no hint of the work that was done to make that happen. It also gives no sense of the struggle and peril inhabitants faced trying to guide a heavily loaded wagon across town in 1700. Back then, Duke of Gloucester Street was more a twisted dirt horse path that followed the high ground. Its path weaved this way and that, trying to avoid the numerous ravines throughout that area. Attempts to straighten out the street were difficult, expensive, and often ineffective. On rainy days, residents had to drive their oxen teams down a muddy path into a marshy ravine then struggle to climb up and out the other side. You have to wonder how many heavily laden wagons overturned and how many people showed up at their destination soggy and mud-caked. I also discovered that the site where Shields' Tavern now sits was once a drainage ditch. It channeled water north across what would eventually be Duke of Gloucester street and dumped it into a nearby ravine. And as to that lovely spot at today's Printing Office, there *were* brick retaining walls put in place there as early as 1722, and an enclosed brick culvert was installed by the little brook to channel rain water under the street. I couldn't determine if it flooded, but I suspect the installation of a brick culvert that far back suggests the drainage there left something to be desired. So, it goes without saying the modern-day CW has in several areas, "smoothed over" the rough spots to make it more amenable to visitors.

And those shady, tree-lined streets of current-day CW? Were they there in the 1700s? To quote CW archaeologist Meredith Poole, "According to firsthand accounts, walking up and down Duke of Gloucester Street was not for the faint of heart...It was bright. So, we know there weren't as many trees..." She indicated that through archaeobotany— a way to study plant material found in archaeological excavations—they learned what the ecosystem of the area was like. Early in the 1700s, the Peyton Randolph house site had plenty of tree cover in the form of oak, pine, maple, and hornbeam. By the time of the Revolutionary war, there were few surviving trees, and by the late 18th and early 19th centuries the area showed a significant rise in goosefoot and ragweed pollens, indicating a weedy environment. Questions posed by these changes include—How did these shifts take place? Were the trees used up or destroyed by the people? And why? What actions took place to bring about such a change? Only more research can answer those questions.

As to what 18th-century Williamsburg looked like, aside from reading reports and documents already on file, or trying to conjure an image in your imagination, there is a new tool that can help you "see it." It's called "Virtual Williamsburg." Modern day archaeologists, working with computer modelers, have taken all of the information from almost eighty-five years of stratigraphic excavations and constructed a 3-D computer model that reveals how Williamsburg's landscape changed over the centuries. On the sites of ravines long filled in with trash, the model can "remove the fill" so you can visualize geographical changes that took place to the locale over time. It would be impossible to do that in real life with a dig without causing major disruptions and destruction to CW. But with 3-D modeling they can remove the layers virtually and thus get a clearer view of 1700s Williamsburg. To see what they did, check out: http://research.history.org/projects/virtual-williamsburg/

So, when you walk through CW today, look around and realize that things have changed, and that there are so many stories just waiting to be told. In fact, CW must have divined that people would want to know more. They published an article—"The Lay of the Land"—which talks about all the changes. It can be found at their history link: http://www.history.org/history/CWLand/resrch4.cfm.

As to that spooky ravine...I still say there's something there. That one will require more research to determine if it's my writer's imagination or not. But even if it is, that's fine. That ravine will definitely play a role in my book!

CHAPTER EIGHT

....

DETAILS: THE REST
OF THE STORY

Spring, 2016

CW program guides for the next four days were spread out on the table. On almost any day during that stretch, I found a program in the daily listings called "Storming the Palace." It was one of those programs where you can not only observe the action, but be part of it. This particular program, which had been offered for many years, was a twenty-minute glimpse into the aftermath of a major mistake made by the then British governor—Lord Dunmore. The mistake was an incident that took place in the middle of the night of April 20, 1775, and it would trigger the start of the Revolution in Williamsburg.

Dunmore had ordered marines stationed nearby on a docked British warship to remove the gunpowder from the town's magazine late one night. Caught in the act, the town's citizens exploded in rage. People gathered to march en masse to the Palace and demand that the governor return the gunpowder. Bloodshed seemed likely and was avoided only by the efforts of men like Peyton Randolph and several other Burgesses. From that moment on, Williamsburg would never be the same. It had been like a powder keg, ready to go off, and now, the governor had set the match.

The Magazine incident. It's full of drama, betrayal, volatile emotions, and confrontation. Every novel set in colonial-era Williamsburg seems to include that incident in some form. It's just too full of great action to pass it up. And regardless of the account you read or the program you view, it seems that Lord Dunmore is the indisputable villain.

I love historical trivia. When I hear those seemingly isolated and meaningless little anecdotes about people from ages past that seem to exist in a vacuum, I wonder where they fit into the bigger picture. Just as pieces of pottery from an archaeological dig can be reconstructed to reveal a bigger picture about colonial life, so too, can the snippets of stories of the people caught up in the turmoil of the Revolution be pieced together for the full picture of their life. A nugget of a personality quirk tracked backwards can reconstruct the larger life story of that person and their part in the events of the time. By connecting the dots of disparate pieces of information, you start to get the bigger picture of the roles those personalities played in altering the very outcome of the Revolution. You also get to see how that effect extends from CW outward, to the rest of the colonies and across the ocean. You have only to start digging around in the documents, news articles, and letters of the time to see personal pain and public drama come to life.

And there is also the question of what the individual, formed by their early circumstances in life, will do when caught in the throes of something huge and beyond their control—like a revolution. That time period was rife with personal struggles—whether it was the decision to rebel or stay loyal, have slaves or release them, aid the enemy to avoid starvation, or risk everything for an ideal. Often the answers found, the decisions made, were not easily achieved, and I suspect they were often not completely satisfying. Very few escaped the soul-searching required to take a stand, and many no doubt went back and forth depending on the day and circumstances. I suspect the British might not have been much different in that, especially one, Lord Dunmore—John Murray, the Right Honourable 4th Earl of Dunmore, AKA, Governor of the Colony of Virginia. And of anyone, he seems to be the person who really stoked the fire of revolution in 18th-century Williamsburg.

We always hear a lot about our American Revolutionary War heroes. Our history books are full of their larger-than-life tales. CW's programming puts us "face-to-face" with the likes of George Washington, Thomas Jefferson, and Peyton Randolph. So, there had to be an equally intriguing backstory to Lord Dunmore that held the clues to why he risked open rebellion the way he did. He wasn't dropped fully formed, into the situation. He had a past that drove his decisions, and a future that resulted from those choices. So, I decided I needed to find out exactly who he was he, and what was his story.

His early years, while part of the nobility, were not free from turbulence. In fact, I wonder if those years didn't set the stage for the rest of his life. While only fifteen, he fought with his father on the side of Charles Edward Stuart—Bonnie Prince Charlie— against the British. That did not go well, resulting in the imprisonment of Dunmore's father in the Tower of London and his family's sentence of house arrest. His father eventually received a conditional pardon, and Dunmore himself joined the British army. From there Dunmore moved on and entered politics. He was eventually rewarded with a governorship in the colony of New York.

Lord Dunmore had been the Governor of New York for less than a year, however, when in 1771 he was reassigned to be governor of Virginia. In spite of being given a higher salary in a more affluent colony, Dunmore was upset and tried desperately to stay in New York. He even offered to trade positions with the incoming New York governor, offering him Virginia while he, Dunmore, stayed in New York. No one will probably ever accuse Lord Dunmore of being gracious. Failing in his efforts to stay in New York, the night he gave up his post, Dunmore got drunk, insulted the new governor, got into a fight with another official, and cursed out Virginia. Dunmore had also sent a letter to the President of the Virginia Council in which he tactlessly shared his distaste for having to move to Virginia. When you add all that to the fact that his deceased predecessor in Virginia, Lord Botetourt, had been well loved by the people, it was no surprise that Lord Dunmore's arrival in the southern colony was not exactly welcomed with open arms by the local population.

In 1774, Dunmore gained some popular support when he waged a campaign to claim some of the Ohio Country land for Virginia. He led a series of battles against the Shawnee Indians and successfully claimed the lands. Even at that, the support was not that strong, as many Virginians correctly understood that Lord Dunmore's motives had more to do with his own accumulation of wealth and power than anything to benefit them. Furthermore, Dunmore's actual leadership in those battles was questionable, further adding to people's distrust of him.

If that wasn't enough, Lord Dunmore had a special knack for dealing with others, especially the House of Burgesses, with condescension and confrontation. He lacked any substantive negotiating skills, and with regularity, he antagonized them, ignored them, postponed sessions with them, or would abruptly dissolve them. This attitude filtered down in his dealings with the local population.

The final straw came in April, 1775, when he had the town's gunpowder removed in the middle of the night. Though he said he would return it and that he had only taken it to protect the local populace from a possible slave rebellion, the truth was, the gunpowder was on its way to a British ship. He had written Lord Dartmouth in London that his motives for the removal were more to prevent the local citizens from seizing it. Rumblings of rebellion throughout the colonies and their general frustration with Parliament's taxes gave him good reason to think this.

However, his plan backfired because upon learning of the theft, angry citizens stormed the Palace and the local militia was mobilized. While bloodshed was averted in April, in early May, Patrick Henry and the Hanover Militia arrived in Williamsburg. This forced Dunmore to move his family, first to his hunting lodge—Porto Bello, near Yorktown—and then to a British warship moored in the nearby York River, for safety. He had eventually followed his family to Porto Bello, where he conducted a series of raids against the local population. When local Patriots attacked his hunting lodge, he was apparently wounded in the leg and withdrew to the same British warship.

Shortly afterward, he sent his family back to England and moved his base of operations to the relative safety of a ship moored in the Norfolk harbor area of Hampton Roads. Surrounded by other ships with loyal followers that the locals dubbed the "floating island," Dunmore continued to mount raids against the local Patriot militias and populace.

Even amongst the loyalists, he was not always popular or welcome. His presence in the harbor interfered with the "handshake agreements" local business and shipping interests had arranged for each other's mutual profit. In November, 1775, he further inflamed the situation when he issued a proclamation saying that any enslaved black man who would come to fight for him would be set free. Before you consider him a paragon of virtue and freedom, consider that he only freed slaves of those who were rebelling against him, and only those that could fight in the army. Thus, he excluded women, children, and elderly enslaved individuals.

All throughout this time, he had been the subject of scathing articles in local newspapers. The last straw was an article referring to Dunmore's father as a traitor in English politics during the 1740s. Furious, Dunmore sent soldiers to the print shop of the pro-Patriot Norfolk publisher, John H. Holt. Viewing the entire episode through a spyglass from his ship, Dunmore watched as his soldiers grabbed two of the printers who worked there, a bookbinder, the equipment, paper, type, ink, and all utensils, and returned to the ship. Shortly thereafter, Dunmore began issuing a newspaper more in line with his own views. John Holt, the publisher of the raided press, had managed to elude capture that day and threatened to open a new press. Instead, he joined the Revolutionary Army and did not return to publishing until after the war. However area newspapers, especially those in Williamsburg stepped up their attacks on him, even going so far as to reveal he had kept a mistress during his stay in Williamsburg.

Undaunted, Dunmore continued his raids against local militias and over the next few months he won various battles in the area. However, after he lost a decisive one at Great Bridge, not far from Norfolk, he retreated to his ships in the harbor and began to work out plans for a withdrawal from the area. He executed that a few months later, with the help of British Naval and Army forces, but not before he inflicted permanent damage on the Norfolk waterfront. Frustrated by Patriot snipers, who used the dockside buildings to hide in while they shot at his ships, Dunmore exacted his revenge. Both sides had been setting fire to various structures around the town, but on January 1, 1776 Dunmore's forces burned down several abandoned buildings in the waterfront area. High winds drove the flames further and then the local Patriot militia joined in the burning. Within three days over eight hundred buildings had been burned to the ground, including the homes, businesses, and public buildings of friends and foes alike.

While this solved the sniper problem, Dunmore only succeeded in unsettling the situation more. For one thing, even though both sides had a hand in the rampant arson that took place, the British received a fair bit of the blame. Also, with the dockside buildings gone, the local Patriot forces now had a great view to monitor the comings and goings of British troops from the ships. The local militias tightened control so it became very difficult for the British to come ashore and restock badly needed supplies, such as fresh water and food. Smallpox and other diseases took hold on the cramped ships. Meanwhile, on the waterfront the local Patriot forces moved in cannon and pointed them at the ships.

By the spring of 1776 it was obvious the situation was untenable and by the end of May, Lord Dunmore and the British forces left Norfolk. They headed out into the Chesapeake Bay and set up camp on a small island called Gwynn's Island. From there Dunmore hoped to regroup so he could retake Virginia, as well as North Carolina, and Maryland. Smallpox, battle failures, and injuries continued to plague his efforts though, and by the summer, with many men dead or dying of disease, Dunmore and his few remaining forces left the Chesapeake for New York City. There he debriefed his experiences with the brothers-in-arms, General Howe and Admiral Howe. While in New York City, Dunmore and his remaining troops helped the British and Hessian forces defeat General George Washington. This drove the Patriots from New York City for the remainder of the war.

Dunmore was not one to give up on his goals, however. The saying "quit while you're behind" had probably not been invented yet, and even if it had, he seemed to have had the sort of nature that he wouldn't have listened anyway. Instead, he continued to lobby the Howe brothers for men and ships to retake Virginia, but there were none to be had. Returning to England, he sought support from political allies and the King, for a return to Virginia. Finally, in 1781, he was sent back as "Governor" since the British anticipated General Cornwallis would win at Yorktown.

However, while Dunmore was enroute to Virginia, word reached his ship that Cornwallis had been defeated. In addition, a new anti-war government was now in power in London. Dunmore's dreams evaporated. Instead, he headed to Charleston, and there worked with other displaced Loyalists to figure out ways to regain footholds in North Carolina, Virginia, and elsewhere in North America. Unlike the history books, which make it seem like the Revolution and all British efforts to suppress the revolt ended abruptly with the loss as Yorktown, that was not the case. Many parties still eager to continue the fight nursed their wounds in places like Charleston, hatching plan after plan to try and retake what they had lost.

Why the determination? In Dunmore's case, due to the Revolution, he had forfeited hundreds of acres of land in both New York state and Virginia, not to mention personal possessions abandoned when he had to evacuate the Governor's Palace in Williamsburg and Porto Bello in Yorktown. Ever the land speculator, he was not willing to give up on the chance for lucrative gains in the colonies. Also, a dogged fighter, he was determined to see Britain and the Crown restored to their full powers in the colonies.

For several years, he tried to interest the British government in plans to retake the colonies and to take Spanish Louisiana as a safe foothold on the Mississippi. However, nothing came of these efforts. To his credit, he did show much honor in working to help Loyalists and supporters of his, including ex-slaves from the colonies, to get assistance when they returned destitute to London. The closest he came to returning to North America was when he was named Governor of the Bahamas. In that role, he also tried to protect the freedoms of blacks and Indians who sided with him. But Dunmore was a person of many contradictions. Over his life, he could be honorable about protecting those who sided with him, even former slaves and Indians, yet he could be equally guilty of enslaving others.

Throughout his many years in the Bahamas, Dunmore never gave up hope of returning to the colonies and reclaiming the lands he had lost. Even as late as the 1790s he kept trying. However, by this point he had made many enemies, especially in the power circles of London. Accused of money mismanagement and other improprieties in the Bahamas, he was recalled to England. It was the last time he would be in North America. His dream of restoring British power in the New World was over. Out of favor, and out of money, his political career came to an end.

For the rest of his life he would struggle to survive. He was heavily in debt, low in income, and at odds with the King and British leaders. In spite of all his losses, and the failures of all his dreams and efforts in life, he remained fiery until the end. When the King insulted Dunmore's daughter over her secret marriage to the King's son and referred to her children as bastards, Dunmore responded by calling the King's children the same name, not once, but several times, right to the King's face. Enraged, speechless, purple-faced, and bordering on apoplexy, the King left the room, ending their conversation, and the relationship.

For the remainder of his life, John Murray, the Right Honourable 4th Earl of Dunmore, lived a more or less enforced quiet life, nursed by his daughter in his later years. He died of "decay" on February 25, 1809, at the age of seventy-eight. Decay, I suppose, is the only way death could catch up with that fighting spirit and silence it.

Dunmore's story is just one of many. Some were famous. Most were unknown. But it is precisely those stories that bring history alive. History is not created by two-dimensional cardboard characters, but by living, breathing, scared, and stubborn individuals. At its core the Revolution was, at the ground zero of peoples' realities, a far cry from what the history books have written. It is only by diving deep into the threads of peoples' lives, researching their connections to places and events, and taking into account their heroic actions, failures, inconsistencies, and foibles, that I think you get the true story of what happened during that or any time.

CHAPTER NINE

....

SOMEDAY FINALLY ARRIVES

Late Winter, 2011

The garden tour started in the David Morton Garden near Christiana Campbell's Tavern. It was soothing and upsetting at the same time. While birds sang and quiet adults wandered the brick or gravel paths between symmetrically-shaped flower beds, I wandered aimlessly, stomach knotted and muscles taut. I felt this edgy readiness to spring into action even though I had no idea what action I should be taking. The guide talked about why Morton planted what he did, and why colonists indulged in pleasure gardens, but it was wasted on me.

I was unused to this kind of an activity at CW. My trips were always "child-based"—either me as the child, or then my son. And I never sat still for any of them. Quiet things like concerts, art museums, and garden tours I viewed as things for "older people," things to go on a list for "someday"—some hazy distant future *many* years from now when suddenly I would know I was old, accept it, and do things for old people at CW. Given all of life's changes in the last couple of years and how I was feeling about them, could it be that someday had arrived? I hadn't expected it to feel like this. And I knew I wasn't ready for "old."

Our next stop was the garden at Christiana Campbell's Tavern. This tavern had always been a treasured favorite of mine, so my hopes rose that maybe this garden would cheer me up. While the garden beds were attractive in their neatness—clean stretches of brown that were spare and devoid of winter's debris—they were equally devoid at this point in late March of much color. There were no flowers, no vegetables, not even green leaves. They seemed a perfect match to the gray sky and the way I felt...empty. But as I followed the group a few of the guide's words caught my attention, things about dormancy, growth cycles, rebirth.

We ended our tour in the Benjamin Powell House garden. This one was less a pleasure garden and more a working kitchen garden. This meant that for the moment, it was even more devoid of any obvious growth than the previous two. However, the guide continued on, cheerily noting that though the garden had been emptied of what had come before, rebirth was near as it was early spring. Even though the plant beds lay bare, beneath our feet roots were busy absorbing nutrients. Swelling buds were getting ready to shatter their seed coats and punch through to the surface. For a plant, this was certainly a time of tremendous upheaval. And it would be even more so in a couple of weeks when new young shoots would be up in the open, soaking up the sun and growing like mad.

It slowly occurred to me that maybe I was no different than those plant beds. I felt empty, but maybe I was really just dormant? Life had certainly disturbed and unsettled all the routines I had treasured and clung to. But could there be new shoots already at work smashing open some unseen emotional seed coats, ready to claw their way to the surface? Maybe in the near future they, too, would reach for the light and create something new and fresh in me?

It's funny, but you do something you like for so long that you assume the experience will remain the same upbeat, fun, relaxing time that it's always been. It's just that that assumption is one hundred percent wrong. While life can remain calm, and even be that way for many years, at some point it *will* change. I just hadn't given much thought as to how. And I guess I assumed it wouldn't be a big deal. But life brings its transition times, those moments when it is a time to take stock and decide if what came before still fits, or if it's time for something new. Transition times require their due, and I have never been good at them.

By this point I had been coming to CW at various intervals for over forty-six years. Being a creature of habit and having had the ingrained habit of associating CW with "family" vacations for almost all of that time—either because I was a child in a family visiting there or because I was an adult with a family of my own—it suddenly shook me to realize that all was different now. My son was off to college, my husband had had a health scare, and I was reeling. I reached for my touchstone, CW, but even there it was unsettling. It didn't feel the same, and suddenly having the freedom to do what I wanted, when I wanted, felt disorienting...almost scary.

I realized it had been years since I had considered *me*, who I was, or what *I* wanted to do. What *did* I want? And to me, the most frightening question of all was: Would my most favorite place on earth suddenly no longer "fit me"? Was CW truly only a place for children and families and no longer applied past a certain age? I didn't even want to think about that. But it was time to find out.

Never having indulged in a "just me" tour at CW since those heady days of ten-year-old adventures with my sister, I decided it was time to step out of my comfort zone. A new direction—a morning garden tour called "Through the Garden Gate"—presented itself. I had been caring for our yard for over twenty years, and before that I had done a lot of vegetable gardening. I thought maybe something connecting my past with my present might feel good, which is how I ended up—with some misgivings and still feeling out-of-sorts—at the garden tour. It didn't help that it seemed like the only others there were other "early-riser types," (read as "older"). But I was glad I stuck it out. It certainly gave me hope that maybe CW and I did not need to part ways just because I no longer had a child at home

I can't say that the realizations from that tour suddenly made all things better. But in looking back on that time I am eternally grateful for it. That tour was my turning point, the beginning of a journey to a more comfortable place, a re-invigoration of long-shelved interests and projects, and a new and richer appreciation for all things in life, including, and especially, CW.

About five years later, we did another spring trip, though a couple of months later in the spring than that 2011 trip. This time I eagerly anticipated my visit, excited to explore some things on my own and partake of everything my son would have rolled his eyes at. That is when I decided I needed to revisit that garden tour. This time, however, I would actually savor some quiet time alone on a misty, gray, early morning, communing with empty garden beds and quiet, older visitors. To my surprise, the morning was flooded with sun despite the early hour. And the group was a mix of grandparents, kids in colonial garb, teens, and their parents. Could it be that all those activities I had judged as being just for old people were really for anybody, and always had been? Maybe my own perceptions had been my mistake all along. It never was about boxing things into separate categories of young vs. old, but about letting your soul soar in its own way, no matter the age.

Again, we started in the David Morton Garden. This time I heard how this was a formal garden, with a design adapted from one in Charleston. It was comprised of four quadrants or "parterres" and edged in boxwoods. All four parterres surrounded a covered well and pump, which gave the garden a hub-like center. When we turned into the garden at Christiana Campbell's Tavern,

I was awed by how incredibly lush and beautiful the young plants were. I don't ever recall seeing such thick, green, ivy-filled beds before. And the vegetable garden at the Benjamin Powell House was in full growth—potato plants, Swiss chard, carrots, herbs, squash, all arrayed on a palette of green, spreading leaves.

Walking back through town after the tour, I wandered past swaths of vivid purple, neon yellow, and scarlet tulips, as well as blossoming pumpkin plants blanketing patches of earthy brown. Everywhere I looked, staff members were busy hoeing, nurturing, evaluating. Spring was in full swing and the foliage was richer than ever. The edginess and fear I experienced on that first garden tour were gone now, replaced by a sense of vibrant urgency—a desire to explore all the things I'd never had time to do before and to do it all *now!* It was such a rush to realize that CW was not just a place for children or young families, but indeed had something wonderful for all the seasons of life. I was just late in realizing that. But I was now ready to make up for lost time.

Spring garden tours are my favorite these days, and I have several "favorite" gardens at CW. In fact, I never realized before just how varied the number and types of gardens there are scattered throughout the Historic Area. Some are large and expansive, some just nooks nestled behind a house, barely seen. A stroll through the side streets and backyards reveals delightful spots, whether formal or vegetable, herbal or floral.

Here are some of the other gardens I enjoy and that are worth a stroll through. Interestingly enough, the Palace gardens, which were the main ones I remember from childhood, are not at the top of my list. They are beautiful and I still enjoy them, but there are some really unique and unusual ones that I seek out now even more.

Always and evermore, the Orlando Jones House, that special place we stayed at many years ago, has the garden that is my first love and the genesis of my passion for boxwoods. An unusual garden design for the 18th century, it is an elongated oval instead of rectangles or hard geometric-shaped beds. Beautifully manicured boxwood hedges form the outer circle, with beds of white tulips and English daisies filling an inner oval bed. The two are separated by a brick path, and innermost is a bed of grass with an off-center, paper-mulberry tree anchoring the entire design. Tucked into the ring of boxwoods, or rather, carved into the bushes, are recesses that hold benches and corkscrew-shaped boxwood topiaries—lovely spots to rest, read, or reflect. It is the best garden in CW to me. While less grand than those of the Governor's Palace, I consider that its charm. The simple but refined design gives it a cozy and intimate atmosphere, the perfect retreat.

*My favorite CW Garden, located behind
the Orlando Jones House.*

The garden that is a close second is one of the three gardens on the special tour, the Christiana Campbell garden. I love the thick ivy beds and the sculptured, tiered, yaupon holly topiary in the center, surrounded by the flowering dogwoods, hydrangeas, and the red cedars which provide attractive focal points and much appreciated shade in the summer. And, of course, I appreciate the emotional memories.

Another favorite is the Colonial Garden and Nursery, located on the west end of Duke of Gloucester Street, across from Bruton Parish Church. Beds of colorful tulips accent one corner of the garden, nestled near other beds of heirloom vegetables and fruits. Herbs, including beautiful lavenders, fill the sides of the space, along with window-frame hot-houses for tender young plants in the spring. An added bonus is the tarp-covered "store" where you can purchase plants, tools, birdhouses, seeds, and gardening books. It's a place I visit every time I am in CW, if only to walk through and appreciate its beauty.

For those who love patterns and order, there is a decorative garden right next door—the Custis Tenement garden. Crushed oyster shells grind beneath your feet as you walk along its angular shell paths that are edged in red brick. Carefully trimmed box-woods line the garden perimeter as well as its beds, which contain white tulips and Johnny-jump-ups in the spring, and blue-and-white rocket larkspurs in the summer. A crab-apple tree orchard sits in the back, which presents as a mass of white blossoms in the spring.

Spring is also an amazing sensory experience in the Alexander Craig House pleasure garden, next to the Raleigh Tavern bake-shop. Its vibrant displays of crimson, bright yellow and purple tulips are arranged in four rectangular beds that surround a central tulip bed. All are framed with brick walkways. The pleasure garden sits in front of the orchard of peach and pear trees. Couple this with the smells of baking cookies from the bakeshop and a cool spring breeze, and it is a delightful spot to be.

Behind Wetherburn's Tavern is a garden that is a visual delight for any vegetable gardener. Mounds covered with wide-leafed squash and pumpkin plants as well as flawlessly weeded rows of onions, carrots, celery, and potato plants are everything you'd expect to see in a colonial garden of that time. And in the early spring, the dark loam just exudes an aroma of rich fertility.

Near the Palace, the George Wythe gardens are another delight, a mix of aesthetic, practical, and color-soaked beauty. The site boasts a kitchen garden, orchard, and farm buildings. A pleasure garden is near the leaf-covered arbors that provide shade and relief from the searing heat in mid-summer.

At the west end of town, the Taliaferro-Cole House gardens host fence-enclosed rectangular beds framed by warm brick paths and beds of fiery-colored tulips. These surround patches of deep green lawn. Benches provide spots to absorb the colorful palette before you, as well as to gaze down steep brick stairs to the rolling green meadow below where sheep graze quietly. The exuberance of this space contrasts nicely with those serene pastures below.

These are just some of the wonderful beds of plantings to be found around the town. CW has a map on their website that you can print and take with you, entitled "Historic Gardens." It lists all the currently open gardens along with a map noting their locations. (www.history.org/history/cwland/gardensmap.cfm) There may also be copies at the Visitor Center as well as the Colonial Garden and Nursery.

Even when you can't be at CW, you can follow garden topics on the Making History Now blog. There you can read articles such as "The 10 Historic Gardens That Make Picture-Perfect Backdrops Every Spring" to "Springing into Chocolate Through Colonial Williamsburg's Gardens." The last one—a chef-led tour of the gardens that includes his ideas on unusual ways to use chocolate in menu-planning—is bound to catch any chocolate-lover's eye.

Also, The Colonial Williamsburg Foundation has published a number of books on their gardens and how to use the fruits of those spaces. Some of my favorites to just sit back and enjoy reading include *The Gardens of Colonial Williamsburg, Plants of Colonial Williamsburg, Vegetable Gardening The Colonial Williamsburg Way,* and *Flowers and Herbs of Early America.* Between the wealth of tips and info, as well as the full-color pictures, they are more than capable of helping you "feel in the moment," even if you are back home in the middle of winter. They help preserve memories of the spring flush that will soon return.

CHAPTER TEN

··

MISSION STATEMENTS AND BEGINNER'S MIND

Spring, 2016

We were full after lunch at Merchants Square's DoG Street Pub. Salad, a hearty burger and an unusual hand-crafted stout left us sated and serene. For a change of pace, we caught the bus to the Visitor Center to stroll around for a while. We did the usual things there—looked for T-shirts in the gift shop, Revolutions, then checked out the bookstore there for any good books we might have missed. Then we just wandered the halls for a bit, enjoying the quiet. Since the morning's crush of people getting their badges and admissions tickets was gone, it was peaceful. There were just a few late-arrivals at the sales counters, finding out how to start their visit. I'd always experienced a comfortable feeling walking through this part of the building. For so many years our visits started right in this room, so the area has been deeply imprinted with many happy memories.

Standing by the information desk, I glanced to my left and noticed the familiar bronze-colored metal plaque above the wooden bench. It had been there for as long as I could remember. I'd walked past it hundreds of times. The words were familiar—the list of prominent donors, and then in large script at the bottom of the plaque, the CW mission statement. My eyes lingered on those words—"That the future may learn from the past."

I had always liked that line. I thought it had a power and brilliance. But this time my reaction was even stronger. This time, for some reason, those words suddenly bored into me with a power I'd never quite felt before. They had been there in plain sight all along, but it was like I'd never truly *seen* them before. But now, for the first time in my life, I was not only seeing them, but *understanding* them. There before me, succinctly wrapped up in eight well-thought out words, was the *total essence of CW*.

**This wall plaque in middle of the Visitor Center shows
the CW Mission Statement.**

There is a concept in Buddhism called *Shoshin*—"beginner's mind." Wikipedia defines it as "...having an attitude of openness, eagerness, and lack of preconceptions...even when studying at an advanced level..." The Zen master Shunryu Suzuki, author of *Zen Mind, Beginner's Mind*, taught that: "In the beginner's mind there are many possibilities, in the expert's mind there are few." I always loved that gentle reminder that if you are open and fully present in the moment, you can be rewarded with new eyes to see familiar things in a new way. That gift provides the opportunity for new insights, emotions, and lessons.

Consider the experience of climbing a spiral staircase. As you climb, you continue to see the same scenery. However, it really isn't the same because each time you look around, you are at a different place on the stairs. You may be seeing the same things, but you are now seeing them from a fresh angle. Observed from a different spot, an object or experience might just reveal an entirely new facet, never seen before. Our lives are like that. So often we find ourselves being brought back to similar memories or experiences, confronting the same issues again and again. We sometimes chastise ourselves with messages like "It's done with, so get over it." Yet the truth is, life is not a straight line. It's not a matter of "experience something, check it off the list, and move on." Instead of berating ourselves for what seems like a failing, might it not be better to welcome the revisiting of the topic as a gift we are being offered? We could celebrate the chance to look again and extract a new meaning from that different vantage point. Those meanings allow us to *grow*. So, it is life's gift to us—if we are open and willing to take another look.

The CW mission statement, "That the Future May Learn from the Past," captures these concepts perfectly. Sometimes mission statements sound forced or sterile, rendered in emotionless corporate-speak. But in CW's case, their statement powerfully nails these ideas. And that is the truth whether you are talking about life or a vacation.

For me, that fateful garden tour I described in the previous chapter—"Someday Finally Arrives"—made me reflect more on all areas of my life; on my attitude in approaching life's experiences. In considering my future through my past, I started to ask myself—"What had I been missing...and why?" Catalyzed by a tour in a place I'd been to so many times before, I found new insights and the path to my future. So, then I began to ask myself what else could CW still teach me that could inform both my present, and my future? One thing became crystal clear to me—far from my time at CW being over, it was really just beginning.

Determined to find anything else I'd been missing there, I spent some time going through all of the various flyers and pamphlets I'd collected over the years. As I flipped through the brochures, tickets, and schedules, I started to realize that all of those things were more than just pieces of paper, they were slices of my life.

I can go back to a brochure from twenty years ago, see a particular margin note I'd written on it, and suddenly I am back there. I can remember what we did on that trip, what my son was like at that age, how hot that day was, when we stopped for soda, or what mood we were in by mid-afternoon on a Wednesday. They were not just notes, but my "emotional paper-based hyperlinks"— a direct connection to a moment frozen in time in my brain and forever stored in my heart.

For example, scrawled across the top of the June 10-16, 1998 Visitor's Companion (the weekly schedule of events) was: "Monday— five p.m. Dinner at King's Arms; Tuesday—five p.m. Campbell's Tavern." I saw that last note and remembered that *that* was the year we *finally* got to eat at Christiana Campbell's Tavern for dinner. Since my teens, I had wanted to eat there, but every time we'd been there before, we always hit it so that Campbell's Tavern was closed. It was either being restored, or was just not open to the public that day. But there on that flyer from Tuesday, June 11, 1998, was the proof that we *finally* made it there! It only took me until age forty-three to get there!

Then there were the 1983 yellowed newspaper ads for a bus trip, as well as an Amtrak "Weekend Escape" to CW. They were from shortly after I had moved out on my own. It was obvious that I had desperately wanted to visit CW, but having just bought a condo, I couldn't afford it. I could almost feel the ache when I looked at those ads with each Williamsburg trip entry circled in red but never acted on.

Moving forward, there was a 2002 visit to CW that focused on the gunsmith, the armoury, and the Magazine because my son was doing a middle-school project on Revolutionary War arms. And in 2007 we'd made *five* trips, because my son was checking out a local university that he later attended. On each piece of paper were preserved the lists of places we visited and with them, the memories of the emotions I felt. As I went through each trip's mementos, I started to realize just how much my visits to CW, and the milestones of my life, were intertwined.

Coming back to the present, I discovered there were a number of things I had brushed off as not worth it, when I was younger. For example, I'd never really spent time wandering backyard gardens practicing macro photography with my camera. Nor in those days, had I ever thought about setting up my oil painting easel in the street to paint. The DeWitt Wallace Decorative Arts Gallery and the Abby Aldrich Rockefeller Folk Art Museum both went unvisited because I thought they would be boring. How wrong I had been to be so short-sighted. I had a lot of catching up to do. So, I had my work cut out for me on future trips.

In thinking through all of this, I also realized that maybe one of the most important things I'd missed in my previous visits was the people who worked there. Why were they there? Had I ever stopped to talk to them? Listen to them? Why did they labor at CW to teach generation after generation of visitors about the past? There was no doubt that their passion fulfilled that mission statement. But maybe that the mission statement didn't just refer to some "abstract" future out there somewhere, but also to the real future in our own hearts. By exploring CW in a much more emotional way, by talking to those people, and observing their dedication, I started to ask myself more and more questions—and along the way discovered new things not just about history, but also about myself. It was those devoted staffers who were the midwives for those discoveries.

The stories I will share in the next few chapters are about some specific people and things that really engaged me. Maybe my choice of who or what I focus on now speaks less about them and more about who I am or who I've become. And maybe now my visits call me to recognize and connect with kindred spirits. No matter what, I think it is in these people's stories that I grow closer to truly understanding CW and its role in my life.

CHAPTER ELEVEN

....

CW HAD A LITTLE LAMB

Spring, 2016

I stood under the canopy of the store at the Colonial Nursery, look-ing over all the books and items on display. I desperately wanted *something* from there to take home with me, a cherished keepsake of a perfect spring day during an absolutely lovely visit. I really didn't need any garden tools, though years of gardening gave me an appreciation of solid-handled shovels and hoes. The clay bottle bird-houses were a delight, but frankly I had nowhere to hang one.

Picking up a small, thin, paper-covered tan booklet bound with twine, I flipped through the pages. Page five caught my eye:

"Though Sheep are the most beneficial Creatures we can raise, they affording us both Food and Raiment, yet there is no dumb Creature taken so little Notice of in Virginia as they; ...I hope it will not be taken amiss if I here give the Readers my Opinion how to manage their Sheep to have more in Number, with finer Wool, and larger Fleeces, than is at present got from the common Flocks."

The entry was from the book—A *Treatise on the Propagation of Sheep*, by John Wily, 1765. I felt immediately angry with the author and protective of the sheep. Maybe it's that early memory of watching sheep trotting up the street when I was a child staying at the Orlando Jones House that makes them extra special to me. I just didn't like him referring to the sheep as "dumb creatures." While I love all animals at CW and am so grateful they take such good care of their livestock, at the end of the day, it's the sight of their small lambs in the spring learning to nibble on buttercups and hopping around in a grass pasture that really melts my heart. In fact, our visit that week was perfectly timed, coinciding with their annual Lamb Week!

Just two days earlier a set of female twin lambs were born and CW was even soliciting suggestions for names. Hoping to get a glimpse of them, we hustled down to one of the nearby fields. However, instead of just two lambs, we found ourselves staring at *many* new arrivals, so it was impossible to tell who was who. It didn't matter though. They were all just so incredibly sweet and peaceful—some nursing, one sleeping, and others curled up against a sun-warmed brick wall in the middle of the pasture.

CW is very picky with their precious babies. These lambs are part of the Rare Breeds Program, the CW effort I spoke about in the earlier chapter—How Do They Do It? Their focus is the preservation of older, more genetically diverse breeds, not just for historical accuracy, but to prevent the loss of those animals through extinction.

The newborn lambs are kept with their moms at the horse stable for a short time after birth. That allows the staff to evaluate the babies' health, behavior, and physical strength, in addition to how well the lambs and the moms are bonding. If they don't bond for whatever reason and the mother rejects the baby, the staff will take on full-time duties to raise the lambs.

Once the babies meet certain criteria and get all their vaccinations, they are released into the pasture to join the rest of the flock. The CW blog, http://makinghistorynow.com/, has a number of good entries about their sheep, including how they are raised, who was born recently, and stories of special ones, like Edmund.

Edmund was born with a birth defect to his leg and rejected by his first-time mother, who sensed something was wrong with him. About half the weight of a normal infant lamb and unable to stand up, it was quickly obvious he would need special care. The CW staff became his "surrogate Mom," and they all took turns bottle-feeding him and caring for him at night in their homes. This care included exercise, snuggles, mopping up messes, and of course, two a.m. feedings.

The vet discovered that the affected leg had weak muscles around a leg joint and splinted it, which allowed Edmund to begin to stand and walk, thus strengthening the leg. Later, he began physical therapy and eventually was able to walk, run, and hop without the cast. He did have a limp but his spunky personality was not to be deterred. With his personable nature, he was on his way to becoming one of the "wethers," a group of castrated male sheep who visit with the public daily on their walks to and from Market Square. Spirited, personable ambassadors, they interact with people and highlight the essential work of the Rare Breeds program.

Unfortunately, it was not to be. CW's Facebook page put out an announcement that shows just how much heart all of those people have. "*In the past three months, Edmund was surrounded by love and had the best life we could give him. He put up quite a fight and appeared to be getting stronger as he learned to be a sheep with all his other lamb friends. But yesterday, he succumbed to those internal complications from birth that ended up causing more damage than we knew. Our thoughts are with our Coach & Livestock family tonight. Rest in peace little Edmund.*"

Reading that, you just know those people were heartbroken. Looking at the pictures of Edmund I could see he was well loved and, though his life was short, the Coach & Livestock staff made it a blessing. To them, it's not just a job, it's family. If you want to see pictures of him with the staff, here is a link: http://makinghistorynow.com/?s=edmund

As for these sheep, they are a breed known as Leicester Longwools. They have a very shiny wool that is considered a "Cadillac" variety. They are bred in the fall and early winter, with lambs arriving between February and May. Most seem to be born during March and April, hence our luck in visiting during Lamb Week.

The breeding methods involve a blend of Mother Nature and science. About fifteen-twenty ewes from CW's flock are bred each year, and most are fathered by CW rams. In September and October, groups of four-six ewes are selectively matched with a male after pedigree records are reviewed. The group spends a couple of months together and then the ram is removed. A second "clean-up" ram may be matched with them in December or January if the staff feel the first male did not mate with the ewes. In the past, artificial insemination was used to bring in new genetic material from flocks in England, New Zealand, and Australia, and this may be used again in the future.

Their wool has a variety of uses at CW, depending on the amount and quality. A young sheep can yield about six-eight pounds of the fluffy material vs an adult that may yield fifteen. The final yield will be less because the wool needs to be cleaned of dirt and lanolin, the oily substance that protects sheep from wet weather. This is removed by washing the wool with either water or water and a mild soap. Old recommendations also include washing the sheep before shearing then housing them in a grassy field, which would help pull out the lanolin.

Soft wool from young lambs is used for things close to the skin, such as socks and hats. The wool on the various parts of a sheep's body has different consistencies, with the rougher types on the legs. Coarse varieties can be used for jackets, blankets, or rugs, while higher quality types can be made into yarns of different weights for knitting, embroidery or needlepoint.

At CW, the wool is used in a variety of locations and trade shops. The Printer uses some of the wool as stuffing in the leather "dabbers" or ink-ball pads—the wooden-handled pads that spread ink onto the presses. Milliners puff up embroidery with wool and make pin cushions from it as well. The lore on this last item was that supposedly the lanolin in the wool prevented pins from rusting. Some wool is used for cushioning saddles, but the bulk of it, in the range of seventy pounds per year, goes to the weaver's shop where it is spun, dyed, and woven into fabric. CW sells some of the wool in skeins for visitors who may want to knit their own items. They also sell woven rugs.

During our stay, we visited the sheep pasture a number of times. I never got tired of watching them. Apparently, that sentiment is shared by a few thousand other visitors—clusters of people constantly lining the fences, phone cameras out and clicking away. For their part, the lambs are oblivious. Though the moms have one eye on us as they graze, their babies are too busy hopping, running, bumping into each other, and "pretending" to graze. It is not actually a pretense so much as early nibbling practice. They get their nourishment from their mother's milk for a number of weeks, only gradually switching to grasses over the next four-six weeks as they are able to chew their cud.

So, about those two twin lambs who needed names? We never did see them specifically, but we did learn that they were named after their "mother"—not the ewe who gave birth to them, but to the woman who has been a second mom to over 470 lambs over thirty years, Elaine Shirley.

As the supervisor of CW's Rare Breeds Program, Elaine Shirley manages the flock of about fifty sheep, including all pregnant and nursing ewes, and their babies. She has been around livestock all her life, growing up on a dairy farm. She is one of those devoted staff members who makes sure all of their four-legged charges get the care, feeding, comfort, and love they need. So, one lamb is now named Elaine, and the other is Shirley.

Unlike John Wily's statement above about sheep being dumb creatures receiving no attention, CW views their sheep as neither dumb, nor something to ignore. Instead they are nurtured, protected, and treated as the valuable gems they are, CW's investment in the future of the breed and of the historic town itself. It is obvious that the people make all the difference in the experience there—for both the sheep and for me. I revel in seeing the love and devotion they shower on all their animals; the heartfelt ethic they each carry as they go above and beyond their "required" job hours to ensure that the animals are well-cared for. They take on the impossible when an animal is sickly, and won't give up. For them, that CW mission statement drives them on and comes alive in all they do.

I did end up buying Wily's booklet on sheep, not because I agreed with the author, but because having it reminds me every day that there are precious people at CW who prove his words wrong each and every day.

CHAPTER TWELVE

....

THE VOICE OF CW

Spring, 2016
The lobby of the Williamsburg Lodge bustled with people coming and going but I was oblivious to them. Sitting across the table from the man, I tried to take in everything about him at once. Some things stood out right away. There were the striking, translucent blue eyes, lively, and accented with a twinkle that suggested an abiding love of mischief and a good joke. Then there were the easy, fluid movements, and the bearing that implied he felt very comfortable in his skin. These were coupled with a quick, broad smile that gave way to a deep, hearty laugh. But it was the voice—like liquid velvet with the cultured smoothness of a fine Scotch—that confirmed for me whose presence I was in.

Here before me, in living, breathing color was the man himself...the "Voice of CW," as we knew him, the man whose voice we heard on the bus announcements every time we came to CW.

As I watched him, I flashed back to a particular summer morning in 1995. The annual passes bounced on our chests as we headed for the staircase at the end of the Visitor Center. The morning fatigue evaporated at the sight of the gray bus waiting outside. My pace quickened as well as my heart rate. No matter how old I got, that particular moment was always the same—a flood of joy and excitement accompanied by an overwhelming impatience to board the bus and get going! We took the seats right across of the back-exit door—our first choice so as to be first off of the bus. People crowded in, some polite, some noisy, some pushing. But the excitement was palpable. After what seemed an eternity, the tone of the motor shifted, the doors closed, and the vehicle lurched forward. I closed my eyes and waited for it. 3...2...1...and then:

> *"This bus is going to Colonial Williamsburg 's Historic Area,*
> *the Restored capital of 18th-century Virginia..."*

The recording crackled as we headed out from the Visitor Center to the first stop in the Historic area:

> *"Among the hundreds of restored and reconstructed buildings*
> *on the mile-long Historic Area you will find over forty exhibit*
> *sites ranging from colonial homes and government buildings,*
> *to trade shops and museums..."*

My eyes still shut, I silently mouthed the words of that next, very special, oft-repeated line:

> *"Each day...the Historic Area c-o-m-e-s alive..."*

From that point on I was deaf to whatever else was being said. I heard what I wanted—the line I waited for *every single time* we returned had just been spoken. That line was etched in our minds and hearts, and those words always marked for us, the *true* beginning of our vacation there.

Why make such a big deal out of seven words? In that recording, the man had a distinct and passionate delivery to those words. His intensity, coupled with the unique inflection on the phrase "c-o-m-e-s alive" just made it seem like he was as excited about being in CW as we were. And so it was that this line became the magical moment we waited for every time we visited. It was the constant of every trip—the signal that *now*, our vacation could officially begin. That greeting always generated a level of excitement in the pit of my stomach because it felt like we were now "home." We didn't know who the man was, so he just came to be known to us as the Voice of CW.

For years, I wondered "Who was he? What kind of person could so infuse those seven little words—'Each day, the Historic Area comes alive'—with all the excitement and promise that CW holds?" Whoever he was, the man was a rock star to me. Time and again I would hear that voice and just wish I could sit down and chat with him—hear how he came to do this, and basically let him know just what his recording had meant to us. With the writing of this book, that wish resurfaced.

Maybe it's also a thing that comes with age—a realization suddenly crystalizes about how precious something has been to you, and you are filled with an appreciation that must be shared. *Things don't last forever; nor do people.* Saying "thank you" before the opportunity is lost becomes important. So, I decided to find him...or at least try. Surely there had to be a way. Somebody had to know who he was.

I love the internet because you can start almost anywhere with a first search term, and go from idea to idea until you find your quarry. So, I began with the John D. Rockefeller Jr. Library's website (http://research.history.org/library/), moved on to CW's Corporate Archives and Records department, and left a message explaining as best as I could—while trying not to sound too weird—what I was seeking. It worked. The very next day, I was contacted by a CW Foundation audio producer and sound supervisor who, though admitting my question was a "head-scratcher," thought he might know who it could be. He emailed me a short sound recording and one listen to it had me 99% convinced it was him. However, the day after that, I received the email that clinched it all:

Dear Deb,

I was the voice on the bus for over 20 years. I would be happy to talk to you.

It was like hearing that not only was there a Santa Claus, but he would actually meet you, or getting the long-sought answer, "Yes," to "Dr. Livingston, I presume?" I had found my rock star! I was so excited, I told everyone I knew that I'd found the man behind the CW bus recordings. Most were happy for me; a few expressed pleased surprise. Even those who had never been to CW politely congratulated me, or at least smiled in quiet amusement. All I kept saying was, "You have to understand. He was *the voice* on the *bus!*" Maybe it was all the more important to me because in recent years CW had replaced him with a variety of others to do the bus recordings, none of which have yet to match the original voice.

If I thought that email response was wonderful, what came in the next one far surpassed anything I could have hoped for:

I have checked my calendar, and I am available to meet with you at any time on the morning of Friday, April 8. I can come over to the Lodge, and we can chat for as long as you wish. Hope this is convenient, and I look forward to meeting you.

I can forego meeting presidents. Seeing a queen pass by in a parade, while nice, I can also give up. But to meet the man behind the CW bus recordings, now *that* is a lifelong gift! We agreed to meet in the lobby of the Williamsburg Lodge at eleven a.m. on

Friday during our coming CW visit. It would be the highlight of our time there and I could hardly wait. I had to force myself to even consider what I would ask him. Just to shake his hand and say, "thank you," would be amazing. To sit there and hear his story would be golden. What I experienced was a glimpse into the soul of a person whose work has been his life's mission—a life reveled in through good, honest work, and the true joy that work brings, a person who *definitely* lived that mission statement each and every day of his many years at CW.

The voice's, or rather, the man's name was John Hamant. His career at CW started in 1977 and he stayed there for nearly forty years. If you search for him online, you'll find the unmistakable footprints of a person entirely dedicated to history, including his own IMDb entry, listing such works as *Founders or Traitors?* and *Washington: Man and Myth*. There are also a number of news articles discussing his portrayal of various historical figures over the years.

From the moment we met, I immediately felt at ease. As we were waiting for him, my husband had asked me how I would know when he arrived. For a moment, I panicked—I hadn't a clue! I realized I had totally forgotten to arrange any kind of signal; I had no "I will be wearing a blue jacket" cue to help me identify the man I'd heard, but never saw, over decades of bus rides. Would he be formal and in a jacket and tie? If so, I was substantially underdressed, as we had already been out hiking the Historic Area. Would he be shy, and not talkative? For a moment, I kicked myself, then just shrugged. I somehow sensed that, when the time came, I would instinctively recognize him.

Right on time, I saw a gentleman stride into the lobby, with that look of "I wonder if they are here yet?" Neither hurried, nor worried, he just amiably crossed the room. He was dressed how I would prefer: Flannel shirt. Fleece jacket. Comfortable. I am a jeans-and-T-shirt sort of person, or flannel, if the weather is cold, so my hope was that this was the man.

I came up behind him and asked, "Are you John?" He whirled around, smiled, and asked, "Deb?" The voice, the handshake, the smile—it all confirmed that my instincts had been correct. I introduced my husband, we sat at the table, and from there the conversation unfolded with an ease that confirmed that *this* was the sort of person who would do enthusiastic bus recordings for twenty years, and do it as a labor of love.

Sitting there, I had to keep reminding myself to catch all the details. I was just in awe of that voice. Descriptive words ran through my mind—liquid, flowing, velvety, resonant, and rich. Images, too: dark chocolate, Grade A maple syrup, and lovingly-aged Scotch. I could have listened to his voice all day.

As we talked, he laughed often, and deeply. He seemed to enjoy his life and appeared to walk easily through it. Apologizing for the length of his hair, he mentioned he was currently performing as Benjamin Franklin in a number of different venues. He shared that the other character he frequently portrayed was President Franklin Delano Roosevelt. With one look, it made perfect sense. Instantly assuming the FDR-esque pose and flawless upper-crust accent, he finished with a full laugh that came right out of a 1940s newsreel.

One of the first things I'm always curious about when I meet someone is how and why they ended up doing what they did. What path does one follow that ends with doing voiceovers on a bus and spending their days as Ben Franklin or FDR? What do you put on a resume or job application for that? As he described it, Hamant started out "as a kid from Baltimore." His college degree was in theater, and he did some work in radio as well. His masters' degree was in acting and directing, and his other love was history. When he returned home, he decided to take a year off to figure out "what next?"

Staying at his parents' rural Maryland property, he taught himself surveying, traced the history of the property back to the original land grants, and developed an interest in historical archaeology. The property next door had an old foundation where he spent many hours digging up specimens with his garden trowel and figuring out what they were. Looking for a more systematic approach to the project, he sought out books on historical archaeology methods. In doing so, he came across books written by Ivor Noël Hume, the head of archaeology at a place called Colonial Williamsburg. Detailed and instructive about archaeological methods, the books were also engaging and hard to put down.

Finding those books must have been fate, because after reading them, Hamant wrote to Noël Hume and asked for a job. Hamant was up-front with him and admitted he had no training and knew little about the subject. But he wanted to learn and was willing to push a wheelbarrow around. Noël Hume hired him at three dollars an hour. Hamant spent his time in the blistering sun, scraping over the hard clay and hauling dirt. He lived in a dorm room in the old CW Annex, along with about forty waiters for the various CW restaurants. It was not a path to riches, but as Hamant puts it, he expected to be there for six months, and then move on. Instead, he fell in love with the place. Within four years, he was senior archaeologist for the CW Foundation.

At that point, he was ready for a change. Returning to his theatrical roots, he began working at CW as a costumed character-interpreter on the street. He played a number of different roles, including that of CW's first Mr. Greenhow—the owner of the Greenhow store on Duke of Gloucester Street. In a 2007 CW podcast, *Playing the Part*, Hamant described the process that goes into portraying a historical figure (in this case, Benjamin Franklin):

"You try to get inside the mind of the man, if that is indeed possible, and to humanize him. To discover his motivations, his thoughts, his fears, and his hopes for his own life, for America, for his fellow citizens. I think you add to that the spice: his incredible humor, his wry wit, his politically incorrect statements on occasion."

He went on to note that doing this work:

"...is part of the magic of what we do, and why it's such a privilege to do it. It's putting the skin on these people, and showing, I think, communicating the emotional turmoil that they go through in making these decisions. We all know how it comes out, obviously. But there was turmoil. There was indecision. There was second-guessing...To show that, instead of these icons that we have in the history text, I think that makes an emotional connection to present-day audiences. People haven't changed. We still love, we still hate, we still lust, we covet—all of those things."

In January of 1984 he moved into management as Manager of the Company of Colonial Performers. The Company did numerous programs around CW. His job title eventually evolved into Manager of Evening and Special Programs, a position he held for eight years.

Finally, it was time for another change; he wanted a new challenge. His wish was granted in the form of "Director of Special Events and Protocol Officer" at CW. It was by no means a nine-to-five job; he was on call twenty-four/seven, always ready to plan for visiting dignitaries and escort them around. But it became quite an adventure, and also led to his role as "the voice."

Even though voice recordings were not a part of his protocol job, he had voice experience from his time in radio and theater.

Add to that the fact that he had "location"—his office for Special Events and Protocol was on the first floor of CW's corporate headquarters in The Goodwin Building, and the AV department was one floor below in the basement. The AV group and Hamant knew each other well, so whenever the AV folks needed a voiceover done, they would call him and ask if he had five minutes to record a tape. He would finish whatever he was doing, and then head downstairs to record.

"It was difficult in those days, because being in the basement of the Goodwin building, it wasn't as controlled acoustically, as the studio over at Bruton Heights. And so you would start recording something and you would get halfway through the paragraph and a bus would go by. The rumble of the bus is in the background and you would say 'cut, cut' and ...do it again!"

In spite of those acoustical difficulties, he always delivered an impassioned and perfect recording. It was a role he would perform for over 20 years. Hamant joked about the far-reaching effect all his voiceovers probably had. "I often bet people that I have talked to more visitors to CW than any other employee." I suspect he was correct.

Hamant spent the next eight years in his position as protocol officer. In that time, he met a wide range of dignitaries and foreign heads of state as well as worked with the Secret Service and White House staff. It was a very, very detail-oriented position and he was often teased about the fourteen-page operations plans he would draft for each visit. The lead Secret Service Agent on one state visit asked him if a degree in theater was any help in such a job. The response was pure John Hamant: "Absolutely. Well, if nothing else, I can act like I know what the hell is going on!" That quality helped too because even with all the planning, as he put it, "you can write it all down, but once the event starts you just better fasten your seat belts…"

In talking of those times, he spoke of it all with a kind of detached amazement and humility:

> "You know, you grow up a kid in Baltimore, and you never imagine you would see a president live and in person, and I've got my picture with four of them and spent time with all of them. How many people can say 'Oh yeah, I took the Queen of Norway in my own car up to Merchant's Square to go shopping?' … I've been to the White House many, many times, in fact I got offered a job at the White House…which I obviously did not take…but it's an honor to be asked. I've toured Blair House from attic to basement more times than I can count. It's just a privilege to have those opportunities…a kid from Baltimore." Hamant added that someone suggested he should write a book, (a view I concur with completely) but he brushed that thought aside with a humble "Naw, nobody would read it."

I have to say that I strongly disagree with him on that point!

He retired from full time employment in the fall of 2002, but stayed on for several years as a part-time regular employee. He worked as a performer, director, and writer for such projects as RevQuest (taking on that role of Benjamin Franklin in a video for that program), educational outreach trips for teacher training, and Electronic Field Trips and podcasts. I even spotted him "locked in the stocks" next to the courthouse, in an ad for the CW Foundation's investment donation program. He also had the flexibility at that point to work on some of his own projects. He wrote many of the stories for the *Ghosts Amongst Us* evening program, coached and directed all its storytellers, and participated in the DeWitt Wallace Art Museum's murder mystery program. That flexibility also allowed him to travel to do his own programming, performing as Benjamin Franklin and FDR in venues around the country.

One particular favorite creation of his was a program he developed and led, called the *Before and After Tour*. It was set in Williamsburg at the end of its golden age (about 1780) to the beginning of restoration in 1927. The focus was on the things that happened during the years Williamsburg was in the background— neither the Colonial capital, nor the present-day tourist attraction. At its core, the emphasis of the program was Williamsburg as a real town.

"That for me is the magic. I tell people on the tour. If you had enough money you could recreate everything that's here in an old orange grove in Florida, but, this is the real place..." He shared stories and pictures of the town from over the years. "In 1918 when World War I ended, they had a big fair, a celebration in Market Square. There's a picture of a French tank, a World War I tank..." For him, this tour had a lot of his heart in it. As he emphasized, Williamsburg has been through it all. "What happened in America happened here. People have laughed and cried and exalted and mourned here for over 300 years."

In keeping with the theme of Williamsburg as a living, breathing town, Hamant discussed the challenge of resolving the tension of time. "CW is a Colonial town, to be sure, but one set in the 21st century. As such, there are always questions of when to allow the present day to creep in, and when to keep things true to CW's 18th-century setting."

He noted that on the one hand, CW strives to be true to its roots. So, there is an increased focus in giving people the physical 'touchstone' items or takeaways—something they can see, feel, and hold—as well as the visceral experiences that connect them to that time back then. The return of activities like the candle-making craft, for example, are:

> *"a memory for a lot of people...they're going back to a lot of the...solid links to this place that evoke memories...the take-aways. I think that's vitally important to bringing future generations back. This is a private institution. We get no state or federal money. It's from people buying tickets, and buying the products, touring the buildings, being in the restaurants, and staying in the hotels."*

On the other hand, CW also strives to make visits welcoming by introducing some modern elements. Halloween's *"Haunting on DoG St.: Blackbeard's Revenge"* was the most recent example. People registered in advance to participate in either the early evening programs for young families or the later evening events for older kids and adults. Family-friendly activities included games, pumpkin-decorating, pirate songs, costume contests, and free Trick-or-Treating at various locations along Duke of Gloucester Street. Older ages participated in *Under Blackbeard's Flag*, which included haunted Gaol cells, games, gravediggers and zombie pirate crews marching down Duke of Gloucester Street. CW even offered the Blackbeard's Revenge Vacation Package, which included all Haunting on DoG Street activities, a two-night stay at one of their hotels, a one-hundred-dollar activity card to use in shops and restaurants, and Bounce Passes to use at the Busch Gardens Halloween event nearby.

Hamant favored these approaches, because they bring modern audiences to the historic town and affirmed his opinion that CW must be a living town. As he said this, it occurred to me that CW's mission statement—That the future may learn from the past—implied this very thing. The statement says to *learn* from the past, *not become* the past. If the latter were true, then there would be no air-conditioning or heat, no light bulbs, or electricity for computer-operated checkout stations. And if that were true we'd all be using chamber pots on our visits, not rest rooms. So *relevance* to the future is the goal, not blind mimicry of the past.

It's obvious that everything in his background—his passions, interests, theater, and radio training—all came together in a perfect mix to make him the man for the job. Add to this his management skills, and easy, competent style, and it was an exquisitely balanced blend. He summed up his life's work in a style that was pure John Hamant.

"I've been very lucky...I've said that to people readily. I was being interviewed by somebody once, and they said 'Well how would you describe your career?' I was sort of taken aback and I started laughing...they said 'What are you laughing about?' And I said 'Well I just realized I've never had one. Because a career is you go from A to B to C to D to E and it's... charted out. And I was just lucky enough to be able to do a lot of interesting, challenging things.'"

Without missing a beat, he then offered his thoughts on why someone would do this sort of job in the first place:

"One of the important things, and I try to stress this to people, it's why people work here. I was only going to be here six months, quite frankly, and at the end of the six months I said to myself, 'This is my life's mission, my life's work. I'll never get rich at it. It's like teaching, it fills the heart. It's noble work. I've always felt that."

With regards to how employees view working at CW, Hamant said:

"It's pride of place. It's generational ... My wife's worked here...forty years. My mother-in-law is retired from here. Our daughter is a manager in the products division here."

In fact, CW is where Hamant met his wife.

Hamant's comments confirmed what I'd read in CW's blog—working here can be a generational thing. It seems to get in your blood. I had read about various employees who started here as children or young adults and stayed on. Often, their parents or cousins or other relatives were here as well. Hamant mentioned one employee, Preston Jones, who worked at the Silversmith's, noting that Jones' dad worked here, and his grandfather before him worked here as well. People love their work and stay. As Hamant put it, "It's what we do."

Throughout the interview, which went by far too quickly, Hamant displayed an ease that I suspect comes from being comfortable in one's own skin...knowing oneself, and being satisfied with that. He just seems like a person with nothing to prove. The joy from loving his life and his work just flowed out as relaxed satisfaction. Even when I asked to take his picture, he was totally okay with that. Most people when asked the same question immediately smooth their hair, struggle for just the right smile, or check themselves to see if they look presentable. He was simply totally relaxed about it and never even worried about his appearance. He was just "himself" and it showed in his smile.

He said he had no plans to slow down. "As long as I can do it I'm going to keep doing it." In typical John Hamant humor, though, he did offer a thought on how he could make his "final" exit. His eyes twinkled again as he spoke:

"*Years ago, we did a recreation of Lord Botetourt's funeral, with the coffin...and the masons...and the whole procession up to the college, and I said the last program I will ever do here is when you recreate Botetourt's funeral again. You can put me in the box...*"

I am sad to say, this did not occur, though he would have fully deserved the pomp-and-ceremony. Yesterday, as I revised this chapter, I learned of his untimely death at sixty-eight. I was and will always be both heartbroken, and thankful; heartbroken because I will never get to see those eyes or hear that voice again in this life, nor will anyone else. I was deeply thankful though, that I had had the opportunity to meet him once, speak to him, and convey to him just how very much we loved his work, and most especially his greetings on the bus whenever we visited. Our son basically grew up hearing him on every bus ride.

So, I am sad but grateful, and I will never forget him, his graciousness, his peacefulness, and his generosity. While he did not get to do Lord Botetourt's funeral procession, I was pleased to read that his final service was being held at Bruton Parish Church. Very fitting. So, to you, John Ross Hamant, I wish you farewell, and thank you. You were the very epitome of CW, and there is no question in my mind that you spent every bit of your time there, living out the words of that mission statement. Thank you, John. RIP.

CHAPTER THIRTEEN

....

A SLAVE'S LIFE

Summer, 2017

I sat on the bench near the outdoor stage behind Charlton's Coffeehouse. Waiting for the program to begin, I read over the play's description again: *Journey to Redemption: Telling the story of enslaved people takes commitment and a calling. Through music, dance, and revelation, witness the conflicting emotions and challenges experienced by our actor-interpreters who portray the enslaved and enslavers.*

Challenges indeed. I pondered the actors who did these programs. This was not mere historical interpretation. The roles they each chose to assume were not easy ones. It was one thing to portray a rich plantation owner or his wife, living in relative luxury. But to take up the role of an enslaved African American every single day, day after day, and willingly step into a role filled with pain? How does one do that and stay sane? And were these new programs or had they always been going on and I just missed it? I hoped the latter was not true.

The topic was at the front of my mind as I had just bought a book that morning from the bookstore in the Visitor Center— *The Art and Soul of African American Interpretation* by Dr. Ywone Edwards-Ingram. It had caught my attention because it was the first time I'd ever seen a book on that topic. I'd seen some on general historical interpretation, but never from the viewpoint of the African American interpreters. I bought the book and planned to read it soon. Maybe it was the heightened awareness from the book that had brought this show to my attention. Perhaps I could find answers to my questions in both the play and the book.

People had been assembling at the performance site and at that moment I spotted the characters approaching. They all walked slowly, eyes straight ahead, as if their focus was somewhere very far away. Two actors were white and three were black. With the exception of the white man with the fine clothes and aristocratic bearing, the rest were dressed in humble clothes. They took their positions on stage and stood motionless for a moment, then began.

They portrayed their station in life through their monologues—each in their turn. It was a staccato performance, one person would speak, then another would cut in, rapidly revealing their stories. They alternated, black with white, aristocrat with enslaved. And while one spoke, the others would strike a pose as a sort of living backdrop. One character, Jack Booker, strode forward and demanded in flawless diction, "Why not *my* signature on that paper? *My* own name? ...instead of some master?" The enslaved character Roger spoke with hostile defiance, each word a verbal punch. Another character, Mingo, let everyone know that he would have been a carpenter even if his enslaver had never told him to be one because he *knew* he had the soul of a master craftsman.

Lydia Broadnax and Mrs. Wager, one black, one white, brought a softness to the performances. The former grieved at being childless—her husband refusing to bring a child into the world of the enslaved, while Mrs. Wager despised the forces in society that made slavery possible. She diligently taught the "Negro slave children" in her care in the hope that someday, those lessons might be the rock in the pond whose ripples would extend far beyond her view.

In stark contrast was the authoritative, almost calculatingly cold attitude of the wealthy Mr. Prentis. He emphatically declared that each slave had a function and should fulfill it, and the only reason he did not break up the families of his enslaved people was because it was the best way to have them accept their condition and do their duties.

It was at this point that all the actors stopped, took a collective breath, then switched back to their 21st-century selves—actors playing difficult and even detestable roles. For the black actors, there was the challenge of portraying an ugly reality every day in their jobs. For the white actor who portrayed Mr. Prentis, he railed against the demands of his role. He felt people's rage, as well as his own pain. These were his real-life friends and co-workers, yet if he were to make this performance a powerful message against slavery, he had to treat them in a repugnant manner. More powerful though, than any of their words, was how they looked as they spoke—faces taut, teeth gritted, and eyes pained. Their emotions with each other ranged from playfulness and hope, to weariness and sorrow. The program ended with the opportunity to speak to the actors about their work and the sense of emotional drain was evident in all. I thanked them for their work, and expressed my sorrow, both for what their predecessors endured, and for what they, now, willingly chose to go through each day.

After the performance, I walked in silence for a bit trying to process everything I felt. Emotionally, I was drained. If that was how I felt, how much more drained were the performers? Questions continued to gnaw at me.

Stopping for a snack at one of the refreshment stands, I thought again about the new book on African American historical interpretation waiting for me back in my hotel room. For sure I was going to have to start reading it that very night. But in the meantime, I was anxious for some answers.

I pulled out my cell phone and searched for articles related to the topic. A Washington Post article spoke to the difficulty of finding people to do that work. It quoted then CW African American initiatives manager Tricia Brooks, who noted that putting on that costume came "with a lot of baggage." If one hadn't unpacked that baggage before taking on such a role they were going to have problems. Her comments were mirrored by the current CW Senior Manager of African American Programming, Stephen Seals, who agreed that "It's not for everyone." Yet that night when I started reading the book I noticed that the six interpreters featured in it spoke of wearing "those clothes" with pride, and that they felt no shame because that was the truth of the history. Interpreter Emily James even spoke of feeling the strength of her African American ancestors' blood in her veins.

As to why they did it, each of the interpreters spoke of a higher goal, of finding a way to connect, engage, and then educate. They were there to start the conversation of how to make racial issues better. A number of them viewed performing as a sacred responsibility, or as an obligation to share the history. James Ingram Jr., in the book, said that interpreting was a mission, "almost a calling." If you can connect, you can possibly change a mind, even a little. And that small start was still a victory.

Several noted it could be an uphill battle at times trying to educate a very diverse audience. Art Johnson told how he was asked during one of his programs if his master was a good master. He turned the question into one for deeper thought. "If he is so good a master, would he still own you? He can't be but so good a master if he still owns you." Some visitors needed help to gain a new understanding. They may have attended the program still carrying with them some long-held, entrenched belief that was challenged by the new information presented. Rose McAphee, a training specialist and interpreter instructor, said that mediation skills are very helpful in situations where you might have to defend your position, and help a visitor see the reality from a new perspective. Many of the interpreters spoke of the need for great patience and humility. Progress in reaching hearts and opening minds comes, but sometimes very slowly. The key was to persist.

In the book, Greg James said that one of his toughest hurdles was interpreting for African American audiences. He spoke of seeing their eye rolls, or their resistance to learning where their ancestors had come from. Their comments and attitudes were not easy to work with. James Ingram mirrored that feeling, noting that some might accuse him of sugar-coating things, dancing around certain topics, or not sharing the horrors of that existence. But he tried to convey that even though the programs don't show profanity or violence, the actors were not giving the horror short shrift. Not all horror was physical or verbal. Not every slave faced lashings, but all of them felt the effects of their reality and the law, which meant that for their entire life they were the property of another.

To create their characters, all interpreters did extensive research. They spoke of the need for meticulous accuracy and felt a personal responsibility to get it right. No one wanted to pass on an untruth and most note that when they find new information, they change their presentation to include it. Several in the book mentioned that it takes years to reach a mastery of their work, and they never stop researching, revising, and practicing, to reveal the souls of their characters.

Even armed with that kind of determination, I still wondered how did they make it through the day? The interpreters in the book spoke to their various ways of coping. Most didn't just get out of their cars, step onto CW property, and go to work. To prepare for her day, Emily James said she clears her mind so she can become that person from the past. With that focus, she can then show how the past still applies to people's lives today. Greg James, a long-time African American interpreter at CW who has since died, talked in the book about spiritually and mentally preparing himself for his day, from the time he awoke until he set foot at CW. He observed that it took him about an hour after his day was over, to relax and return to the present. Even after that, he still carried the experience home, thinking about the people he'd met, the impressions he'd made, and considering how he might have made a difference in a visitor's day.

As I read through the book, I found myself wondering if these programs had been available all along and I had just totally missed it. When I first started going to CW in the sixties and seventies, I was young, and oblivious to the whole aspect of slavery in Colonial America. And I can't recall whether Williamsburg put much emphasis on that part of the history at the time, even though it was an important part of Williamsburg's history. That 1700s town did not have a white majority. At least half of the population was African American, and there were also a number of American Indians. That awareness fed a constant fear in the whites, of slave uprisings and of being slaughtered in one's bed. As this did at times occur, it had to be a major influencing factor on the quality of everyone's life, from enslaver to enslaved.

Unable to remember what, if anything, went on for programs in the sixties, I started digging through all my old brochures and guides when I got home from that trip. From what I could see, it wasn't until the late seventies that I could find any actual African American content and characters present in the offerings. One article I had from the Summer, 1982 issue of "Colonial Williamsburg Today" featured the work of Dr. Rex Ellis, a theatrical arts professor from Hampton Institute who had embarked on a revolutionary concept—to actively portray the life of enslaved individuals in colonial America. He did a tour called "The Other

Half," which not only worked well, but he continued to create and deliver more programs in that vein. A 1992 brochure I had listed twice-daily offerings of *The Other Half: African American Colonial Life*, as well as other African American programming each day. Some examples were: *African American Life in the Eighteenth Century; Night Walking: Evening Activities of Slaves; The Runaway; Slave Cate; and Black Music*. Each of these shone a light onto various aspects of the life of the enslaved in CW that no one had ever talked about before.

In 1994, CW's African American Department took the incredibly brave step of staging a slave auction. As the *New York Times* described on October 8, 1994, "...four blacks—two men and two women—are scheduled to be auctioned to the highest bidder. They will stand outside a tavern while a dozen people look them over and call out how much they are willing to spend." The response was strong. The Virginia NAACP protested and said people were outraged. Christy S. Coleman, the director at that time of the CW Foundation's African American Department, defended it as the natural progression of their efforts to educate. She acknowledged that the issue was fraught with sensitive and emotional themes. But she also noted that as very real history, she was distressed if people wanted that history to be kept hidden. She felt that only by openly confronting this past could people, all people, have an understanding of the degradation and humiliation endured by blacks under slavery. During the program, she had to confront protestors who broke through and she challenged them to watch and judge with honest hearts and minds. Afterward, some of those protesting had a change of heart and even retracted their objections. Others still struggled with the topic and how best to educate others about this issue.

By 1995, there were at least fifteen African American-themed programs throughout the week and in 1999, CW launched a major interpretation initiative—*Enslaving Virginia*—that put even more realistic slavery stories out there for the public. Others followed in the early 2000s with *Voices in the Bushes*, and *Liberty for Whom, Freedom from What?* They even tackled the slave auction subject again in 2009 with a program that portrayed the volatile emotional moments right before four slaves were to be sold.

I thought back to my own embryonic awareness of the topic over the years, nurtured only because of the efforts of these interpreters. I remembered spending a day in June, 1998, following one of the African American interpreters around from one spot to another as he wrestled with the question—should he risk it all and run away to Lord Dunmore's army? Or should he stay? It was an eye-opener. Intellectually, I knew running away was risky because to be caught could mean death on the spot if the wrong white person caught you. Yet to see the reality portrayed before your eyes really intensified the experience. Also, it brought up questions people often overlook. What if the enslaved man had a spouse and children? If he ran, would he ever see them again? If they all ran away together what happened if they were caught? It was a much more agonizing question that any of us realize. In that moment, following the actor as he went from enslaved person to enslaved person seeking answers, it was obvious there was no easy or set answer even among the African Americans. They had conflicting opinions on the subject. I questioned what I would have done in the same position.

After that particular program, I started to think more about what life must have been like for the enslaved in CW. I had always assumed it was a hopeless existence. Yet a recent CW podcast proved me wrong. Stephen Seals, the Senior Manager of African American Programs at CW, had some very unique observations:

"It's very important for guests, for everyone to understand just how varied the lives of the enslaved and the free blacks

of the Americas were. People were enslaved but they weren't. That wasn't what defined them...these enslaved members of society were people...They had just as much of a varied way of being, and being with each other and society, as the whites... They had a culture...a life. They had hope...victories...things to look forward to...These people survived...and that to me is a triumph ... something that needs to be celebrated."

Seals also had another strong point—that today's programming needs to be integrated, white with black. It cannot be "separate but equal." The public has to understand that while legally blacks and whites were separate, "life made them intertwined," and we all have a shared history. I thought back to my February, 2017 trip during Black History Month. We saw that goal being put into action in a number of new programs. One program demonstrated how enslaved African Americans used the Virginia court system to try and obtain their freedom. Another revealed how the various royal governors over the years actually sought out the help of free and enslaved African Americans to succeed in the New World. The program I attended on that trip was at the Peyton Randolph House—*The Job They Didn't Choose: Resistance, Community, and Healing.*

Peyton Randolph was a wealthy and prominent Williamsburg citizen, speaker of the Virginia House of Burgesses, president of the 1st Continental Congress, and the owner of many slaves. Unlike previous tours of that house, this new one did not focus on him, but spoke from the perspective of the twenty-eight-enslaved people who lived and worked there. The delivery was different from *Journey to Redemption*. It was a tour, not a dramatic performance, so there was only one person involved, our guide. Given that it was about the lives of the slaves in that household, I guess I had expected the tour to be led by an African American interpreter representing that perspective, versus a white man in colonial-style garments. Also, he was not there in any historical persona. Instead he spoke to us as a present-day guide. He brought the enslaved of that household to life by sharing some of their names and life roles. We heard about Betty, the cook; Aggie, the laundress; and Secordia, an older, infirm, enslaved woman.

His approach was unique as well. Using a "Socratic" style he would give us some information, then pepper us with questions to make us think more deeply about the situation. For example, in talking about how little time the slaves had to themselves free of their masters, he asked: "Can you think of any coping mechanisms the slaves might use in the morning to help each other get through the day?" When he raised the issue of "resistance" by the slaves, he posed more questions. "Do you think the slaves had some negotiating power...some options to get back at the Randolphs if they were upset? "What about running away? Why would a slave run given the threat of punishment?" Or he tested our awareness of what effect patriotic rebellion had on the slaves. "If boycotting English goods like soap was the patriotic thing to do, who carried the burden for that? Lack of imported articles in the stores meant more work for the slaves. No English soap? Slaves would have to add soap-making to the list of their many other jobs."

When we got to the subject of violence—by the owners against slaves and vice versa—he did something I've never seen before. He warned the group that he was about to bring up very serious and violent things. If that would upset anyone, they had the option to leave the tour right then. No one did, though, which heartened me. The questions continued. "How do you as a slaveholder deal with a lack of total obedience by the slaves?" It was a chilling concept to consider—just how far would someone go to make another "submit"? And then there were the theoretical, ethical, and legal questions: "So, who is enslaved? Can a Christian be enslaved? Can a Christian enslave another Christian? What if a slave's father was a free man? How do you prevent free blacks from helping slaves rebel?"

My husband and I talked about that particular approach versus the one used in *Journey to Redemption*. He observed that maybe a white man speaking of those things possibly gave a bit of distance for some visitors to hear and absorb the story. Furthermore, by not being "in character" as an enslaver, he also didn't become a focal point for either audience hate (by the racially sensitive) or approval (by any with opposing views). Either way, I understood the commitment these performances took and I felt tremendous gratitude for the people who put themselves in these roles every day.

Coming back around to that original question, "Why do they put themselves through this?" I think two CW staff members associated with these efforts sum it up best. CW's Stephen Seals stated in a recent interview that:

"My goal has always been to make the story of the Africans in America the story of America ... If one day the average American could look at a person that was in chains and go, 'Those are my ancestors, those are my stories,' then we can truly be one country. That's what I'm trying to do with African American programming."

And Mary Hardy Carter, assistant director for *Journey to Redemption*, wants the audience to consider the question: "Who is responsible for this mess?" By "mess" she means the history of our racial divide. The hope is that everyone will come to understand that we are all responsible and we all have to work together to fix it.

We may all have our individual pasts, but we also have a *collective* past, a *human* past, and an *American* past that affects us all. To quote Seals:

> "Those stories, those experiences, everything that happened back in that time with free people and enslaved people, all are part of what makes America what America is today. You will not be able to understand who you are or where you come from if you take that part of the story away."

So this effort is a plea to the audience to help heal the divide that still plagues us today. As Seals puts it, it is about "*making sure everyone is welcome to the table. 'The African American story is not a black story. It's an American story ... No matter what you look like, it's a story of your ancestors, it's a story of your people.'*"

CHAPTER FOURTEEN

·····································

A BUILDING OF MYSTERY

Summer, 1968

I eagerly ran forward in the direction of the Capitol building at the east end of Duke of Gloucester Street. Maybe this time it would be open! I stopped in front of the shuttered building, which was my destination. The map indicated I was at the right spot— Wetherburn's Tavern, one of the original structures in CW. Located near the Capitol, it is across the street from the Raleigh Tavern. It was also one of the most prominent businesses in 18th-century Williamsburg, second only to the Raleigh Tavern in its renown and quality. But just like our last visit three years ago, the windows were still covered with white paper, and there was that annoying little note on the map that said the building was not open to the public.

"Come on!" I grumbled. I understood on our first visit that we couldn't get in. I figured maybe they were working on it. But *still* closed, three years later? In all that time they couldn't get it open? What *were* they doing?

Aside from my frustration, I was also intrigued. The place called to me, and it positively reeked with mystery. I could sense it had a "story" behind it, and I wanted to know what it was.

I peered closely at every window, but they were sealed off well. Not a glimpse could be had of the mysterious interior.

What could be so unusual about this place to warrant keeping it closed? Was someone murdered here? Was it haunted? What was in there?!

Fast forward a few years and the building was finally open for tours. You could even explore the backyard and its out-buildings. Everything looked in order. Frustratingly normal. Benign even. There was not a trace of a clue to suggest what all of the mystery had been about. Then I came across a book, *Archaeology and Wetherburn's Tavern*, by a man named Ivor Noël Hume, and discovered my answer.

Who was Ivor Noël Hume? For thirty-one years, he was the director of CW's archaeology research program, the person who really created it, and brought it up to modern standards. He directed the digs, wrote the reports, instituted the lab procedures, and determined everything from vision to meaning. And he did all of this without ever having acquired a degree in archaeology.

He was originally from London and grew up in the bombed-out rubble of World War II. Originally, he wanted to be a playwright, but a passion for collecting historical artifacts along the shore of the River Thames turned him into what he called "an accidental archaeologist." Years of collecting bottles and working in various archaeological, museum, and public relations positions gave him considerable experience and a reputation as an expert in old bottles. A National Park Service archaeologist who had sought out Noël Hume's expertise on a project during a 1950 visit to England, ended up recommending Noël Hume to CW in 1956 when they needed an archaeological consultant. That temporary stint resulted in Noël Hume being offered a position the following year, to head up archaeology at CW. Accompanied by his wife, Audrey, a classically trained archaeologist whose own experience and talents were impressive, they made the move. In some ways, the two were almost like foster parents for CW—so much of their work, leadership, analyses, and vision formed the backbone of what's been recreated and restored there.

Archaeologist. The word brings up images of Indiana Jones crawling through pyramids or jungle-covered temples. Many would not associate CW—a relatively "young" place compared to the pyramids—with archaeology. However, as Noël Hume once noted, archaeology doesn't just happen in places where buildings have disappeared or are in ruins. Noël Hume understood how quickly "time mutilates even recent history." Written records alone can't tell the whole story. In fact, there may be no records for some things. What did they eat? How often? Did they use a knife and fork? Were their backyards tree-shaded? How were the various buildings used? Often answers are only found buried where the buildings used to stand, at the bottoms of wells, or hidden in a backyard garden. Noël Hume was determined to find these answers and he had some revolutionary new ideas for how to make that happen.

The state of archaeology at CW in 1957 was, as Noël Hume described it, "atrocious." From 1928-1957, the main focus was architectural—to locate the foundations of the various structures that existed in 1700s Williamsburg, and then recreate them. Often new structures had been built over sites and had to be removed. Then the original foundations had to be located. A man named Jimmy Wright came up with a very efficient way to find these foundations. Given that at the time it was the height of the Great Depression and help was plentiful, Wright employed teams of laborers to dig trenches across the various lots in town. The trenches were dug at either ninety-degree or forty-five-degree angles to the street, and stretched from one end of a lot to the other. The trenches were about a foot wide—about the width of a spade—and were about five feet apart. CW now generally refers to this initial work as "excavation" and not archaeology. It was incredibly successful in helping locate the foundations and getting over 300 buildings reconstructed. But even though almost seventy-five percent of the Historic Area had been cross-trenched in this manner, this process was missing the heart of archaeological purpose—gaining information on the people who lived there, what they did, and how they lived. As far as collecting any artifacts, most were either reburied when the trenches were filled in, or tossed out to end up in the local landfill. The few things they did keep had to fit in the three, fifteen-by-twenty-eight-by-fifteen-inch artifact boxes allotted to each property. Further, the items were collected by untrained laborers who selected unusual things that caught their eye, or things related to architecture rather than anything with a historical purpose. With random scraps of things stuffed into boxes, and no information on where exactly they were found, what was found with them, or any kind of contextual information, the bits were not very helpful.

Hence, when Noël Hume arrived, he instituted a world of changes. Considering himself a historical detective, he took a forensic approach to site interpretation. His goal was to tell the stories of Williamsburg's 18th-century people. To achieve this, he used methods he had learned in England that would reveal the people themselves, as well as what activities took place on a site and when. He was instrumental in creating the approach called "historical archaeology" at CW, which he described as "hunting for physical evidence and reviewing it alongside the testimony of people who knew or saw what happened." In essence it matched the archaeology of the people and their culture with any written records that could corroborate what was found in the ground.

His first major change was in how a site was excavated. The lots were set up in grids and dug up in ten-foot squares. Instead of shovels they used trowels to carefully remove the soil. The workers used the "open-area, stratigraphic excavation" method.

In this manner an entire yard might be opened up and slowly excavated downward to reveal the different layers of soil built up over the years. As they slowly dug down through these layers, they discovered numerous things that had been missed in previous excavations—post holes, trash and fire pits, gardens, and even privies. The deeper the layer, the older it might be. When dating these layers, the rule was that the layer could be no older than the newest object found in it. That is a principle called *terminus post quem*, the date after which the most recent artifact was thrown away. This means that the date can be any date after, but not before, that new artifact's date. For example, if most of the objects found together suggested a date of the 1750s, but another object located with them in that layer was from the 1770s, then the layer could be no older than the 1770s.

Another innovation Noël Hume implemented was the extensive and systematic collection of artifacts found. Anything found was labeled as to its exact location on the lot. Using this method, meticulous records were established, including "crossmend forms."

Crossmend forms document not only that an artifact is found at a site and its location on the site, but also what is found *with* it. By studying that object in the context of the items found with it, the archaeologists often could glean much deeper information about the people who lived there, what they did, their station in life, what they ate, and so on. Essentially, the context of the findings, as captured on the crossmend forms, would help reveal the story of the site.

It was at this point that a chance to try out all these new archaeology methods presented itself. Enter Wetherburn's Tavern. In 1964, CW had acquired the tavern property under a long-term lease and it was decided to do a full-scale archaeological investigation. Before any site work could take place, however, a thorough study of any and all documents and records had to take place. This would provide the chance for the people who lived then to "speak" through whatever was available in the written records.

Artifacts found in CW sit with their associated "crossmend forms"—the sheets that contain location data and contextual information. These will help interpret what the item is, its age, and what is was used for.

Hunting down every existing record on the tavern, Noël Hume's team tried to determine when it was built, as well as what additions took place and when. Using historical, architectural, and archaeological records, they hoped to assign dates to the various structural changes. In the tavern's case, instead of the usual approach of searching for clues in the basement and the ground then working upward, they actually had to start with the roof and work down.

There had been a number of changes to chimneys, replastered attic walls, and destruction by rats and squirrels, such that many artifacts were found buried in walls behind laths and floor joists. It was actually these things that proved most useful in determining the evolution of the building, which took place in three stages. Between this information and the fact that detailed inventory records existed from 1760 when Henry Wetherburn died, they were able to decide on the 1760 date as their target period for the restoration of the building.

Full-scale archaeological excavation of the site started in 1965. In keeping with his efforts to upgrade CW's methods, Noël Hume employed 16mm movie cameras to document the stages of their work. First, they had to remove modern-day additions and changes to the building that were not in keeping with the 1700s-time period. As they dug, they unearthed a 19th-century root cellar, at least five different porch stoops, and a variety of trash and rubble, all of which needed to be sorted to determine what belonged to the colonial period and what didn't. Along the way, they also found a bricked-up entrance to the basement that they had not previously known about. As they dug, they unearthed discolored patterns of soil layers, which indicated the locations of such things as trash pits, fence posts, and ornate gardens that once existed on the site. They also discovered the foundations of several additional buildings, including a dairy, multiple smokehouses, and a kitchen. Near the kitchen, they uncovered a mystery.

Excavating behind the tavern, they had unearthed a large deposit of ashes. There did not appear to be any clear reason for its presence in that spot. The team was able to determine that the ash was placed on the site when very hot, as the earth layer below it was scorched from the heat. This meant the fire had taken place right there, as opposed to the ashes coming from somewhere else in the town. Also, there were melted wine glasses, bottles, and brass buckles. These latter items gave testimony to the intensity of the fire. However, the actual date or cause of the fire could never be found. It remains a mystery.

Another odd finding was an unexpected discovery along the kitchen foundation. Buried there were no fewer than eighteen glass bottles clustered in groups of three, five, and ten. The bottles were half full of a brown liquid, as well as intact cherries, cherry pits, or stems. While historical documents existed about the practice of burying bottles, about the methods for how to cut cherry stems before bottling Brandied Cherries, and about how to bottle cherries dry, none of these could explain what these bottles were for, or why they were left in the ground.

One area at the tavern site that yielded rich returns was the well behind the tavern. Noël Hume knew from his days digging on the Thames, that sites located under water can yield many interesting, and well-preserved objects. He and his team dug down over forty feet into the well and discovered everything from ashes, papers, and old leather shoes to a wide range of seeds, pits, and plant material. All of these things were transported to the Archaeology lab where they were cleaned, sorted, and catalogued—each and every specimen or broken bit receiving a number that connected it to a set of crossmend forms.

Even the plant material was analyzed. The variety of seeds, pits, tree branches, and cuttings found there told the story of what was grown and eaten at the tavern, and even allowed landscape architects to reconstruct what the terrain was like in Wetherburn's time. They found evidence for everything from peaches and gourds, to red oak trees, Virginia pines, mountain laurel, and red maples. This approach—analyzing any discovered plant material to identify what plants grew at a given site and how those plants were used by the site's inhabitants—fell into a branch of archaeology called "archaeo-botany." These methods were used at CW in many future digs.

For example, on a later excavation at a site behind the armory, archaeologists discovered a very large number of blackberry seeds in the soil. The question was: Why were so many blackberry seeds in this one location? They knew, from medical science, that this kind of seed travels through the human body without being digested. From the number of seeds found there, along with the other materials present, they were able to determine that the site contained fill from a privy.

An even more novel example involved studying the pollen found trapped in the mortar of various CW buildings. Tree pollen counts in the mortar of different buildings constructed at different times, told the archaeologists how many or how few trees were in the area at each time point. They discovered that a marked change in the amount of tree pollen mixed into the mortar of CW buildings took place over the 18th century. By the late 1700s, the amount of pollen in the mortar decreased compared to earlier in the century. This pointed to a decrease in the overall number of trees in the area over that period. This was further verified by first-hand, writ-ten accounts from the time that noted that Duke of Gloucester Street was a "brightly lit, rather open area," in contrast to its tree-lined appearance today. Archaeobotany was an important tool at the Wetherburn site.

While Noël Hume and his team were not able to answer all the questions raised at Wetherburn's Tavern site, they learned a great deal, and his methods developed there continue to be used to this day. For a good read and a better understanding of just how much information they learned at Wetherburn's site, I recommend the book that I mentioned at the beginning of this chapter and the one that ignited my interest in archaeology—*Archaeology and Wetherburn's Tavern.*

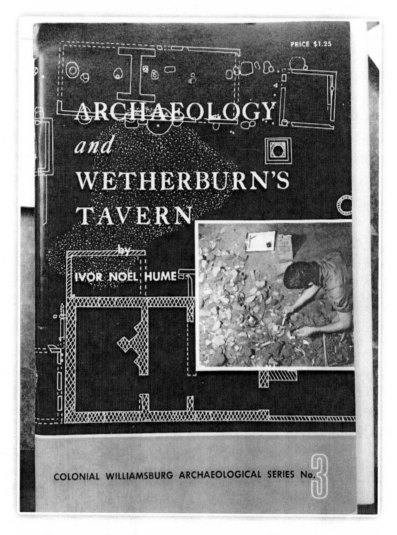

One of my favorite CW books, by the former head of the CW Archaeology Department, the late Ivor Noël Hume.

Written by Ivor Noël Hume, it was originally published in 1969 by the Colonial Williamsburg Foundation. Though I think it is out of print, old copies may still be available on Amazon. It's an engaging read, as are many of his books. Even as a child I loved them. I considered them as good as my Nancy Drew mysteries and maybe even better because these stories were real. He could make the story of finding an old leather shoe alongside a busted oak barrel at the bottom of the well a mysterious adventure, and leave you craving more.

Ivor and Audrey Noël Hume both retired from CW in 1987, after thirty years of work there, and Audrey, his beloved partner of forty-three years died suddenly in 1993. Ivor Noël Hume died in February, 2017 at the age of 89. But his efforts didn't die with him.

Later researchers at CW have built on his methods, and integrated new technology as it became available—ground-penetrating radar, soil chemistry, resistivity testing, neutron activation, and most recently, computer modeling and cataloging, and CAD-drawn maps. They also added an anthropological perspective when interpreting artifacts, which led to new discoveries. This meant that when they evaluated a site, they not only analyzed it for what was found *there*, but they then would compare it to another, similar location and pose a number of questions. Things they might ask included: "How did the diet of a 17th-century rural elite family differ from an urban elite one in the 18th century? Or, how did the clientele of various taverns compare to each other?" This kind of approach could give researchers an even deeper understanding of what the people were like and what the colonial residents did at each site. And because of the fifty years' worth of archaeological specimens and knowledge accumulated under Noël Hume, CW archaeologists had enough material to start making these kinds of comparisons.

I had a chance to learn about this approach on a recent tour of the Archaeology lab. The guide led us to a glass case that held different groups of excavated objects. He had us consider each group, one at a time, and then render our thoughts as to the kind of people that had lived at that site and what their social status might be. One group of items consisted of a three-legged vessel called a "pipkin," along with an unglazed ceramic chamber pot, and a tobacco hoe blade. Those items came from a dig at the quarters for enslaved people. The materials and simple nature of the items reflected a very basic existence. We then contrasted that with a collection of items that included shoe buckles, forks, spoons, knives, Chinese porcelain, and sheep jaws. From these we could determine that the people at this site were from a much wealthier social status.

In the faunal lab, we examined food research displays that held bones excavated from different sites and time periods. An early 17th-century arrangement from a rural elite estate held large bones from cattle, sheep, and pork. These indicated a wealthy existence with the individuals being well fed on a diet high in meat. In contrast, the display from the 18th-century enslaved persons' quarters held almost exclusively chopped up bits of bones—anything from chicken, mutton, or pigs, to wildlife, and fish. From this they determined that those people had to use whatever was available to them in their environment; if they were given any larger animal pieces, these would be chopped up to get at the marrow and to make soups and stews.

For a nice overview of the process of CW's archaeology work, here's a great link: http://research.history.org/research/archaeology/

As you can imagine, the amount of material accumulated from over fifty years of archaeological digs is now so large that on that tour of the lab, I couldn't help feeling the storage room was going to burst at its seams.

Rows of neatly labeled artifact boxes fill the archaeology lab almost to bursting. The new lab can't be built soon enough!

The tour guide noted with excitement that they would soon begin construction of a brand new, much larger set of archaeology labs, thanks to a multi-million-dollar gift from August Mars, heir to the Mars candy fortune.

Not only do the current-day archaeologists at CW carry on the vital work Ivor and Audrey Noël Hume started, but they are also working to excite and recruit a future generation of scientists. Even though the staff labor under the sweltering sun all day, or climb forty feet down into a well to be, as archaeologist Meredith Poole describes it, "armpit deep in muddy water," they still go back out as a labor of love...for the kids. Poole created a hands-on program in 2015 called *"Dig! Kids, Dirt & Discovery."* The goal was to give a taste of archaeology to the large number of young visitors that came through CW every year.

The program is still going and is run during the summers at the site of the Archibald Blair Storehouse on Duke of Gloucester Street, just west of the Prentis Store. The young visitors, ranging in age from five to sixteen, work that site and learn to do what the archaeologists do. To these kids, the archaeologists and staff members are rock stars: role models to emulate. Eagerly, they wait in the long line for their moment "in the sun" to work in the specially prepared excavation area. There, they are instructed in the proper methods to search a patch of soil for any artifacts, as well as how to take note of the different colors of the soil, and what those color changes mean.

It is not busywork, either. The site was chosen carefully for specific research goals. It had been excavated two or three times in the past, and archaeologists knew that there were building foundations there. But it had been decided not to reconstruct the building. The artifacts found there were reburied when the foundations were covered over. Poole and other researchers first wanted to see what artifacts were there and what they could reveal about colonial life at that location. They then wanted answers to the questions: "Why did the previous researchers chose not to keep any of those specimens?" and "What criteria did they use to determine what was important and what wasn't about that site?" Poole also realized this was a great way to get kids actively involved, and to learn about archaeology in the process.

The effort was such a success that the following year Poole expanded the program to include *"DUG!: The Cleaner Side of Archaeology."* Here visitors of all ages wash the artifacts, then examine and evaluate what they have before them. Shaded by a tarp, they wash and mend ceramics, learn how to judge the plant and seed material unearthed, and understand what archaeological lab conservation and interpretation is all about. In these two programs, *"Dig"* and *"Dug,"* visitors of all ages get a glimpse of both the field work as well as the lab work, both of which are now the basis of all modern-day archaeology.

Why does the staff do all of this extra outreach? It comes back to the fact that letting someone actually *do* something is a much more powerful way to excite them about that work, rather than talking about it. Nothing fires passion like "action." So, the staff willingly spends extra hours to give these young scientists-in-training the chance to experience the techniques first-hand. Instead of *telling* them, or even showing them, they instead *let them get out there themselves, get dirty, and learn by doing.* To see details on its success, just search on the term, *"KIDS' Dig!"* at the following blogs:

http://discovery.history.org/
http://makinghistorynow.com/

What began in 1965 with mysteriously blocked windows, a building that seemed perpetually closed even as it beckoned to me, and the vision of a man from England who spent his youth collecting bottles from the mud of the Thames, has grown into a world-class archaeological operation that continues to expand with every year. I highly recommend the tour of the facilities if you get a chance. It's one of CW's behind-the-scenes tours and is called: *"Rubbish, Treasures, and Colonial Life: The Archaeology Labs."* It's incredible what they are able to do!

Oh, and one improvement CW has made in recent years is to now tell the visitors what is going on when they are working at a location. Whether it's an archaeological dig, or a plumbing repair, they post signs to tell you what they are doing, and why. So at least you don't have to wait years to find out what the mystery is all about!

CHAPTER FIFTEEN

....

NOT ALL FACTS ARE
IN THE GROUND

Summer, 1998

Awed by the rows of bookshelves around me, I was mostly oblivious to the tour guide's voice, at least until she started describing the library's reason for existence: "...the focus of this library is the history and culture of colonial British America, the American Revolution, the early United States, and the history of Colonial Williamsburg's restoration." Basically, I pretty much love *any* library. But one devoted to my favorite topics? I could barely contain my excitement.

We were on last stop of the behind-the-scenes tour at CW's Bruton Height's research campus—a tour of the John D. Rockefeller Jr. Library. We'd already toured the rest of the campus with its conservation lab, education sound studio, and museum about the building's history as a segregated school for African American children. But like a special dessert, we'd save this part for last, and I was glad we did.

The tour guide continued to talk. As fast as she pointed something out, I tried to make mental notes of where it was so I could come back to it later. My eyes rapidly scanned the room, desperately trying to take it all in. There was so much to see and I wanted to see it all at once. I thought my head would explode. By the end of the tour, I felt like I'd gorged myself on historical facts and details and couldn't possibly absorb another bite. That day, anyway.

Essentially, I'm a book lover. My idea of perfection is a house with wall-to-wall bookshelves everywhere, except maybe the bathroom—and that's only because the steam would destroy them. My home is filled with books, and I even have an entire bookcase just on CW. But this was an entire *library* on the subject. Needless to say, I wasn't able to absorb it all that day, or even a fraction of it. It would have been impossible, anyway, as I found out later. Wondering just how extensive their resources were, I did a bit of digging on CW's website and learned that the Library's collections now include "some 65,000 volumes, 43,000 manuscripts, 12,000 rare books, 50,000 architectural drawings, and hundreds of thousands of maps, photographs, videotapes, and microforms." They have original political pamphlets, religious tracts, newspapers, playbills, cookbooks, and histories.

It's an amazing place with the depth of historical resources most academics can only dream about. Along those lines, the library's website description notes that their primary mission is to be a resource for CW staff, visiting scholars, and the faculty and students of the College of William and Mary. That said, they have also fielded over 6,000 visits a year from the general public. They continue to serve the public as they can. Since the staff is limited, and very busy, they require an advance appointment to come into the library, or to access the special collections.

Recently, I had the opportunity to stop in again and spend a little more time in the main collections area. Those stacks span two floors. All was quiet, almost church-like, and we leisurely inspected the various titles on the shelves. Tomes such as *Documents Illustrative of the Slave Trade to America*, with records dating as far back as the 1400s; the multivolume set of *Correspondence of King George III;* and multiple volumes of *Virginia Journals of the House of Burgesses* dating back to 1658, spoke to the unique focus of this library on all things colonial. The staff has a gold mine of resources right in their own backyard.

Who would be interested in these resources and why? Well, one group for sure, would be the archaeologists. Before they dig anything up, they research all the old records to find anything that can inform their work. Even after their dig they need to come back to research the numbers of artifacts recovered. With the help of those documents, they then try and identify just what they have in the lab.

But even that isn't the end of their research. Ivor Noël Hume taught that the picture was not complete until you had the testimony of the people who lived then and saw what happened. Otherwise, how would you understand how an object might have been used, or what significance it had in everyday life? Since those people are long gone, your only alternative is to hunt through the records they left behind. Important facts are often buried in things like bills of sale, death notices, marriage certificates, or even tavern menus. Land records, farm ledgers, and even weather data can add more. Those contextual clues are not found in a ditch or the lab, yet they are vital to letting those earlier people "speak" about the things found in archaeological excavations. Hence, the archaeologists spend a lot of time perusing these records.

Consider the stories of two taverns—Wetherburn's and Shields taverns, both at the east end of Duke of Gloucester Street right near the Capitol. Extensive work had already been done at both sites to excavate the plots. At both, many artifacts had been found, along with the foundations of various outbuildings. As expected, that information was documented in several research reports. A visit to CW's research link—http://research.history.org—revealed just how much information they had on hand. At that link if you select "Library," then "Digital Library," then "Research Reports," there is a description of the types of materials available for review, as well as a handy search function. Typing in "Shield's Tavern," or "Wetherburn," yields a multi-page listing of reports and information on each that fleshes out an elaborate picture of the two places.

For example, the search on Shields Tavern brought up a number of reports, including a 1986 document on the "Social and Architectural Context of the Shields Tavern Property." Using historical, architectural, and archaeological data, they attempt to reconstruct the chronological story of the site and the people who lived there. The 1990 archaeology report covered several time periods up to the present day, and for each period, provided data from historical documents, archaeological excavations, laboratory methods, artifacts, spatial patterning, and even zooarchaeological findings. That last one investigated the 6907 bones found on the site—some 1485 that were identifiable and 5422 that were not. It noted there were thirty-one different identified species including "one crustacean, nine fish, one amphibian, nine birds, and eleven mammals." It went on into greater depths from there, but you get the picture.

By the way, in case this list seems macabre, it is actually quite helpful. Collecting this information in each excavated layer told, for that layer's time period, just what the people were eating and possibly implied their social status. The same was true of the various tableware, vessels, and utensils. The report documented not only objects, but what they might have been used for. From that information, they could infer whether the building was a private home or a tavern, whether the occupants were wealthy or not, and so on.

In another example, when I typed in "Wetherburn," no less than 161 items came up in the list. There was Ivor Noël Hume's

1968 report documenting how they dug the site and what they found. A 1970 report by his wife, Audrey Noël Hume, focused on identifying the various ceramic-ware found there. Two 1986 reports focused on how to interpret the site—including whether there was a stable located there—as well as a phased plan to move these initiatives forward.

However, perhaps the most extensive stories of the people and culture at that site were found in two 1965 reports by Mary Stephenson. Her reports included things like personal property tax records, lists of owners from the 17th century through the present, biographical sketches of those people, estate inventories, ledgers, wills, land and marriage records, and even diaries by George Washington and William Byrd. This was the material that added the "meat to the bones" of the excavation records. And in some cases, they left you looking for more.

In one of the reports there was a statement indicating that Henry Wetherburn was married to Mary Bowcock, the widow of a tavern keeper. She later died and a mere *ten days later*, he married the widow of a rival tavern owner. The 1968 report by J. Douglas Smith stated:

"On July 1, 1751, Mrs. Wetherburn died, and on July 11, 1751, Wetherburn married Mrs. Anne Margot Ingles Shields, widow of James Shields. We have almost no information on which to base a judgement of Henry Wetherburn's character; however, his unseemly haste (even for the 18th century) to remarry may reflect an unattractive, opportunistic facet of his life."

Apparently, Henry Wetherburn's contemporaries did not miss this aspect, either. Both this report and a 1966 one by Mary R. M. Goodwin, remarked on a diary entry by the Honorable Henry Blair, a noted Williamsburg citizen at that time—"...on July 3 he wrote—'Very rainy while at Mrs. Wetherburn's funeral,' adding, 'He has found her hoard they say.'" This last statement referred apparently to a stash of money that she had been keeping. Blair then noted on July 11, 1751, "H. Wetherburn married to Mrs. Shields."

The account leaves the readers wanting to hear more and probably wondering—what exactly was going on here? These tidbits make you realize that historical people weren't just names on a two-dimensional page or a list of biographical dates, but real, fully-developed, living, breathing, flawed human beings with emotions and backgrounds that drove their decisions and actions. The point of all of this is, that there is a heavy investment in preserving not only objects and buildings at CW, but people—the people who brought those buildings to life and whose tales *really* tell the whole story of the place.

So, is this an archaeologist-only facility? Not by a long shot. Any historical interpreter over the years has had to research the character they will present, in great depth. They spend countless hours finding every detail they can to bring their person to life in the most accurate way possible. All programs at CW are heavily researched in order to create something both engaging and correct. As mentioned earlier, anyone in the conservation lab entrusted with restoring precious items, uses these facilities before beginning their work. And then there are the beautiful and historically accurate reproductions made by the tradesmen at CW. They too make use of these resources. In fact, the list can go on and on, with outside researchers and academics, and even book writers, such as myself, looking to be certain that whatever they use in their stories does not upset a more knowledgeable reader with an incorrect bit of information. I have consulted the research librarians there on occasion and they have always provided me a quick, courteous, and fact-filled reply to my questions.

So, is the Rockefeller Library the only place there to get information? There are a few more resources to consider. First, there are two incredibly good bookstores at CW. One is the bookstore at the Visitor Center, a place I visit on every trip to see if there's any new historical treasures. The bookshelves in the front of the store are full of the CW-published books. Along the right side of the store is a most extensive selection of local and colonial topics of any bookstore I've seen. Topics range from colonial life, medicine, gardens, and slavery, to trades, architecture, military techniques, and reproductions of 1700s newspapers. On that last one, nothing tells you more about a time than what people were actually saying in newspapers. Most times, I never get any further than those two spots. And when I leave I am almost never empty-handed. The bookstore also has a children's section of fiction and non-fiction to feed all the young history lovers. Teachers and home educators can find resources there as well. You can also access them online, and that makes me *very* happy.

Aside from the Visitor Center's bookstore, there is also the College of William and Mary Bookstore at the west end of Duke of Gloucester Street, right at Merchants Square. There too, you can find a number of books on colonial history, copies of the books that CW publishes, and many books by authors interested in local history.

A place that is an absolute *treasure trove* of CW-specific historical information can be found without leaving your own home. Two CW-run websites can keep you reading historical info for days. The first is the site: http://www.history.org/. Its home-page contains such tabs as history, education, research, publications, and multimedia. The wealth of resources available under each tab is extensive. The research tab, for example, takes you to several options that include links about the areas of CW's historical research projects, online resources, corporate archives and records,

The variety of books available on any number of historical subjects is impressive.

and learning resources. There is a link to the research library, and the online resources include such things as an online library and a virtual Williamsburg site. Multimedia options include everything from podcasts, videos, a variety of blogs, and several webcams, to an online photo store, jigsaw puzzles, and games. At last check, I spotted thirteen different blogs listed there.

The second site is their main blog—Making History Now: http://makinghistorynow.com/. It is written by a variety of bloggers and has pieces on all the latest goings-on, as well as a lot of how-it-works or what-was-that-all-about type of articles. It also has a search function, so every article they have ever written on whatever topic you are searching for is only a couple of keystrokes away! I have spent hours there soaking up tons of details on everything "CW."

Lastly, one of the quickest, and best ways to get information is to participate in the programs and talk to the historical interpreters. On both counts, the heavy research has already been done and you can learn quite a bit about a topic from either one. The interpreters are especially pleased to be able to engage in such conversations and they love to share the many bits of information that they've found.

So, if you want the full story of Williamsburg and its people, the resources are almost endless...and you don't even have to get your hands dirty to use these.

CHAPTER SIXTEEN

··

SHEER DELIGHT: MY OWN VERSION
OF BEHIND-THE-SCENES

Spring, 2016

Single-minded of purpose, I headed for the Raleigh Tavern Bakeshop. At that moment, nothing distracted me as I was on a quest for some of those gingerbread cookies that I remembered from my very first visit. Even before I could see it, I could smell the bakeshop. The sweet, light, smoky aroma beckoned and drew me to it. My pace quickened as I turned the corner from Duke of Gloucester Street. Overhead squirrels skittered through branches, accompanied by the abruptly shifting melodies of a mockingbird. Soft breezes fluttered through the yellow-green leaves on the trees. The uneven bricks of the narrow walkway led past a flood of color on the right—the Alexander Craig House pleasure garden. Its rectangular expanse of tulips momentarily arrested my attention. The explosion of beauty was overwhelming, but even that deterred me only for a moment. My quest was the entry door to the bakeshop, and a display of "mere gorgeous nature" would not waylay me.

The slam of a door drove me on. Deftly I slipped past a group of distracted visitors. They were blocking the path and seemed to be in no particular hurry to go in, something I simply could not fathom. Rounding the corner, I saw the screen door straight ahead. Like a pilot with the target in my sights I moved forward to grab the handle. The door was like something out of my childhood—wood-framed screens, opaque and slightly torn, and a spring hinge to pull the door shut.

The place was mostly empty as it was still early. The inside area was split between two rooms. Both were a homey mix of warmth, smoke-streaked bricks, and age. The back room housed two brick ovens on the right, which were being used for making fresh cookies. Nearby were familiar 21st-century items—refrigerators stocked with lemonade, bottled water, an assemblage of colonial tavern-branded sodas and beers, salads, and sandwiches. Except for these and a soda machine near the ovens, the rest felt circa 1775.

I spotted the baker in his red hat as he entered the oven area carrying a wooden bucket full of water. The back door was open, probably to let in a breeze. One oven had a roaring fire, the other, glowing coals. Speaking slowly with an easy drawl, the man began to share tidbits about what he was doing. I found myself slowing down to wait patiently for his next carefully chosen words. His thoughts were deliberate and considered, and he edited himself well, saying neither too little nor too much. He just flowed from topic to topic as he explained his process.

His love for his craft was evident as he related stories from his visits to other locations that used brick ovens. You could tell he lived, breathed, ate, drank, and slept this work. In the middle of his story, he stopped to point out very matter-of-factly, the differences and similarities between his processes and those of others. He explained the reasons behind his choice to do something a certain way, and you could tell that nothing about his current work methods was an accident or a guess. Each step in this operation had been consciously chosen.

He resumed his story, sharing details of how the staff at a palace he went to, would burn a small bundle of sticks in a brick oven then let the heat radiate from those bricks, keeping the place warm for several hours. He started to go on, then caught himself and asked if he was boring us with all these tales. I shook my head. Frankly, I could have listened to him all day. He was truly a Zen master of the brick oven.

Using these brick ovens in the Raleigh Tavern Bakeshop to bake the gingerbread cookies was standard operating procedure through the 1980s. At one point the bakery's ovens even produced about 1,000 cookies a day. I don't know why they stopped, but apparently over the last thirty or so years, the cookies have been baked in ovens elsewhere in CW, including at the kitchen of the Williamsburg Lodge—a nearby CW hotel. The decision to reverse course on this and go back to baking onsite, at least for the gingerbread cookies, came from the top down and involved a whole crew of people to make it happen. Everyone from the CW President and CEO, the Director of Historic Hospitality, the Historic Foodways Journeyman cook, and the Head Pastry Chef, to the Master Blacksmith, Manager of Building Trades, Manager of Mechanical Trades, and several others got involved. There were a number of obstacles that had to be overcome, one of the biggest ones being the uncertainty about how well the chimney would work after thirty years of no use. There was also the 21st-century concern about whether or not the refrigerated drink dispensers could stand up to the level of heat those ovens would generate. After many tests, trial runs, and kinks worked out, the process got started and was so well received that they now bake gingerbread cookies seven days a week from nine a.m.-noon.

It is a hot process and though he stops baking by noon, the baker is not done until he's cleaned out the hot ovens and prepared them for the next day's work. The baker must stand almost the whole time right next to a blazing fire and is constantly leaning into the hot oven, either to attend to the fire, or to check on the cookies. Though the building is air-conditioned, one of the staff mentioned that it doesn't really matter once the hot summer months set in. There is no escaping the heat on those days. Hearing all of that, I could almost understand why they had moved to baking offsite in large commercial ovens. It was quicker, easier, more automated, and probably cheaper. To bake them onsite in the brick ovens was by comparison, a labor-intensive, manual process at the mercy of the quality of the fire and how the oven reacted to conditions that day. For sure it was a much less predictable way than the modern method. Yet there was a quality to the cookies, to the experience of seeing such craftsmanship happen right before you, and the ultimate ecstasy of biting into a warm fresh gingerbread cookie, that just couldn't be replicated in the modern process.

The baker reached down and selected a few chunks of wood. Before he could bake cookies, he had to prepare the ovens. So his first task was to light a fire in each oven and get it blazing. I was fascinated watching him, both by the intricate process the baker had to use to do his work, as well as by the man himself. What kind of person took that much interest in a long-forgotten art? It was obvious from the care he used, that this was not a job, but a form of artistic expression for him. Here again, as in other locations throughout CW, was another person who pursued his work not just as a job, but as a labor of love and commitment. Seeing his dedication and hearing his stories, I could not leave. I was determined to watch the whole process, beginning to end, and honor his work.

The first oven, which he had started earlier, had a pile of glowing coals in the center. The second now had roaring flames that were hitting the top of the oven's interior. Each oven had a circular base whose sides rose up to a domed top, something like the dome in a rotunda ceiling. It was meant to resemble an 18th-century beehive. He explained that he only needed a tiny bundle of wood to raise a very intense fire, noting with some amazement how much heat could be obtained from such a small amount of fuel. If the wood was a bit damp, he would add some fat to the wood and that would get the fire going. He usually used oak, hence it yielded a lot of heat. To make the fire even hotter, he sought out pieces with knots in them. As he talked the fire continued to burn. By now all of the oven's walls were white hot. He explained that temperatures reached about 900 degrees and one hour of a burning fire yielded two-three hours of baking time. So, he would stop feeding the fire at the end of the hour and let it reduce to a pile of hot coals. His method was to start a fire in one oven, then an hour later, he would light the second oven. By staggering the starting times, he could expand the amount of baking time he had. For most of his baking period both ovens would be going and later, about the time the first one was cooling off, the second one could still bake a couple more batches.

Noticing the nice pile of hot coals in the first oven, he took a metal rod that bore a resemblance to a hoe, and used it to spread out the coals over the entire circular brick baking surface. He carefully pushed the coals right to the edges and left them there for several minutes so that all areas of the oven floor heated evenly. Then, picking up a shovel-like implement, he scooped up the coals and dropped them into a metal tray on the shop floor. Those would be used to either start fireplaces elsewhere in CW, or collected for use in pottery- and soap-making.

Next, he reached for the wooden bucket of water he had carried in earlier and set it down on the floor next to the ovens. Using a long pole with a cloth attached to the end, he soaked the cloth in the bucket then began to clean that oven floor. Each time he pulled the cloth out, it was steaming hot and covered with leftover ashes. He would then rinse the cloth in the bucket, deftly twirl the rod so as to rewrap the cloth around the top of the pole, and wipe out another spot in the oven. Once he had washed out all the surfaces in the oven, he used a straw broom to sweep out any remaining traces of ash.

Timing is everything in this process and he seemed to flow from one task to another so as to be ready for the next step, just in time. Before he could prep the cookies to go into the oven, he needed to be sure the temperature of the oven was cooling down to the perfect baking temperature. He told us that the washing and sweeping actions dropped the oven temperature down to about 500 degrees. Though he had no thermometer, I didn't doubt him. He just seemed to know when things were ready, as if his hand was a calibrated instrument. Every so often he would extend his hand carefully into the center of the dome to check on the rate of cooling. Once assured that he had the right amount of time left to work his process, he began readying the cookies to go into the oven.

He reached for a tall narrow cart sitting in the corner of the room that was covered with a large sheet. Pulling the covering aside, I could see that each level on the cart had a metal tray with twenty-eight cookies on a paper sheet. The cookie dough had been prepared earlier in the kitchen of the Williamsburg Lodge, then sent over here for baking. The raw cookies had continued to rise while they sat on the covered cart. Pulling a tray of cookies off the shelf, the baker tipped the pan up at an angle and slid the paper sheet holding the cookies onto a wooden peel.

One last time he checked the temperature in the oven with his hand. If the oven was too hot, the paper holding the cookies would burn. Again, showing his love for his craft through his intricate knowledge of the details, he shared with us that paper burns at 411 degrees and at that temperature the cookies would bake too fast. That meant they would crust over before the rising had finished, causing the cookies to crack. To me, cracked, delicious cookies were no big deal. But he was an artist at work, a maestro of the operation, and cracked cookies would simply not do. He waited a few more minutes. What he sought was a temperature a bit cooler, about 400 degrees, which would allow the cookies to finish rising before they started to set in the oven. If the process was done correctly, they would have a firm but pliable maple-colored exterior and only a few tiny craters where the air bubbles were still emerging during baking.

Assured that the oven was ready, he inserted the peel holding the cookies and gave the peel a snap. This caused the cookies to slide into the oven. For the first batch, he only put one sheet of cookies into the oven. For later batches though, he put two sheets of cookies in at a time. He was able to do two-three more batches of cookies in each oven. On an average day, he said he could bake about seven sheets of twenty-eight cookies each, per oven.

Once the cookies were in the oven, he monitored the temperature to decide when they were done. Just by tapping the cookies to feel their consistency, he could determine if they were ready or not. The baker said that the cookies average about twenty minutes per batch. Once he decided they were ready, he slid the peel underneath them and lifted them out of the oven. Setting them down on the nearby brick counter, he let them cool for a bit. At this point it had taken about an hour and a half to get the first batch of cookies out.

By now a crowd had gathered around the man. Seeing the cookies lifted from the oven, people pushed closer. Their eagerness was palpable. The baker noted that on a busy day, he can sell out of 500 cookies by one p.m. As he spoke, visitors eyed the cooling cookies like hungry vultures. I was no exception. I had gotten here

The baker carefully checks the cookies before
starting to bag them.

early and watched it all from beginning to end, so I was not letting anyone else beat me in line. He swiftly bagged up the cooled
cookies and set a tray of them in front of the nearly frenzied group.
The cookies barely landed on the counter before hands shot out

from the crowd to scoop up cookies. Observing the effect his work had on all the visitors, the baker smiled in silent satisfaction, then turned away. He had done his job.

Quickly gathering up a few of the warm bags, I headed to the front room to pay. To my left was a long table filled with thick brownies, chocolate chip cookies, Sally Lunn bread, Queen's and apple crumb cakes, all of which looked mouth-watering. But I couldn't have cared less. I had the treasures I came for. My only stop was to get a cup of chai tea, the perfect complement to hot gingery cookies. The payment line, which actually moved fairly quickly, seemed to take forever given my eagerness to enjoy the cookies. At one point, I cracked open the bag while I waited in line and was immediately enveloped in a cloud of ginger fumes. Pure heaven. However, I quickly crinkled the bag shut and distracted myself by looking around the room so as not to be tempted to eat the cookies while standing in line. I focused on the tall fireplace across of me, brushed clean but obviously used in the past. The size indicated it was certainly capable of holding a hearty fire and a large cauldron of boiling stew. Food. My stomach growled. Would I ever get to the register?

Finally, I reached the cashier (cash registers are another 21st-century accessory that just seems to blend into the background in CW), paid for the cookies, then I bolted for the exit. Outside of the bake shop is a brick-floored patio area with a number of benches, some tucked under shady trees. There is also seating on the back porch of the Raleigh Tavern just across from the bake shop. As I scanned the area for a good place to sit, I noticed a bird sitting under a nearby bench who eyed me critically. I can only assume it was assessing if I was a good, or rather, a generous, prospect. The wildlife here isn't spooked at all by the presence of humans. In fact, I think it's the humans who should fear the ire of the wildlife if the humans fail to drop enough cookie crumbs on the ground.

I walked past the trash can, drawing the attention of a cluster of yellow jackets hovering above it. A warning about yellow jackets and trash cans. The yellow jackets are especially fond of partially-filled soda bottles. If you come to close to the trash receptacle they will assume you are there to steal their treasure and may react. So, don't linger. And if you throw your bottle into the trash do not attempt to reclaim it. The wasps do not share.

Deftly evading several people who couldn't decide where to sit, I grabbed my favorite bench near the well. Tearing open the paper bag, I pulled the cookie out. So, what of those cookies that I waited so long for? Were they really worth all this effort and time?

Even in my eagerness to eat it, I took a moment to appreciate the man's work. The cookie had a "thick" sensation in my hand, not so much a heaviness, as a feeling of substance. It was a maple-colored hue, with a perfectly arched top. Its shape looked almost like someone had lopped off the top of a muffin, except it was much smoother, with just a few craters in the surface. As promised, he created a perfectly formed cookie whose craters were just right in size and number.

With my taste buds practically screaming and my salivary glands working overtime, I bit gently into the firm crust. It offered a little chewy resistance but was not hard. As the cookie yielded, my teeth sank into the soft warmth. Gingerbread cookies that are not right out of the oven are good, though sometimes a little dry. Even dry, they will still melt into a delicious syrupy consistency. However, when you are eating gingerbread cookies that are right out of the oven, the experience is in a league of its own.

The inside of the warm cookie transformed into a soft, sweet, gingery paste. I closed my eyes and savored the aroma. Batter-coated, my taste buds were in heaven. It was an explosion of sheer, spiced delight followed by a smooth caramel-flavored finish. Between the color, texture, flavor, aroma, and warmth, there was nothing I

Before devouring these cookies, one must take a moment
to appreciate the sheer perfection of the creation!

could compare it to. It was just sensory bliss and emotional contentment. And it was gone in seconds. My only decision at that point was whether to have more cookies, or avoid the temptation and start hiking the town. This was merely a joke though, because there was no decision. Hiking could always wait. Fresh cookies from the bakeshop could not.

Others may wonder what all the fuss is about...though given the reaction of everyone around me as they bit into warm cookies, I think they understood. The flat-out fact is that those fresh gingerbread cookies really are that good. But for me, it extends even beyond that. They are a multi-level joy.

They are, of course, a reconnection to those fifty-year-old memories of running through CW with my sister, and staving off our hunger with these cookies. I will grow to be a very old woman and will still treasure that day and that memory. But even beyond taste and memory, there is that one last quality that makes those cookies, like so many other things here, special. It is that man—the baker. Like so many other employees here, he doesn't just do a "job." Instead, it is a calling, an art, a passion. Every intricate process, every detail incorporated into a particular effort, shows as a labor of love. At CW, whether it is covering weighty topics like slavery and injustice, or simple topics like baking cookies, each task is treated with pride, care, and accuracy in its delivery.

The future can learn from the past here too, as you can learn to make these cookies yourself, at home. They may not have the master's touch or come out of a brick oven, but still, you can try. Just search the blog, Making History Now, or pick up a copy of *Recipes from the Raleigh Tavern Bake Shop*, and you can find the recipe. Even easier, several of the stores in CW sell the cookie mix. So, after that, all you'll need is your own oven peel and the red baker's hat.

CHAPTER SEVENTEEN

....

ART IS NOT JUST FOR THE OLD

Summer, 1972

The voice on the bus announced the next stop—the DeWitt Wallace Decorative Arts Museum. It sounded about as boring a stop as I could ever imagine, so I just continued on. In fact, I did the same thing at Merchants Square. Those particular places just seemed like they were "not me." That whole area of CW seemed like it was meant only for "old people with more money than me." So, I just passed it by.

Even as an adult I wasn't that interested in the art museums or the hotels there, and once I had a young child in tow, I never figured there would be anything there that would be fun for him. We were more likely to be found outside the Magazine pretending to be soldiers as we marched with shouldered sticks that served as our pretend flintlocks. Or we might be running around with cameras for a school project or riding a carriage through town.

I'm not sure why I was so closed-minded about those museums. It wasn't like I didn't have an interest in art, having taken oil painting lessons for a number of years in my childhood. But whatever the reason, "someday" does finally arrive and you stop and ask yourself, "Am I missing something?" I remember going up into our attic at home one day during that same time period and noticing just how many packed-away boxes of my life were stored there. For years I had ignored them, figuring that at some point I should really just get rid of all that junk. But on that particular day I realized I no longer even remembered what I had packed in those boxes. It's remarkable what you find from your life that you had totally forgotten about. One box in particular caught my attention—the one with art supplies that I'd used so often in my childhood. Holding up a paint brush, I wondered, "Do I even remember how to use this?"

On a trip to CW just a few years ago, I was listening to the bus recording as we circled the Historic Area and my ear caught the mention of a lecture on colonial spy methods called *"Crack the Code."* It was going to be held in the Hennage Auditorium... in the DeWitt Wallace Decorative Arts Museum. Given that I was researching that very topic for my novel, I knew I couldn't miss it. It was at that moment, too, that I suddenly realized that in all of my visits to CW, I'd never set foot in either one of their art museums. Ever. Why? And what was I missing? So, I decided to find out.

Both museums are housed in the same structure and you enter through a building called the "Public Hospital for Persons of Insane and Disordered Minds." The Public Hospital, which opened in 1773, was the first facility in North America that focused on "care" for the mentally ill. It was a stark and depressing place, mostly reserved for those considered dangerous or who could be treated and released. The harmless and incurable were not admitted. I toured the hospital that day, to honor the memory of those who had to survive there. But it was a hard place for me to visit, and I did not linger.

I headed for the art museums and was surprised to learn that you had to take the elevator down to the basement level to enter the art museums. I also realized at that moment, that I didn't have a clue what either decorative arts or folk arts actually were. Were they different than fine art, which is what most of us expect in an art museum? So, before we headed downstairs, I pulled out my phone and did some "quick digging."

What I learned is that *folk art* is "work," not "fine art," and is done not so much for aesthetic reasons but for utilitarian or decorative purposes. It has a "naive style" with no use of rules for proportion or perspective. This type of art is often done by tradesmen, peasants, or indigenous cultures—essentially productions created by artists untrained in the fine arts. The nature of the topics found in this type of art varied considerably, and included everything from religious or cultural items, things specific to gender, age, or geographic locations, or items that had an ethnic or tribal identity. Items could include quilts, weathervanes, carvings, store signs, milk cans, game boards, and carousel horses. Common materials used included cloth, paper, wood, metal, or clay. *Fine Art* on the other hand, includes items, such as paintings, drawings, photographs, or sculptures created by someone trained in artistic methods. The creations themselves have no other use than to be viewed and appreciated. And unlike the previous two categories, *decorative arts and crafts* are concerned with the manufacture of beautiful objects that are also functional. They can include jewelry, textiles, glassware, ceramics, furniture, wallpaper, interior design (but not architecture), metalwork, including things done by goldsmiths and whitesmiths (silver or tinsmiths), and some paintings and prints.

Satisfied that I now had a general idea of what I would be looking at, I headed downstairs. And that's when I realized just how much I had been missing for so many years.

Emerging from the elevator, we walked down a darkened hallway and emerged into a wide atrium, brightly lit by the daylight filtering down from above. Before me, a palatial staircase rose to the next level. Beyond the stairs was a lovely cafe area and all around were halls leading off in different directions to the various galleries.

A tour guide standing there told us that the DeWitt Wallace had fifteen galleries that displayed an amazing array of British and American silver, coins, ceramics, maps, weapons, furniture, painting, toys, costumes, tools, and textiles. Turning to my phone again, I consulted CW's website and learned that "The Colonial Williamsburg Foundation's vast collections comprise more than 70,000 examples of fine, decorative, mechanical, and folk art." The objects were displayed in the various historic buildings throughout CW and in both the Abby Aldrich Rockefeller Folk Art and DeWitt Wallace Decorative Arts Museums. (To give you a taste of the immensity of the collections, CW's website has something called EMUSEUM, where you can go and view several thousand items online.)

By this point, standing in the atrium, surrounded by centuries of history on all sides, I froze, uncertain where to begin. Surprised by what I had been overlooking all these years, I now wanted to see it all at once, every artifact. But I also knew I would only be able to take in a fraction of it, which meant lost opportunities. So, I was actually grateful we were there to hear about colonial spy methods. That simplified the decision of where to begin.

Heading left toward the auditorium, we walked through a display of old coins—doubloons, coppers, pieces of eight—all real, just inches from my face. If even one of those coins could have spoken about where it had been, the transactions it had been used in, or who its owners were, it could have no doubt shared some amazing stories!

Entering the auditorium, we spent the next hour at the program, *"Crack the Code,"* which was about the codes and ciphers used by Washington during the Revolution. The program itself was great and was not a lecture so much as a "laboratory exercise." They gave a bit of background information and some instructions, but then we had to actually work out some ciphers and solve some coded messages. All of the activities were in a little booklet that we could take home with us...in case we ever had need of coding a message again! I loved the hands-on aspect. Everything made so much more sense when you had to *do* it, not just hear about it.

Afterward, we came out of the auditorium, still facing the same questions—where to start, what to exclude? Fortunately for me, my husband chose, so we began with the display of building materials, tools, and weapons. Then we wandered through gallery after gallery of fine glassware and china, cutlery, and coffee urns. So many little details were printed on cards in the cases, each one a clue to the past lives of these objects. Room led to room led to room, all with display cases of beautiful items gently lit. Locked drawers in each gallery gave testimony to just how vast the collection was and that there were so many more items that weren't able to be displayed.

After a while, I felt saturated mentally, unable to absorb another piece of information even though I tried. But like that banquet, you finally cannot take in another morsel and it must wait for another day. I have since been back to the art museums several times, each time taking in as much as I can. But still there is so much more to do.

Maybe "do" is the operative word in that sentence. While you could certainly spend your time just quietly wandering and looking, the museums also have a wide range of programming to participate in. The ones I particularly love use that behind-the-scenes tour approach. Those have an intimate feel that suggests you are getting something special that is not ordinarily seen. For example, they offered a "*Backstory*" tour that introduced us to various pieces on display in the museum by sharing the stories behind each item, such as who made it, why, how it came to be at the museum, and tidbits of historical trivia. By the time we finished that tour, we felt personally acquainted with several pieces in the collection. On another tour, *"Behind Closed Drawers,"* we had the rare and tantalizing opportunity to explore items hidden away in some of those locked gallery drawers. And one they more recently added was *"Ceramics Up-Close."* This one offered a discussion of ceramics along with a behind-the-scenes view of the ceramics storage vault.

Other programs allow you to "meet various American Founders," see a depiction of Martha Washington as she evolves into her role as George Washington's wife, or learn about what was going on in Williamsburg from the end of the Revolution until the time of the restoration in 1927. African American programming included things like: *"Princes Without a Palace: Tracing African Princes and Captives in Williamsburg,"* about two African princes who negotiated their return to their homeland; *"To Be Seen As An American,"* the story of three black women in different centuries, who rose above society's limits; and *"Every Piece Tells a Story,"* where a 1960s black woman and an early 20th-century white woman consider the importance of quilts in their lives.

Love a good mystery? They also offered *"An Art Museum Mystery"*—an interactive mystery experience where you are the investigator and have to solve both an art theft and museum murder mystery. As you wander the museum, you and the other visitors have to figure out clues, and interview suspects, to solve the crime.

There are also general overview tours of the place—*"Introduction to Folk Art"* and *"Decorative Arts Highlights."* Then there are more narrowly focused programs, such as *"Busting Myths,"* that takes on questions—Were quilts used to send messages on the Underground Railroad? Were people shorter in the 1700s?—and teaches people how to tease out truth from myth. And if you have younger children and wonder whether they will be bored, there are programs such as *"Toys!"* which explores the toys of the 19th and early 20th centuries and then includes the opportunity to create a toy inspired by the exhibit. They have even set up programs specially designed for families with children on the autism spectrum. Those programs are set to give those families and children flexibility in how they tour the Museums, as well as offering them special tours, activities, and crafts.

As of this writing, CW is embarking on an expansion of the art museums. One big change is a grand new entrance directly into the art museums instead of going through the Public Hospital exhibit. Other changes include:

- The addition of 8000 square feet of gallery space
- A more spacious lobby and grand entranceway leading into the two museums
- A new mechanical plant to upgrade the mechanical and environmental control systems
- Enlarged areas for programming and activities
- A larger, updated café and museum store

I look forward to all the new things they will be able to do with these changes and I am especially intrigued by the mention of "enlarged areas for programming and *activities!*"

As I was leaving the museum that day, I realized that I had no idea who the people were who so generously created these two museums. Again, I did some digging. Abby Aldrich Rockefeller was the wife of John D. Rockefeller Jr., heir to the Standard Oil fortune and the philanthropist who funded the massive restoration of Colonial Williamsburg. She was a philanthropist in her own right and was the driving force behind the 1929 creation of the Museum of Modern Art in New York City. In addition, she had a collection of folk art, some of which she loaned to CW for display. Four years later she made the loan a permanent donation. She died in 1948, and in 1957, the Abby Aldrich Rockefeller Folk Art Museum was founded to house her artworks. Additional pieces she had previously donated to the Museum of Modern Art and Metropolitan Museum of Art were brought to the collection in CW by her son, David Rockefeller. Her 424 objects form the core of the collection, which now exceeds 3,000 pieces and is one of the largest collections of American folk art in the world.

DeWitt Wallace—or to use his full name, William Roy DeWitt Wallace—was the founder of *Reader's Digest* magazine. It succeeded beyond his wildest dreams, so in his later years he was a philanthropist, donating large amounts of money to various institutions. One of those happened to be CW, where his donations funded the creation of the art museum that bears his name.

In any event, I was totally pleased with my visit to the art museums at CW and only regret that it took me so long to go there. Now whenever I visit, part of my planning process includes checking out what they are *doing* there...because in fact, the CW art museums are not a passive experience. So, if you want to be part of that action, take a break from the hustle and bustle outside and check out the art museums. You won't be disappointed. Overwhelmed, maybe, but not disappointed.

As to the Public Hospital—it will still be there once the art museums' renovations are complete. I do suggest visiting it, at least once, if only to honor the memory of the people who had to be there.

One last note about "doing"—regarding all those paint brushes and art supplies in my attic and the question of "Could I still remember how to paint?" It was through doing that I found the answer. I could not remember how to make the brushes work. It was only when I picked up the brush in my hand, put some paint on it, and started to move it around on the canvas, that it came back to me. Little by little my hand remembered—tactile memory. By *doing* the painting, I remembered *how*.

CHAPTER EIGHTEEN

....

A NEW PET

Summer, 1968

My sisters and I stepped off the back porch and explored "our" backyard. Staying at the Orlando Jones house in the center of CW, we felt like the pampered daughters of a wealthy burgess or a prominent planter. The yard—which at least for the duration of our vacation, was our yard—felt palatial. It had neatly painted small structures that included a dairy, a smokehouse, and a well. Even more luxurious was the finely manicured pleasure garden beyond the well-house. I couldn't imagine living in a place that had a fine brick garden path to "stroll" on during pleasant sunny evenings, or benches for us to sit on and view the sunset. This was certainly different from any yard we had back home. And the idea of taking some air in a back garden was definitely different than our usual after-supper, Wiffle-ball game in the street with the neighborhood kids.

The garden was beautifully designed and gave a peaceful, luxurious sense of seclusion in nature, even though we were in the middle of the downtown area. It had many unique elements, but most alluring to me were the hedges. As I sat on the bench I noticed an unusual scent when I leaned close to the leaves. I'd never smelled anything like it before. I could only describe it as a cross between spicy wood and pine. I didn't know what the bushes were called, or anything about them. All I knew was that the only place I'd ever encountered them was in Williamsburg, and so forever after I would always associate those bushes and that smell with CW. For years I just called them "CW bushes."

As an adult, I finally discovered that they were actually English Boxwoods, a slow-growing, attractive hedge, used extensively to mark property edges and define aesthetic gardens. And as to their unique aroma, which I still love, I have to admit being puzzled that so many gardeners hate that smell. Many describe it as akin to cat pee. Frankly, and happily, I can't make that connection at all, and there is a rare gardener here or there that shares my love of the plant and its scent.

Over the many years since that stay, I've had the opportunity to have many gardens of sorts—mostly utilitarian ones like vegetable gardens or herb gardens. While I always thought it would be lovely to have a finely-designed herb garden perhaps even edged in boxwoods like that one at the Orlando Jones house, there was never quite the time or place for it. And by this point in life, I had run out of energy or enthusiasm for digging up backyards to create such a garden.

Also, over those same years we'd had several pets—a few dogs, and the occasional gerbils and hamsters. However, when our last pet, a dog, died, we decided to stop with pets. Other priorities—aging parents, a son at college, jobs—and the opportunity, for the first time in many years, to get away on the spur-of-the moment brought us to that decision. It wasn't an easy one, but it just seemed selfish and wrong to have a dog, then constantly have to board it. However, thanks to CW, we discovered a low-maintenance, yet satisfying solution to both the lack of a pet and the lack of a pleasure garden.

On a trip to CW in 2011, I was wandering the crushed-shell paths of the Colonial Garden and Nursery, thoroughly enjoying the cool, sunny afternoon. As always, I enjoyed looking over that garden and admiring the layout. It is my idea of what a proper 18th-century garden would have been like. I like to think that my previous herb and vegetable gardens looked like this one, but alas, I know that is not the case.

Unlike the rocky, clay-based soil of my New England gardens, these beds were filled with rich, dark loam. You just knew they had to be filled with many happy earthworms chewing their way through the soil and leaving behind lots of nutrient-rich castings. I found myself wanting to scoop up a handful of the dirt and let it sift through my fingers as I'd done so often in my own gardens over the years. There is no mistaking the feel of fine soil once you've worked with it.

The beds were so neatly organized, and tree-branch trellises on one side held up lush, broad-leafed pole beans. Along the fence of the nursery, glassed-in, straw-insulated boxes cradled new seedlings, while out in the main part of the garden, green, blown-glass bell jars protected tender young shoots on cold nights.

At the other end of the nursery was the little open-air store tucked under a canvas awning that sold everything from birdhouses and flower pots to books and garden tools. I picked up a couple of the tools just to hold them in my hand, and remember. There is nothing as satisfying as the feel of a well-made garden trowel.

As for the books, there were historical tomes like *John Prentis' Monthly Kalendar & Garden Book*, or the reprint of the 1793 pamphlet: "*A Treatise on Gardening*, Written by a Native of this State." Its yellow crinkly pages had the words pressed so deeply into the paper fibers you could feel their imprint on the next page. It was coverless, bound together with taut string, and printed right on

site at CW in the Printer's shop. It was a tiny gardening encyclo-
pedia whose pages were filled with cultivation tips for a variety of
alphabetically listed plants. It started with artichokes and ended
with turnips, and also included a variety of herbs as well. It also
gave a month-by-month set of gardening tasks so as to ensure
that every vegetable would be planted at the right time.

Then there was the olive-green-and-sienna-marbled paper-covered booklet: *"The Gardener's POCKET-BOOK; or, Country Gentleman's
Recreation. Being the Kitchen, Fruit, and Flower Garden Difplayed in
Alphabetical Order,* by R. S. Gent." You just have to love entries such
as: "ELECAMPANE, *Helenium,* is a medicinal plant, the root of
which is much ufed by the Apothecaries," or "SHALLOTS, Bulbous
Roots, fee GARLICK." As an aside, note the "f-like letter" used in
the text to replace an "s." In actuality it is not an f, as the cross-
bar on the letter does not go all the way across the long bar as it
does in the letter f. This substituted form was called a "long s,"
and was standard practice in printing until the late 1700s. It is a
Latin-script known as Roman type, which became the new norm in
printing during the 15th century. Previously the common type used
was "blackletter," most frequently associated with old English and
Germanic printed documents. However, by the 1790s the use of the
long s was gone, replaced by the short s in all uses. So, there's your
moment of trivia on typeface in 18th-century booklets.

In any event, the Colonial Garden and Nursery was enough of
a joy right there, but there was another reason I enjoyed the place.
The word "nursery." Plants. They sold plants. On this particular
day as we strolled the garden's paths, I noticed some tables off
to one side that held all different-sized potted plants for sale.
Looking closer my pulse quickened. They had *boxwoods* for sale!
Suddenly a lightbulb went off in my brain and excitement flooded
through me. I could bring a bit of CW home with me in the form
of my very own boxwood plant!

It was a *great* idea...until I saw the price. I was already over-budget from buying too many books at the Visitor Center's book-store and had little spending money left. Getting a decent-sized plant was out of the question. Then I spotted another table with smaller pots of boxwoods that cost half the price of the larger ones. I consulted my wallet and confirmed that I had enough for the little plant. So that day we acquired a small boxwood, which became my own little pleasure garden in a pot, as well as our new pet of sorts!

It lived for several years in a shady spot under a beech tree in our backyard, and it did reasonably well there. But when we moved to our current home, I set it out on our front porch. The conditions—sheltering and light—must have been better, because it has *thrived*! I feed it once or twice a year, water it every week, and other than that, just enjoy it.

Here is a picture of the boxwood when I bought it, sitting in a little plastic pot on the bathroom counter of our hotel room. You can compare it to the hairdryer on the wall behind it for scale.

This next picture is of the boxwood about seven years later, where it now lives in a big pot on our front porch. It appears to be happy there, if I say so myself, with its billowy branches spread out to catch the breeze.

It is now more friend than plant, more a comfort and giver of pleasure than a photosynthetic life form. I've never felt this way about a plant before. In fact, it's a joke in my house that any plant in my yard has to be self-sufficient because once planted, it's on its own. But this one is my pet, alive, with its own personality. Call it silly, but it is one of the simple pleasures of my life to "visit" the boxwood on the porch. Running my hands softly through its branches, I sniff its leaves and greet it with an affectionate, "Hello, plant!" It is my constant companion, and my connection to my other love, CW. I couldn't ask for more.

Here is the brand new boxwood sitting on the counter of our hotel room, next to the hair dryer.

Here is the boxwood seven years later, much larger,
reveling in its large outdoor pot.

CHAPTER NINETEEN

....

TIME OUT: THE SPA

Summer, 2014

It was typical for a CW August afternoon—hot, humid, some clouds in the distance that suggested "interesting" weather could visit in a couple of hours. My focus, though, was the brick walkway before us. In my usual manner, I marched briskly through the arbor as if on a mission. Shaded by lush green vines dangling from the beams above, the location is an invitation to slow down and indulge the senses, something I am often oblivious to.

My husband, on the other hand, always the more even-paced of the two of us, took my hand and smiled. This is his way of reminding me that not everything needs to be fast-paced, or a rush to check off on a to-do list.

Approaching the door, I felt slightly tense, yet hopeful. The brick column held a sign that read: The Spa of Colonial Williamsburg. It suggested a level of pampering that neither my husband nor I were accustomed to.

It felt both a little weird and exciting at the same time. Entering the brightly lit lobby, we were hit with a flood of wonderful scents that suggested cinnamon, nutmeg, and lavender. The pressure of my husband's hand, mixed with the soothing fragrances in the room, eased some of the tenseness in my muscles. Perhaps this would be okay...maybe even fun.

The entry sign outside of the Spa of
Colonial Williamsburg.

I am not a spa person. It's not that I dislike them, it's just that I rarely get to go. Somehow massages with spiced rubs never quite make it onto the shopping list along with milk, eggs, and fruit. Also, I guess I've often approached places like this with a sense of "This fanciness must be for someone else, not me." But this August trip was in honor of our 25th wedding anniversary, and sometimes you can rationalize doing something for that occasion that you might not ordinarily have the guts or the money to do. I glanced at my husband—not exactly the luxury spa type either—and noticed he seemed quietly intrigued.

For our afternoon, I had selected some sensory delights to indulge in, a couples' experience. We checked in at the spa's front desk—not too scary there...in fact, everyone was very nice and welcoming. After confirming reservation times and details, my husband and I were led downstairs, each to our respective locker rooms.

As I descended the stairs I couldn't help but notice the beautiful stonework on the walls. I let my fingers slide along the rough surfaces as I passed by and felt a growing wave of peace and joy. I am and will remain, a New Englander at heart, and New England is the "land of rocks," a leftover gift from the glaciers thousands of years ago. They are part of my soul. I think I have always understood the symbolism Zen Buddhists attach to the rocks in their gardens—that of representing the journey of life. So even though I've lived in the South now for almost thirty years, I am still soothed by displays of beautiful stonework. Looking at the wall as I descended the stairs I felt something in me ease.

The locker room glowed warmly in gentle light, accompanied by soft music. One side of the room had a setup with various herbal teas and a glass decanter of iced lemon water. A potpourri, again those tones of spices and florals, accented by the citrus fragrance from the water, surrounded me. Already, I was loving the indulgent touches.

The hostess who escorted me, told me to change into a lush terrycloth robe, use the whirlpool in the locker room, and the sauna if I wanted. She added, "Take your time." Imagine...*take your time?* Whirlpool? Sauna? Yes, things like that happen to me every day, not. The attendant said she would be back in about forty-five minutes. What gym had I ever gone to where I got forty-five minutes just to get ready? I was so primed to just keep moving, that I confess I didn't use the whirlpool or sauna, but I did luxuriate in the sensation of soft plush terrycloth on my skin, and warm, herbal tea. It felt odd to "stop" and have nowhere to get to. But, I decided, "why not give it a try?" There's a first time for everything.

Eventually one of the attendants returned and I was led down the hall to the elevator. On the next floor we strolled, and I do mean s-t-r-o-l-l-e-d, down a sunlit hall past softly lit, immaculate massage rooms. Strangely, her slow pace didn't bother me. I felt a part of me slipping into a languid frame of mind. We arrived at an intimate lounge, where my husband was waiting. Similarly attired in robe and slippers, he was sipping a glass of iced lemon water, and seemed thoroughly delighted by everything. He had of course, used the whirlpool and sauna.

I walked over to the table where another arrangement of teas and fruit waters were set up. The room had soft couches with pillows, and end tables. The windows were discreetly covered on the bottom with wooden shutters while light drapes allowed sunlight in through the tops. You had the feeling of being in a warm, safe cocoon, and nothing outside the window could touch you. One or two other couples were there, quietly chatting. I sat with my feet tucked under me, sipping my drink. As I allowed the relaxed pace of the place to slowly seep into my usually taut nervous system, I remember thinking, "I could stay here forever."

Again, after a somewhat lengthy time—which I uncharacteristically didn't even mind—the attendant brought us down to a room with subdued lights and a huge whirlpool tub. Across from the tub were two massage tables. The treatment I had selected for this visit was the couples "20th Century Williamsburg Water Therapy Spa Experience. It involved soaking in a whirlpool bath of "soothing extracts of rosemary, basil, and bay laurel" followed by a "healing Arnica deep tissue massage."

I had made the selection earlier, while still at home. As I studied the options on the website I'd had a hard time selecting that "perfect one." There was such an array of options, most sounding so exotic I wanted to sample them all. Here are a few shortened descriptions from their website, of some of the special treatments they had available that year:

Sarsaparilla Espresso Mud Treatment

A combination of volcanic pumice and warm sarsaparilla clay, combined with the earthy fragrance of Arabica coffee, to cleanse and soften the skin. It will increase circulation and is followed by a Sicilian and Bergamot moisturizing lotion.

Seaweed Body Detox Treatment

The skin is treated to a dry-brushing exfoliation, followed by a nutrient-rich warm seaweed mask to detoxify your body. It also includes a head and neck massage and a foot treatment.

Lavender Lemongrass Stress-Reducing Scrub

Receive a refreshing scrub with oils of lavender and lemongrass followed by a gentle exfoliant.

18th Century Orange & Ginger Scrub & Massage Spa Experience

Feel your overall wellbeing improve with this orange and ginger body scrub. Soak your feet in an aromatic bath and top this off with the "Williamsburg Massage."

Aside from selecting the treatment, I had to decide how long each part would last. You could opt for a fifteen-minute indulgence, but there were also options for thirty minutes, or the ultimate in decadence—an hour! And that was just for the bath. The massage had its own array of choices for type and durations. Some of those selections included: Arnica Deep Tissue, Aromatherapy, Hot Stones, Williamsburg Classic, Sports, Foot...God, which one to pick? The only one I could easily rule out was the Pregnancy Massage.

The Spa also offered a dazzling list of other indulgences—including a variety of hair, nail, or day packages. I noticed there were some mothers and daughters there for the mother-daughter package, as well as groups of women savoring a friends' day. It struck me as a lovely idea—slow down, savor, be pampered—I just never do it. So today would be one for the memory books.

Our whirlpool bath was aromatically sensual, candlelit, relaxing, and ...hysterical. Yes, as in funny. The refined imagery conjured up by the bath description gave way to a comical reality. After all, you are climbing into a *deep* water-filled tub, with powerful air jets pushing at you. The tub surface itself was smooth and slippery to start with, then add to that the *really slippery* oil extracts. Instead of leisurely soaking, we got an athletic workout trying not to slide under the water every time we moved. We both just started laughing as we tried to anchor ourselves to something so we could just hold still in the water. Another earlier time in our lives we might have gotten frustrated that the whole illusion had been destroyed by trying not to drown. But that is the joy of many years of marriage—you are with your best friend enjoying the experience, *and* can have a sense of humor about things. It was perfect.

After about forty-five minutes of "swimming," we then had our massage. It was beyond wonderful. The masseuse worked the tissues hard, but for a stress-filled body, it was s-o-o-o-o-o soothing. You never realize just how tense muscles are until someone works them over. I left the room wondering how we ever managed to live without this. In the glow of the moment I dreamt of doing this as an every-week experience. Not to worry though. I knew that once back out in the sunlight, fiscal responsibility would return to my brain.

After the massage, they led us back to the lounge with the plush sofas and teas and told us to stay as long as we liked. Again, I would normally be pacing the room ready to move on to the next activity. But after such a luxurious experience, we just sat there, our muscles like gelatin, hoping the afternoon would never end. I was vaguely aware of a thunderstorm outside—the storm promised by those earlier dark clouds on the horizon—but frankly, I didn't care.

Maybe it was the special treatment, or the fact that we don't get to do this as part of our regular life, or both, but it was worth waiting years for this and every penny we spent. Maybe my out-of-character acceptance and enjoyment of this experience was due to being older—the body demanding time to slow down. But I think it was something more. There are many times my body requires rest that I still ignore it because my mind wants to keep going. It seems to have retained that ten-year-old's exuberance that revels in everything Williamsburg. So, getting the two factions in me to agree on how to respond has never been an easy deal. But this time was different. Somehow the whole experience captured and engaged my over-active mind and imagination with all the detailed touches, as well as relaxed the rest of me with the lovely sensations. For once, both parts of me could be at peace.

Needless to say, it's on the wish list for another anniversary. I will just make sure it isn't in another twenty-five years. And next time we'll know to bring along an anchor or life vests so we can have less of a workout when enjoying the whirlpool bath!

CHAPTER TWENTY

••

A FAT CANARY

Summer, 2014

We stood in the patio area of the restaurant studying the place. We'd not had good luck with restaurants on this visit to CW. My husband had been having some serious digestive issues, such that we were very concerned about what he would be able to eat on our visit. Most of the foods he used to enjoy he could no longer have and the things he could tolerate were very limited. We had visited different restaurants in Merchant's Square, including a rather expensive one. Yet either we could not find what he needed, or the chef was unwilling to alter his creation to accommodate my husband's needs.

Enter the Fat Canary. We had eaten there once before, about three years earlier. It was a lark because it was expensive and the menu was unusual, but we'd had a great time. However, that was before all the dietary issues.

As we approached the front entrance, I noticed some gold-leaf writing over the doorway:

"Oh for a bowl of
fat Canary, rich Palermo,
Sparkling sherry..." John Lyly

I did not know who John Lyly was, nor had I ever heard those lines before. I thought they seemed quite unusual—odd even—but I figured if they went to the trouble of stenciling them on their doorway, the lines must have been important. So, I pulled out my phone and did a quick Google search of John Lyly, and the Fat Canary website.

John Lyly was a 1500s poet, comedic playwright, and wit whose works predated and influenced ones by William Shakespeare, Christopher Marlowe, and others of that era. His poem above the door referred not to the bird but to a fortified white wine found in the Canary Islands, a stopping point on Atlantic voyages, where early seafarers would dock to resupply. The blog, A Poem Day, describes Lyly's poem as a humorous celebration of indulgences in wine, women, and food, such that Jove himself would find it excessive. You have to admit, any restaurant with that kind of a lead-in *must* bear investigating. But it was the statement on their website that clinched it: "Please let us know if you have any special dietary requests. We are happy to accommodate."

We arrived with no reservations, which in itself could have been a serious problem. The Fat Canary is usually packed, and as the evening goes on, even the bar is standing-room only. However, I guess the Universe was smiling upon us that day because, for whatever reason, at that moment they had a table for us. Before we even agreed to be seated, however, I questioned them about their policy of flexibility regarding dietary requests. If they weren't going to accommodate what we needed, I had no intention of staying. However, their response was totally positive. They assured us that whatever we needed, they would do. And they were *cheerfully and totally true* to their word. I quickly understood why the place is *always* packed. It is an *absolute delight,* and in terms of being able to have what you need and still feel indulged, the Fat Canary lives up to its name.

Also, the Fat Canary confirms that the attractions in the Historic area are not the only places committed to providing a great experience and a sense of history. You don't have to be 18th-century in origin, to connect to CW's quality and vision. The Fat Canary has its own story, roots, and ethos that ensures that the experience you receive is top notch.

First, their story. In 1971, Thomas and Mary Ellen Power started with just a small cheese shop in Newport News, Virginia. While some thought such a gourmet establishment in that location would never work, the entire family including the children pitched in. Through hard work, passion, attention to detail, and *great* customer service, they not only succeeded but then were able to move to Williamsburg. There, they eventually expanded into three businesses—the cheese shop, the wine cellar, and their high-end restaurant, the Fat Canary—a dream come true.

Today, the children who worked in that original store are just as passionately involved, running the businesses and focusing on that same wonderful customer service. For my money, the Fat Canary is our go-to place for culinary splurges when in CW. In fact, the Powers received the 2017 Prentis Award given by the College of William and Mary to recognize members of the local community for their strong civic involvement and support of the university. It was a touching tribute that came just in time. A short time later Thomas died in a swimming accident in Bermuda. While devastating, the family took some comfort knowing he was in a place he loved, doing what he deeply enjoyed. And they make sure that his legacy is well-preserved by continuing to ensure that same level of quality that he and his wife started so many years ago. Their establishments are places that convey the values of their family origins. It is no wonder that the Fat Canary has received the AAA Four Diamond Award every year since their opening in 2003. For their complete story, check out the "About" tab at their website: http://www.fatcanarywilliamsburg.com/

Aside from the devoted efforts of the family, there's also their staff. That dedication to great customer service is not just the ethics code of the owners but is demonstrated by every single staff member. They are professional, attentive, and fun. If you are a return visitor, they—not just the hostesses—but the wait staff and kitchen staff, remember you and welcome you back. Even those who are new and don't know you...yet, are a joy to talk to.

Now. About the food...and drink. First, I'll give you the short version: the food is creative, unique, and prepared to perfection; the desserts' decadence justifies every single calorie; the depth of the wine list makes it interesting without being intimidating; *and* they have a fully-stocked bar with an excellent list of single-malt Scotches. So that's the short version. Now for the slightly more elaborate one.

Let's start outside. The Fat Canary is nestled in the historic Merchants Square at the west end of Duke of Gloucester Street near the College of William and Mary. The approach is brick-walked, tree-shaded, and adorned with umbrella-covered tables out front. The 1930s-era building has the flavor of the nearby colonial homes, accented by the curvy front facade with black-and-white trim and gold-leaf letters above the doorway that reminds me of a Dickens' Christmas collectible house. Lastly, honoring that attention to detail, on either side of the Fat Canary name are the lines from Lyly's poem.

Entering, you are immediately greeted by the staff, who make you feel welcome even as they bustle about answering phones, seating people, and writing the nightly specials on the chalkboard. The Art-Deco-style interior is soothing in a soft pastel green and subdued lighting. Along one wall is the bar...and that sounds so plebeian a description. It is more an inviting nook with an entire wall of top-shelf liquors in front of you and crystalline glassware dangling above the bar's surface. To look at it is to know you'll find some true classic choices along with the latest cocktails.

The rest of the restaurant is tables, many nestled into nooks and corners for a secluded feel. An open kitchen is tucked in the back, allowing full view of the chefs at work. The moment I sit down, I experience this tingly, happy feeling that comes from a mix of anticipation for the culinary delights that await, as well as the sense of being in a friend's snuggly home as opposed to a cold, overly fancy restaurant. It is not that the restaurant doesn't have elegance, because it does, but it is a confident, understated feel that does not distract from the food but rather, complements it.

I happen to love simple romantic table settings, and from that first moment I sat down there, I fell in love with the fresh flower vase and faux-candlelit bowl. But my absolute favorite touch on the table, which I seek out and smooth my fingers over whenever I return, is the Fat Canary logo stamped onto the paper tablecloth covering.

You are well cared for at the Fat Canary. A young waiter constantly ensures your water glass, or iced tea or whatever, is filled—a must if you've been hiking CW on a hot day. The other waiters and waitresses greet you promptly and take time to connect with you and make you feel at home.

The wine list has a number of unusual and quality choices. Aside from a fine list of bottled wines, they also offer, at last count, eighteen different by-the-glass or quartino selections, many from small boutique wineries. If you'd like to see what they offer for cocktails, aperitifs, draft beers and wines, just go to their website, http://www.fatcanarywilliamsburg.com/.

Aside from reading through the options on the wine list, another joy is perusing the menu. The descriptions are spare and to-the-point and that is their brilliance. It reads more like haiku—not a word wasted—and within moments your mouth begins to water.

*The familiar Fat Canary logo stamped onto
all of the paper table covers.*

It is a celebration of local ingredients delivered in a palette of
Asian, European, and American cuisines with a garnish of history. There is no question from the description what is included,
but immediately as your brain takes in each item, it is already

racing to anticipate the explosion of flavor you will enjoy. And enjoy you will.

With that preface, let me now take you on the "beginning-to-end, multi-course sensory journey" that was my dinner that night. I will also answer the question of whether they adequately created something my husband's restricted diet could handle

A fresh flower always adorns the intimate table light.

The waitress came and took our order. After much struggle with so many good options, I finally made my choices. I will share those in a moment. She then turned to my husband to discuss what he could have. Some places, when requested to prepare things simply, just seem to throw things together with little care or attention. But not at the Fat Canary! The waitress listened to what my husband needed in terms of certain foods and preparations. She asked questions and offered suggestions for substitutions, carefully noting what garnishes and spices to avoid. She left, and we held our breath. Hopefully, if he could just receive a plainly grilled dinner that would not give him problems afterward, we would be happy.

Shortly afterward, my appetizer showed up. I had chosen the gingered barbecued pork ribs with marinated cucumber salad. Words fail me other than to say that first, the ribs literally draw you in. There is no "daintily" approaching them because they are s-o-o-o-o good, you just *have* to use your fingers to get every last little bit. There's a reason they serve that dish with a heated hand towel. You cannot *not* use your fingers. But even more is the genius of matching the ribs with marinated thinly sliced cucumbers. With their light taste, they complement rather than compete with the intense sensations of the ribs.

For my entree, I had chosen the Pan Seared Sea Scallops, Couscous, Smoked Tomato, Snap Peas, Green Beans, and Pork Belly. Scallops are a treat to me, no matter how they are prepared, and pan-seared is my favorite. I'm not as crazy about green beans and snap peas, and had planned on just ignoring those. When the plate arrived, I have to admit to being mystified. No piles of "greens" appeared anywhere. Instead, there was a ring of perfectly browned sea scallops sitting on top of a bed of cooked tomatoes. In the center of the ring was what I thought was an "off-color" scallop, until closer observation revealed a large portion of pork—the pork belly. Lifting it up with my fork, I discovered fluffy couscous with small pieces of snap peas and beans mixed in. There was no question but that the presentation was amazing.

Putting a forkful of tomatoes and couscous in my mouth, I had to just close my eyes and savor the sensations. Tomatoes can be boring, but these were a pleasant surprise. Smoky notes joined forces with the sweetness of the mix. The couscous and vegetable blend was light in texture and flavor. And the pork belly; if I thought the smoky flavor of the tomatoes was wonderful, the pork belly was even better. Needless to say, there were few words spoken during this time. Just the sounds of forks hitting plates, and groans of delight.

When it came time for dessert, the selections were just as hard to narrow down as the previous courses were. The options change frequently and equal the rest of the menu in creativity and execution. For that night, I chose the Macadamia Nut Pie. It sounds simple enough. But let me add in the rest of the title: With Pineapple Brûlée. Now it gets interesting. I assumed that meant there would be some diced up pineapples in a sugar sauce or something along those lines. But I was totally unprepared for the experience I was about to have.

They set the plate down in front of me. There before me was another simple arrangement—a delicious-looking, round, single-serving pie. It actually resembled a small pecan pie sized for one person, except with macadamia nuts. I love pecan pie, so I was intrigued. A generous scoop of vanilla ice cream rested on top. Again, it was another favorite of mine, so I figured this would be a decent, if not over-the-top dessert. But knowing how the main course had arrived looking unassuming on the plate, only to defy all expectations, I wondered what was in store for me with the dessert.

Looking closer at the "adornments" on the side of the pie, I realized they were the pineapples. But they were not cut up fruit in sugar syrup. No, these were thick slices of brown-sugar-crusted pineapple, toasted to perfection like a Crème Brûlée would be. My mouth watered. Then my eyes spotted the numerous lines of caramel sauce swirled all across the plate. At that moment, any semblance of self-control disappeared. I dug in. Decadent waves of vanilla, complemented with caramel, augmented by the sensation on my tongue of macadamia nuts encased in gelled sweetness all came together in an explosion of delight. There were no words to express the pleasure of that dessert. All I could do was let the sensations wash over me, then take another bite. And another...

After a dinner and dessert like that you would assume there were no more good things in store for you, but wait, there's more. For anyone who likes unusual after-dinner sherries, or a well-aged, single-malt Scotch, their menu does not disappoint. Add to that a cup of coffee or tea and you are left floating in a sea of satisfaction.

Now, how did my husband's special-request dinner turn out? What we received was a work of elegance. Though his entree required eliminating some of the ingredients that no doubt gave the entree its special qualities, they delivered a dinner that was as artfully crafted as one could make it. Not only did he get exactly what he needed, but every special touch they could add to make him feel cared for was added. The salmon was flaky, browned, glazed, and just the proper moistness. His asparagus spears were sautéed to tenderness, but not soggy, and the potatoes were crisped up and browned. It was beyond anything we could have hoped for. If that wasn't enough, they even created a simple Crème Brûlée dessert that he could have! They also put his information on file so that now, whenever we go back, they can look up what he needs and be ready to prepare it for him. Needless to say, he enjoyed that dinner so totally, that we made a point that week of going back several times.

So, for those moments that require special touches, we head to the Fat Canary. It has time and again been a place we can count on for celebration, romance, artful cuisine, and simple warmth. I cannot recommend them highly enough.

As to that robust enjoyment of total excess and indulgence spoken of in the poem? I think John Lyly would agree, that The Fat Canary is the embodiment of his words.

CHAPTER TWENTY-ONE

....

IF IT'S THURSDAY NIGHT
IT MUST BE TELEMANN

Summer, 2014

Walking up Duke of Gloucester Street at dusk, my husband and I approached the Capitol, hand-in-hand. Crushed oyster shells crunched under our feet as we took our place at the gate of the building's outer wall. Inside the Capitol courtyard lights glowed, candle-like, surrounded by bright orb-like halos.

We didn't say much, being in kind of a quiet reflective place. This was our first time attending an evening concert at CW and we were both looking at this as a special treat. I had dreamed of attending a concert ever since I was a child and heard the music played for us in the King's Arms Tavern. But concerts were one of those things I had written off as being for older people and, alas, I passed on the experience until now.

We entered the darkened building, our eyes struggling to adjust to the dim lighting. Two men in colonial garb directed us into the chamber where a couple of centuries ago burgesses would have argued weighty matters of taxes and war. But tonight, dissension and hostility were not to be found. Instead, we entered another world, sequestered from whatever turmoil lay beyond the walls of the room. That candlelit room, like an inner sanctum of safety, exuded a warmth and serenity that erased all other cares.

People had started filing along either side of the room to take a seat on the cushioned benches lining the walls. In the center of the chamber two pairs of chairs faced each other, like silent guests with stands of sheet music and candles arranged between them. They seemed "expectant" just sitting there all properly set out, and I felt a sense of anticipation for what was to come.

Candlelit sheet music waits expectantly for
the musicians to arrive.

It would be a chamber music quartet, a musical genre we both loved. Twenty-six years ago, we had such a quartet playing Mozart at our wedding. Now we were enjoying a belated 25th-anniversary trip, and the music by Telemann, another favorite, seemed like the perfect choice to honor that achievement.

The sounds in the room were not unlike the soft murmurings heard in the church of my youth when people would assemble before Mass. There you didn't talk out loud. It was hallowed reverence, only hushed whispers allowed.

Across from me was a very young child with his family. I remember worrying that he would get bored and end up losing it in the middle of the concert, destroying the peace of the evening. But for the moment, he just sat there, snuggled up against his mom and taking everything in.

As daylight from the circular windows disappeared, the tan walls took on more umber-shaded tones, illuminated only by the glow of the candles. In the back, one of the men who earlier had seated everyone as they came in, stood by the door, guard-like, scanning the room as it filled. Meanwhile, two men dressed in formal 18th-century attire slowly made their way toward those four empty seats. One carried a flute while the other clutched a bow and violin. Two more musicians joined them a few moments later.

After several minutes of tune ups, the musicians settled down, motionless and quiet, in a kind of pregnant pause. The audience took their cue from them and also grew silent. No one moved. Just when it seemed like we would hang on the edge of that silent cliff forever, the musicians picked up their instruments and began to play.

Strains of sweet notes spread through the chamber. Like Da Vinci wielding his paints and brushes, the musicians wasted not a move as they delivered the velvet sounds that filled our ears. As I listened I couldn't believe I had never chosen to do this sooner.

Total joy at the experience filled my heart and I experienced the sense of a special life moment, just as I had the first time I set foot in CW as a child.

Speaking of children, the young boy across of me that I had worried about earlier, seemed equally entranced. His eyes glowed, barely blinking as he watched every move of the violin bow and of the musician's fingers on the flute. Apparently, music aficionados can come in all ages. Piece after piece, the musicians played on that night. Telemann filled the room, my heart, and my soul.

Georg Philipp Telemann's music is a cross between the sanctified and the playful, alternating between moments of subtlety and then total majesty. Aside from Mozart and Bach, Telemann is a particular favorite of mine, a man after my own heart. He supposedly had a good sense of humor and a friendly demeanor; listening to his music, it was clear to me that this was certainly the case.

Speaking of time, even though the concert went on for a couple of hours, to me it seemed both timeless and too short. As they played, it was as if we were in that spot between the minutes of the hour, and time stood still. I could have stayed there in that peaceful, darkened chamber soaking up Telemann's creations forever. Alas, time was not standing still, but instead very much moving on. When the concert ended it just felt like only a moment had gone by. Sighing, we exited the building and quietly strolled back to our hotel. Words were unnecessary after such a beautiful time. In fact, they seemed like a grating annoyance—like fingernails on a blackboard—and I think we both sensed that. So instead, we just walked, arm-in-arm, letting the echoes of the music play back through our memories for just a little longer. If there was any thought beyond the memories of the sounds we had heard, they were simply to make a mental note to find out when the next of these concerts would take place, and to sign up for it. Hopefully, it would not require another fifty years.

EPILOGUE

....

S o, what do all of these stories mean in terms of my question—why do we fall in love with the places we do? In
looking over the topics I chose to write about, I realized
they were all things that defined me. I am a detail-obsessed lover
of behind-the-scenes information, who craves to understand the
passions, motivations, and mythology of a culture whose people
risked everything to undertake an epic battle, all for an ideal. In
short, I am a history geek!

The reason we connect with certain places and not others,
comes down to the bolt of cloth we're cut from. It's our history,
our passions, our souls. Those destinations touch a spot inside
our hearts where we hold our deepest questions and struggles,
values and expectations, goals and longings. Those places are not
random but are in fact very specifically chosen, because at their
core...those places *are* us.

To anyone contemplating a visit, I suggest you take CW on
your own terms. Let it be for you, whatever it is meant to be based
on who *you* are, and not who *I* am.

To assist with that, I have provided a number of tips in the next
section of this book. They can help you create your own precious
memories, and have a wonderful time doing so.

Rather than give the latest "time-specific" details, my comments will cover topics from a thematic perspective, such as how
to plan a visit there, seasonal variations in activities, special needs,
or how to get there. Like life, things at CW change regularly.

That's been a constant over the entire fifty-plus years I've been visiting the place. They try to stay relevant and responsive to their audience and the times. They are always updating and adding new things. So, if you want the most current prices, special offers, hotel information, and schedules, do an online search or visit the CW website. "That the future may learn from the past," isn't just a cute saying, it is something CW does every day and will continue to do so.

So now, on to the tips.

PART II

TIPS

CHAPTER TWENTY-TWO

....

WHY ARE YOU GOING?

Unless a trip is supposed to be an indulgence in the unexpected, I like to know why I am going and what I will do when I get there. Call it my flaw, but I just don't like "totally open-ended" situations. Give me a good plan and I will show you a vacation that maximizes access to all the possible experiences that I want. I realize that this attitude may not be what many aspire to on a vacation—relaxation, no set schedules, go with the flow—but I was just never that type. That said, as I've gotten older, I have been known to actually "kick back" and only plan "a few things" per day, and leave the rest open. Getting wild in my old age, I know. But since for years I was the queen of multi-page itineraries for our vacations, one could actually say I've gotten really lazy these days!

In any event, whether you plan a trip to the last detail, or commit to nothing, I suspect everyone at least needs to know why they are going. What do you *want*?

- Excitement or quiet?
- Gentle or raucous?
- Peaceful and lazy, or constant motion?
- Total sports, resting at the Spa, or somewhere in between?
- Fancy or casual?

What do you *need*?
- To reflect, recover, rebuild?
- To have new experiences?
- To hide out from the 21st century for a little while?
- To mark a milestone and celebrate?
- To just cut loose and have fun?

Our trips have covered the range from soul-searching to family reunions, school projects to anniversaries. Given all that I shared in Part I of this book, it is obvious that CW can offer a lot of a variety in a vacation. So, once you know what you want, then it's time to consider the when and the how.

CHAPTER TWENTY-THREE

....

SEASONS OF CW:
WHEN ARE YOU GOING?

Most of my visits until later in life, seemed to have landed in the main tourist season: summer. That made sense for all the years our son was with us because of summer breaks from school. The other times we might end up at CW were holidays, or family events.

As I've gotten older and have had the opportunity to visit at other times, I've had a chance to get a "taste" of all the "seasons of CW." The following is a review of the goings-on at CW at different times of the year. These "seasons" are not the usual winter, spring, summer, or fall ones. Instead they are based on the flow of visitation and activities I've experienced on many trips at different times of the year. They are not based on any official data; just the things I've observed. I found that matching my expectations to the time period ensured I had a great time and wasn't disappointed.

Summer (mid-June to early September)
This is the "in-season" time of the year. It offers all of the craziness, fun, and excitement of a tourist season as well as many benefits. All the venues are open, the days run long and bright, and even if a storm breaks into the day, it's usually due to the heat

and humidity, so the weather changes rapidly. Because it's warm, you don't have to worry about carrying around coats, gloves, or sweatshirts. Just water bottles and umbrellas should do the trick. Because it's vacation time for most schools, that means no homework to do, no school projects to work on, and everyone can stay up late and get started late in the morning. That certainly makes for a pleasant time for everybody. And of course, there are the big July 4th festivities and fireworks. What better place to celebrate the birth of our country than in the Revolutionary capital?

Early Fall (early Sept to mid-October)
At the other end of the spectrum, early September can feel like a car traveling at eighty m.p.h. suddenly slamming on its brakes. It is definitely a complete change from the hustle and bustle of the summer. However, if you want time to just relax and to explore at your leisure minus the crowds, this is a *great* time to come. Most schools are back in session but not ready for field trips yet so there's no large groups to compete with.

While the weather can still be hot and humid at times, most days are breezy, sunny, and just lovely to be out and about in. Even as you move into mid-October and some cooler temperatures, it's still glorious and at most a light jacket will keep you comfortable.

Halloween (late October to early November)
The quiet of September and early October starts to dissipate as excitement builds for the Halloween festivities, and later, Thanksgiving and Christmas. In addition to their regular programming, CW has been hosting special Trick-or-Treat events for young children as well as haunted Halloween events with pirate- or zombie-themed activities for older kids and adults. It is also prime season for walking through crunchy piles of brilliantly colored leaves as you tour. Crimsons, brilliant yellows, and deep oranges adorn the trees

and practically glow against beautiful blue skies. Even the overcast days have a beauty to them, with those same multi-colored leaves framed against steely-gray skies. Add to those visuals the scents of moist, sweet, over-ripe fruits and vegetables, moldy leaves, and rich dark humus in the cleaned-out garden beds and it is a sheer sensory pleasure.

Thanksgiving/Christmas (late November to late December)

I will expand on this time of year a little further down in this chapter. For my comments here, just consider this time of year at CW like a mini-summer in terms of big crowds and lots of activity. This is especially so right around Thanksgiving and Christmas, and especially during the Grand Illumination festivities in early December. The only differences are the temperatures are colder, the weather more unpredictable, and everyone is bundled up in jackets, hats, and gloves. These times also seem to bring their own gaiety. People are gathering with family and friends, there are lots of shopping opportunities, and there is that sense of abundance that comes in the form of package deals for hotels and admissions and special holiday meals to savor.

The weekend of Grand Illumination (the first weekend in December) has its own magic and the excitement is palpable. The ice-skating rink at Merchants Square is open. Fifes and drums are playing, fireworks are going off, and blazing cressets line the streets to provide illumination. Cressets are baskets on top of tall poles that hold burning fat wood. On cold nights, you can stand close to one and feel the warmth on your face, smell the aroma of burning wood, and hear the crackles and hisses as the flames hit the pine sap. It is rustic and lovely. And there is something about the short days and the cold temperatures that makes the season complete.

*The brilliant flames in the cresset baskets cut the
darkness of a CW Grand Illumination night.*

January

Except for locals, William and Mary students, and die-hards, CW
is mostly deserted in January. It is definitely the hibernation time
of the year. At this point, most venues are either shut down or

have shortened hours. It is a time when CW is busy behind the scenes, restoring, retraining, and restocking before the new year of visitors in the Spring. January can be gray, cold, and snowy. Generally, only the stoic, or those who love a brisk walk, will probably enjoy this time. However, don't worry. This "hibernation" period is what prepares CW for another busy year. But I would consider skipping January unless you're into solitude.

Winter (February to early March)
While this is still off-season and cold, some of the buildings have begun to reopen, even if hours are limited yet. They offer some special winter programs, and CW has a number of package deals for this time. February is the time of love and for sure there are Valentine's Day and other couples' weekend offerings. It is also Black History Month and there is an increased focus on the lives of the enslaved and free blacks in 18th-century Williamsburg. However, there are still a number of places that don't reopen until March. On our recent February, 2017 trip, the Raleigh Tavern Bakeshop, Blacksmith Shop, Market House, and all taverns except for Chowning's were still closed for the season. Also, getting into the Visitor Center to buy tickets for a nine-a.m. carriage ride was a no-go. The Center itself didn't open until eight-thirty a.m. to go in, and no ticket sales were available until nine. Also, no buses were running until nine. So, plan ahead and try to get any tickets the day before, if you're trying for an early tour. The schedule in March gets better as operations begin to return to more normal operating hours.

Early Spring (late March to early May)
Just like an animal peeking out and then pulling back inside its nest, the late March period can still be a little tentative. However, as April starts to dawn there are many exciting signs of life at

CW. Barren gardens that were prepared in the late fall are starting to show some early sprouts. Other patches are being tilled and planted with vegetables. Many of the early crops really start to take off, and flowers are in full bloom in early-mid April. There are wide swaths of brilliant yellows, reds, and purples in flowering tulip beds. Another sign of life is in the pastures. April is lambing season! Around this time, newborn lambs are making their appearance and visitors get to participate in naming some of the new arrivals. There are local garden festivals, special weekend programs, and people are starting to appear on the streets, biking and jogging. Even though the outside tables at the taverns and restaurants are not yet available, there is a definite feel of life in the air. And it is a special treat to take an open carriage ride in the crisp breeze. Cleans out all the mental cobwebs from winter.

Late Spring (early May to early June)

It is finally time to welcome the warm weather and the imminent arrival of summer crowds. This is a perfect time to have an "almost" summer experience, before it gets really hot and crowded. People are dining at open tables in Merchants Square. Runners are out in large numbers especially on weekday evenings after work, and many end their run outside DoG Street Pub to savor a cold brew. Local gardens are past the brilliant tulip displays and are now on to later-season flowers. The musket range is open and the weather is not likely to interfere with your reservation. Also, there are still special prices and pre-season package deals to be had, at least for a little longer. And if you like more hustle and bustle, there are a *lot* of school field trips at this time. So, while the huge influx of families may not be here yet, there is a definite buzz of activity given the number of school and other groups making their way around the Historic Area.

Some special comments about Thanksgiving and winter holiday times:

I've visited during the holidays and the line from Dickens' *A Tale of Two Cities* comes to mind: "It was the best of times, it was the worst of times." Now first, let me qualify my comments by noting that I am an introvert. Therefore, for me, being *anywhere* during a major holiday is an energy-draining ordeal and an acquired taste. So, please don't go by me for whether visiting places during a holiday time is good or bad. I'll just give you the good and the bad here as I see it. If you're an extrovert, you will find all of my comments a positive. If you're not, you'll be forewarned to prepare yourself, so you can still enjoy your time there.

The good news: Holidays can be special in a way the rest of the year can't match. To be there with all the hustle, bustle, decorations...it has a magical quality. The entire place is decked out in the majesty of the season, and if you are staying onsite, that means you don't have to contend with traffic, trying to find parking, or later trying to get out of Williamsburg traffic to get back to your hotel. The onsite hotels and restaurants really make it a memorable time, and the menus sometimes have seasonal options to try. It can be a joy to wander around on Grand Illumination night—an event that mirrors the Illumination events in the 18th century to celebrate a military victory, a monarch's birthday, or other special times.

The bad news: Schedule *months* in advance for Thanksgiving and Christmas lodging, restaurant, and activity reservations. And it's very difficult getting dinner reservations in Merchants Square. It's not quite so bad for just getting Thanksgiving dinner reservations for a colonial tavern, but I would still get them as soon as you know you want to go, and at least a couple months in advance. Other observations? It is packed. It can be very cold. There can be torrential rain or heavy snow. The regular activities are not going on during this time. And, this is a difficult time if you have any special needs. People can be rude, or at least oblivious. It is not CW's fault. They can't control crowds and who may or may not be polite or considerate.

So, are holiday visits hopeless? Absolutely not; in fact, they can provide some of the most cherished moments if you do two things: know yourself and your comfort limits, and do your homework. And this applies no matter the time of year you plan to visit. Ask yourself what activities you like and what you hate; which situations you love and which drive you crazy. Also, take into consideration any special needs or wishes. (I'll write more about this topic in the chapter on advance planning.) Then use the website or even call the Visitor Center to get the answers you need. Armed with this information, you stand a really good chance of having the visit you want...and creating your own special memories of CW. Good hunting!

CHAPTER TWENTY-FOUR

··

WEATHER IS YOUR TOUR GUIDE

I have been to CW in all seasons. While most of my visits have been in the summer and winter, there have also been the occasional fall and spring trips. The variation in the weather is as wide as the faces of the visitors. But for every bad weather day I've had there, it's resulted in some new, unexpected, and often pleasant experience. For example, in the winter, people huddle outside the taverns while waiting to be shown in, often commiserating about their mutual sense of chill. This then opens the door to conversations about themselves, where they are from, and what brought them to CW. I find that weather is often the mutually shared circumstance that encourages people to connect with each other, even if just for a brief moment.

In addition, weather can introduce you to some new experiences when it forces you to duck into some spot to escape the elements. Whether you need a reprieve from the heat, the cold, or the rain, you've only to step into one of the trade shops, stores, or museums for a respite. The weather is actually the most creative of tour guides, setting up new discoveries you would ordinarily miss. So, whatever happens with the weather at CW, I have learned to just go with it. That said, a few suggestions for what to bring with you might make those experiences more pleasant.

CW is located on the Tidewater Peninsula of Virginia, on a strip of high ground between the York and James Rivers. It is situated at the base of the Chesapeake Bay, just inland from the Atlantic Ocean to the east. While the spring and fall are generally sunny, cool, and mild, with gentle breezes, singing birds, and varying shades of plumage everywhere, the area does experience its share of changeable weather. Sudden storms, crushing humidity, and high heat in the summer are not unusual. Nor are hurricanes in the fall, wind and snow in the winter, and Nor'easters of various types throughout the year. Yet to be frank, that's not very different from what I can encounter at home, so I'm not giving up a trip to CW to avoid weather. I've learned how to adapt my days to enjoy them no matter what.

For the heat and humidity there's some things you can do. Plan your activities for early in the morning, late afternoons, and evenings. During the height of the heat, be back at your place of lodging for a swim in the pool, in a restaurant for a long, late lunch, back in your room for a nap, or—and here's the one time I'll recommend this—go shopping. Now, I hate clothes-shopping, but stores are air-conditioned, and if you enjoy looking for new things and consider that a treat, mid-afternoons are the perfect time to do that.

During the heat, there are a number of refreshment stands with the appropriate refreshments—ice water, soda, chilled or hot cider, and snacks—to keep you going. If you're willing to spend the whole day out on the streets, sun block, ball caps, or light umbrellas help keep the sun off you (or at least diffuse it). And the last two do double-duty for those late-day downpours on humid days. You can pick up a CW umbrella at just about any gift shop. I have about five in the back of my car. They are compact and fit easily in a small backpack.

Speaking of backpacks, if you put all your belongings into one you won't have that feeling of 10,000 sticky things hanging off of you. Yes, your back will get sweaty, but you will have a lot more freedom to move around. Not to mention you won't have to keep stopping to pick up all those odds-and-ends you keep dropping. Also, most backpacks have a pocket for water bottles, so you can easily stay hydrated. It's a small thing but it helps.

The right clothing helps, too. Light-colored clothing and drip-dry hiking attire are a definite plus, as are sun block, hats, and most especially, *good shoes.* Yes, you can wander in sandals and maybe they are open to the air, but unless they're the very supportive type of walking or hiking sandals, you may not appreciate them. With cobblestoned streets, horse droppings, sand, and oyster shells to walk on, and running kids to step on your toes, you may want to think practical vs. fashion statement, at least in the middle of the day. Save the dress sandals for dining out in the evening.

*Cobblestones provide a touch of the historic and are
beautiful to behold...but tough on the feet.*

As far as winter, *dress warm*. That is not the time for a light jacket. Come with a hat, gloves, scarf, and a good, warm jacket. You'll remain comfortable for the rest of the day. Besides, they've added an ice-skating rink near Merchants Square at Christmastime, so if you are dressed warmly, you can enjoy that, too.

Winter is a perfect time of year to wander around, soak up the season, and wonder what it must have been like to live in a time with no central heat—ever. When the cold starts to get to you, "hopscotch" your way through the Historic Area—jumping in and out of trade shops, gift shops and stores, touring houses and museums, or stopping at a tavern for lunch. The Blacksmith Shop is one of my favorites to visit in the winter. You're enclosed in a room with at least one coal-heated forge going—the perfect place to thaw out. Best of all, hot chocolate and hot cider can be found at booths on the streets or in the taverns, and let's face it, hot chocolate never tastes so good as when you're cold.

In short, to have a good time at CW, regardless of the season, focus on comfort, ease, and a practical approach, and you'll never go wrong.

CHAPTER TWENTY-FIVE

....

LET'S TALK
ADMISSION PRICES

Before we go any further, let's talk tickets. I am not going to get into the costs of hotels, the pros and cons of onsite vs. offsite lodging, or the food costs. Those topics depend on a lot of factors, such as personal preferences, priorities, and budgets. What I will talk about is admission tickets.

CW receives no government funding. For them to keep the doors open means they must take in enough in admissions and product sales to cover all their costs. That said, CW has many different admission tickets to choose from. There are single-day tickets, multi-day tickets, annual passes, special package deals that include lodging, some meals, and admissions passes, and lastly, combo tickets for CW and other places in the area. For example, CW, being the official hotel for Busch Gardens has currently worked out special shared admissions tickets and shuttle bus routes between the two. They also offer military and senior discounts, as well as different price ranges depending on the time of year. The decision for what you choose will really depend on what you want to focus on in the area, what time of year you are going, how long you are staying, if you will return in the next twelve months, and whether you want a package deal.

For us, the best value is an annual pass. We want to be able to access everything at CW, we live within a four-hour drive, have family in the greater Williamsburg area, and so we know we'll be back. Therefore, it makes sense for us to just get an annual pass. Even if we only return one more time in the year, we've gotten a good deal. And, I guess, speaking of priorities, even if we only went that one time during the year, we still get our money's worth considering how much we do when we go there.

I just renewed annual passes for my husband and me at CW, and the total for both of us was $123.00. That means unlimited admissions for the next twelve months for both of us. And in that twelve months, there are things open and accessible pretty much every month except January.

So just what do you get for that price? Let's look at it this way. What if you had to pay a separate admission for everything you do at CW? That would mean a separate admission to each major building—the Palace; the Magazine; the Capitol. Then add on another admission price to cover the many smaller buildings, houses, and gardens you can tour, which number in the dozens. Then include a package price for all of the live trade demos, as well as admission to each of the three museums—two art museums and one Public Hospital museum. In addition, include a price for the many hands-on activities, programs, and the services of historical interpreters, and don't forget to include bus fare for *each* time you ride the bus. Lastly, multiply that by any number of return trips over twelve months should you do that. That is a tremendous amount of value for the price.

The one-day admission fee currently runs between $25 -$40, depending on whether you want access to just the four main attractions or all of them. Both prices include all-day, unlimited shuttle bus service.

So, whichever way you go for admissions tickets, know you will get a *lot* for your money.

For the latest ticket prices and package deals, consult: http://www.colonialwilliamsburg.com/plan/tickets/

CHAPTER TWENTY-SIX

....

ADVANCE PLANNING AND
SPECIAL NEEDS

Because I am always planning for "my next trip to CW," I keep a running "wish list" of things I want to do next. But even if that were not the case, whenever I visit anywhere for the first time, I research it and make a plan. I call it "maximizing and anticipating." Some could say that planning ruins spontaneity and that sense of adventurous discovery, but that is my style. I feel best when I have a plan.

First, if I am going to spend money to travel, I want to maximize my time there. Even when I want to be "flexible," I still want to know what options I have to choose from. I'd hate to miss out on something because I didn't do my research to see what's there and what's possible. I can choose to pass on something, but if I miss something because I didn't look ahead I will regret it.

Second, researching a destination gets the "anticipation juices" flowing. As I research, I get more and more excited about all that is possible. Planning gives me a "taste of the place" long before I actually set foot there.

Here's where 21st-century online tools can really make travel research a pleasure, even for a "visit to 1775." For my CW planning, in the past I would eagerly anticipate the arrival in the mail of the latest version of the CW vacation planner, the multi-page booklet filled with beautiful pictures and the latest prices and package deals. Now, however, I can go on my computer any time of the year, and even any time of the day, to see what's new. I can do an online search and in seconds, access beautiful pictures and an abundance of the latest information. Everything I need is right at my fingertips.

CW's online presence would have impressed our forefathers: webcams, blogs, research sites, and the main CW travel and reservations site. If you go to the main website: http://www.colonial-williamsburg.com/, you'll find links for eating, accommodations, playing, learning, and their current schedule of programs. You can buy some program tickets ahead of time, set up hotel reservations, or arrange a tavern dinner, all while sitting at your computer in your pajamas! The link for "Learn" gives you a list of choices: History, Education, Publications, and Research, as well as the blog, Making History Now. Each link takes you to a wealth of information and offers several more topics to choose from.

Need to have a glimpse of CW just to tide you over until you arrive? The webcams can be found by clicking on the "History" link, then selecting the "Multimedia" tab on that page. With the push of a button, I can be at the King's Arms Tavern, gazing across the street at the Raleigh Tavern, watching some mom break up a fight between her two colonially dressed sons. It is as close to being there as you can get from a few hundred miles away. Another button push and I am at the Market House...or the Court House, the Armory, or the Capitol.

In addition to webcams, there are podcasts, slideshows, audio clips, virtual tours, maps, and games. Also, kids have their very own sites to plan from:

- http://www.history.org/kids/has games, activities, history and tips for teachers.

- http://www.history.org/kids/visitUs/index.cfm has the history, details, and town map
- http://discovery.history.org/about/ is an archaeology blog for kids. Catch up on the latest discoveries made by the younger visitors to CW.

Then there's the CW's blog, Making History Now (http://makinghistorynow.com), which is *great!* You can search on a multitude of topics and they'll no doubt have something helpful:

- Top 10 Things to Do
- Top 10 Things for Families to Go to
- Top 10 Things for Couples to Do
- Family Tips
- Kids' Hands-On Experience in The Trade Shops
- Deals and Discounts
- Mistakes to Avoid
- Guide for Gun Enthusiasts
- Guide for Photographers
- Pokémon Go
- Mom's Planning Guide

Have a question about CW? Just search that topic on the main website or their blog. Anything from food to archaeology, package deals to Halloween, it's all there. There is even a Frequently Asked Questions page: http://www.colonialwilliamsburg.com/plan/faq

In addition to all you can do at CW, there is also a wide range of places to visit and things to do in the greater Williamsburg area. Again, online searches are your asset here, too. Here are some search suggestions and no doubt these will lead to others:

- Jamestown
- Yorktown

- Water Country
- Busch Gardens
- Factory Outlets
- Campgrounds
- Richmond
- Norfolk—Navy Base tour; Waterfront Museum; ships to board; harbor tour
- Newport News—Mariner's Museum; Virginia Living Museum
- Virginia aquarium
- Horseback riding
- Williamsburg Winery
- Alewerks Brewing Company Tours
- Jamestown Discovery Boat Tours
- Ripley's Believe it or Not
- Williamsburg Ghost Tours

Special Packages

CW offers a wide variety of package deals throughout the year. Many are related to specific themes and some may be season-specific. Often, they include a hotel stay, meals, admission tickets, and access to special events. Some examples of past package deals include: an Autumn Couple's Weekend as well as one in the Spring; a Taste of Taverns Package; spring Garden Packages; Halloween packages, including the *"Haunting Package"* with an option to stay one night in a Haunted Colonial House, and *"Blackbeard's Revenge Vacation Package"* for a true zombie experience.

Also, there are more general-themed, family-targeted packages, such as the *"Revolutionary City Package,"* as well as the *"Spring Bounce Package."* The latter includes free tickets for both CW and Busch Gardens.

There are also discussions or deals in the works to provide special offerings for parents, alumni, staff, and faculty at both the

College of William and Mary, and Christopher Newport University in nearby Newport News.

The bottom line is that CW is always trying to expand their offerings to not only their visitors but to their community as well.

The packages and what they include change from year to year, so check the CW website for current offerings and promotions.

Special Needs

After a recent foot injury that required me to temporarily make my way around CW with a cane, I started to think about what I would do if this became permanent or I had more troubles getting around. The thought of giving up CW visits seemed terrible. But knowing how much walking, stairs, and crowds one can encounter there, I had to admit it would be a challenge. I have a lot of respect for anyone willing to brave it all when they don't get around well. And mobility issues aren't the only special need visitors may have to contend with. Hearing and vision impairments can pose problems, as can language differences. And visitors on the autism spectrum have specialized needs, too. In that vein, here are some thoughts about how to deal with some of these things to make a trip possible and hopefully a bit easier.

First, let's talk about mobility problems. As mentioned earlier, carefully consider the time of year to go and the size of crowds expected. Aside from the quiet of fall, early spring is another good time to visit. Both of these seasons offer pleasant weather, smaller crowds, all venues are open, and there is just more opportunity to take one's time. The buses aren't packed, and since all of them are kneeling buses with seats for seniors and those with mobility issues, as well as stations to anchor wheel chairs, getting around the area is definitely possible.

As for building access, there are a number of places in the Historic Area that have limited accessibility due to the age of the buildings. CW does offer a discounted admission ticket for guests with special needs, but be aware that not everything is accessible. One *nice* thing that's really helpful is that the CW website, http://www.colonialwilliamsburg.com/, provides a "Special Conditions" section at the bottom of the various page entries. These indicate accessibility availability or issues for each location, as well as any other helpful information. For example, here is the note at the bottom of the page for Wetherburn's Tavern:

> *"Wide doorways, spacious rooms; grounds and garden accessible. Six entrance steps with railing; outbuildings have one or more steps; most can be viewed from outside."*

These tidbits help in deciding what to visit, when, and what can be easily navigated. These entries also provide hours of operation as well as days closed.

Places that are accessible include the Visitor Center and the CW hotels (including some of the colonial houses). Some of the restaurants and taverns are as well, but I would check ahead of time to ensure that. Regarding bathrooms, the Visitor Center can provide information as to ones that are especially designed to provide easy accessibility. I also talk more about bathrooms in an upcoming chapter.

Mobility issues are not the only needs that people may have. There are resources for visual and hearing disabilities as well and CW recommends calling about a month in advance if signing interpreters or guides for the visually impaired need to be scheduled. CW can also help with some language differences. They have guides and information available in several languages. Just ask for these in the Visitor Center.

Also, there is a well-written entry on the CW blog by a young woman with autism, Kristy Makuta, about her visits to CW.

(Go to http://makinghistorynow.com/and search for: "Colonial Williamsburg: Experienced Through the Eyes of Autism.") Unable to visit with a school group, she and her family prepared carefully and went on their own. She had a wonderful experience in spite of some of her struggles, and found the staff very helpful. In fact, she wrote thanking a particular staff member for the kind way she made Kristy feel at ease, without even knowing of the girl's autism. As a result, CW contacted Kristy about revisiting the Historic Area and perhaps sharing some helpful insights with various staff members to teach them how to better work with autistic visitors. Together they crafted a special trip with a variety of experiences all designed to minimize anxiety and stress. The article is a delight to read.

So, if there are special needs for a visitor, my suggestion is to consider what time of year might work best, and contact CW ahead of time to indicate what your needs are and see what special assistance may be available. They can arrange for special parking passes, wheelchair rentals, portable ramps, buses with lifts, and so on, and may be able to point you to further resources, or make you aware of any other limitations to take into account.

You can contact CW at:

The Visitor Center Administrative Office
Colonial Williamsburg Visitor Center
101A Visitor Center Drive
Williamsburg, Virginia 23185
(757) 220-7205

More information can be found at:
http://www.colonialwilliamsburg.com/plan/accessibility/

CHAPTER TWENTY-SEVEN

....

HOW TO GET THERE

So where exactly is CW and how does anyone get there? CW is located on the Tidewater Peninsula in Virginia. It is about an hour east of Richmond, and about the same amount of time northwest of Norfolk. It can be reached by highway, bus, train, or plane.

Highways: Given that most people have a GPS, this part is probably not needed, but here's a recap anyway. From the northern or southern U.S., you can approach via I- 95 north or south toward Richmond, follow I-295 around Richmond, and then take I-64 east. At that point, just follow the signs to CW. From the east or west, you can approach on I-64 and again, follow the exit signs to the CW Visitor Center.

Traffic jams are frequent on I-64. Also, road construction to widen I-64 from Newport News to Williamsburg is underway and is expected to continue for some years to come. In short, expect delays. Alternate routes are a godsend, and they're usually more "scenic." This includes Virginia Route 60, the old main highway from Richmond to Williamsburg, which parallels I-64.

If you are driving between CW, Historic Jamestown, and the Yorktown Battlefield, there is a lovely road that connects them called "The Colonial Parkway." It's a slower pace but a beautiful ride on pebbled concrete roads CW built back in the 1930s. Just a tip—the Colonial Parkway has three unmarked lanes, one for each direction, and one in the middle for passing *where allowed*. Many visitors to the area tend to drive more in the middle of two lanes, preventing anyone from passing. Whether intentional or not, please avoid this because, at best, all it does is slow down traffic, and at worst, I've seen some near accidents. Stay in your lane on the right and only get in the middle lane to pass.

Bus: I have seen many bus trips advertised by various private bus companies over the years that include CW as part of their trip itinerary to the area. Check with your chosen bus line or newspaper ads to see what trips are available and how long they will be in Williamsburg.

Train: Amtrak's website gives details for how to travel by rail to CW: https://www.amtrak.com/home.html

Plane: There is a major international airport in Richmond, one in Norfolk, and a smaller one in Newport News, just east of Williamsburg. From those airports, you can rent a car and head to CW on I-64.

No matter how you approach, if you are anything like me, there is that final moment of excitement when entering the traffic circle just outside of the Visitor Center. At that moment, you have arrived! You can then cross from current-day reality to the place of historic dreams where new memories are born.

CHAPTER TWENTY-EIGHT

....

THE VISITOR CENTER

You would know it was the Visitor Center even if the sign didn't tell you. From the cars hunting for a parking space, the people streaming toward the Center's entrance like determined bees returning to the hive, and the steady parade of shuttle buses stopping at the building, you can't miss it.

While you can enter from the side where the shuttle bus drops riders off, that would be an underwhelming first impression. To experience the Visitor Center at its best, follow the winding walkway (and all the people) to the back of the building where a terraced garden flanks a cascading waterfall. That leads to the main entrance. In front of the building is a huge cast-metal map of the Historic Area spread before you—your first hint of what awaits you.

Across from that, the glass entrance is open and welcoming. I particularly like that even the local birds find shelter there under the high, extended roof of the entranceway. It is as if the place has opened its arms to all, including nature.

Once inside, the sensation is airy vastness—a wide open, high-ceilinged hall, bright with natural light. Colorful colonial flags adorn the sides of the hall and contrast nicely with the gray tile floor and columns. Your senses are alive and responding to voices, lights, people, colors, and music. There's a large bookstore on the right and a well-stocked gift shop on the left. Next to the gift shop is a small cafe with light meals to stem any hunger.

The Information Desk is in the middle of the building, with rest rooms to either side. The helpful desk staff are ready to answer questions, get you started in the right direction, and hand out daily schedules of activities or information pamphlets available in several different languages.

Then, there is the rest of the building, the portal to it all, the beginning of your adventure. Once you cross over that threshold, you are on a quest with hundreds of others, to get what you want for your time there. It is a huge hall, packed with people, especially in the mornings. But it is not chaos. Just standing there looking out over the furor, I feel a mix of things—anxiousness to get going, peace at the familiarity, and gratitude that after all these years people are still drawn to the place. It's the one time as an introvert that I love a crowd because these are the sights and sounds that tell me that yet again, I am in my favorite place.

There are the sales counters to get your admission badges and any event tickets you'd like. There's also a desk for any special-needs services. If you need help with mobility issues, hearing-impairments, wheelchairs etc., the people at that station can help you. At the other end of the building is the theater playing the classic orientation film, made especially for CW: "Story of a Patriot."

Beyond the theaters, you reach the end of the building, and a decision. You can take the staircase that leads down to the shuttle bus pickup point—our traditional way of approaching the Historic Area. Or you can head to the town by walking across the "Bridge to the Past"—a 500-foot walkway that opened in 2002. It doubles as a "timeline" to lead you from the present day, back to the 18th century, with various historical events noted on it as you "walk back in time."

On a sunny day with no particular to-do list in mind, a stroll across the bridge down into town is lovely. Its tree-shaded path under warm skies, with birds singing and a cool breeze brushing away buzzing insects, is heaven. On days when I can't wait to get started, I opt for the shuttle bus. But either way, once we have reached this point, as Sherlock Holmes has said, "The game is afoot."

Just a few ending tips:
For additional information on The Visitor Center, go to the link: http://www.colonialwilliamsburg.com/plan/visitor-center/

The Visitor Center's bookstore has a couple of helpful things you might consider buying before you get on your way. One valuable aid for navigating the Historic Area is a copy of the *Official Guide to Colonial Williamsburg*. The almost 300-page guidebook has a lot of helpful information on just about anything you can think of, including special tips for first-time visitors. For something more compact, there is a 96-page pocket guide that has essential information on all the locations in the colonial town, as well as details about special events, night programs, and other activities.

If you are staying at any of the on-site CW hotels, you can choose to do all (or most) of your ticketing arrangements at your hotel. We often stay at either the Woodlands, or lately, the Williamsburg Lodge. Many of the admission passes and program tickets can be obtained right there. There are also locations within the Historic Area, such as the Lumber House ticket office or the one in Merchants Square, where you can get tickets to various activities and general admissions passes. Sometimes these other ticketing places are a little quieter and less crowded than the Visitor Center.

Lastly, CW's website has a FAQ page that can help with some basic information. Check out: http://www.colonialwilliamsburg.com/plan/faq/

CHAPTER TWENTY-NINE

....

PLAN OF ATTACK

C hances are you've probably done at least some research on the website ahead of time. You may have your to-do list, and maybe even purchased some of your tickets in advance. On the other hand, maybe you've shown up on a whim with no preset plan. Either way, to get the most out of your visit you will need some kind of "plan of attack."

The first thing I do is get the daily *Program Guide* from the Information Desk at the Visitors Center, or from any of the hotel front desks. And for those who don't do paper and prefer to use their phones, CW has mobile apps for Apple and Android devices. I found the old version of their app to be somewhat frustrating because the information was limited. However, the new one includes interactive maps, multi-day schedules, and more information on the various sites.

For those who are "paper-based," the daily guide sheets list everything happening that day, by the time of day. Consider it your "menu" to choose from. I usually get the guide for each of the days that I plan to be there. This way I can see what programs are offered across my whole visit and spread out my schedule. Many programs are offered multiple times a day, or at least multiple times a week. Also, some of the craft shops, taverns, and other buildings are not open every day. By viewing the guides for different days, you can check out exactly what days or times various spots are open or closed, avoiding disappointment. Even if you are like me and arrive with a detailed to-do list, you still have to match that up to the reality of what is actually being offered once you get there.

Either way, phone or paper, my suggestion is to take a moment to go through the listings and select what strikes your fancy for things you want to do. Make sure to note how long a particular program is, whether it is offered more than once that day, and where in town it is located. For example, if two programs that you want to see overlap, then you know you'll need to catch one of them at a different time or on a different day. Knowing the location is just as important as the time offered. If two programs run back-to-back and they're both at the same end of town, you can probably fit them in. But if they are located at opposite ends of CW, accept that you'll never make the second one in time even if you're an Olympic sprinter.

Regarding the programs, there is an extensive array to watch or participate in each day and also several in the evenings. Some of the programs are ongoing and just require the general admission ticket. Others are limited in time and the numbers of visitors that can participate, so they may require an additional "free, with an admission badge" ticket. That one is all about keeping participant numbers manageable. And there are some programs especially in the evenings that will require purchasing a special ticket.

Some of the things you'll see offered can include joining the army at the military encampment or being part of an angry mob storming the Governor's Palace to demand he return the gunpowder stolen from the Magazine. You can be present for the dissolution of the House of Burgesses by the Governor's decree, participate in a court trial, or be part of a bucket brigade in an

18th-century fire-fighting team. Experience the dramatic tensions that arise over race, gender, class and culture, when three enslaved women go into labor and an enslaved midwife must accept help from a local white midwife *and* the male doctor. Later watch General Lafayette interrogate a spy, then finish the day with one of several "behind-the-scenes" tours to learn how a place like CW functions.

And don't forget the ghosts. Both the George Wythe and Peyton Randolph houses, as well as a number of other sites in CW have a reputation for being haunted. Staff working late at those sites have reported odd activities, such as doors closing, scraping chairs, furniture turned upside down, and voices in a locked house. Visitors too, have reported seeing images of women in long gowns or colonial soldiers passing through a room. One can learn more about these occurrences by taking one of the ghost tours or evening ghost programs. The Visitor Center's bookstore, as well as the College of William and Mary Bookstore in Merchants Square, also carry a large selection of books about these occurrences. And in 2016, CW offered Halloween packages that included an overnight stay in some of the haunted buildings.

A fairly new offering is the chance to fire 18th-century firearms in the *"To Fire a Flintlock Musket"* program. Anyone fourteen years of age or older can purchase tickets to participate. You learn about the firearms, their history, how to operate them, and then have the opportunity to target shoot with two different firearms. They have also just introduced ax-throwing as well.

In addition to the structured programs and activities, there are other experiences available to you. Take a stroll down any street in CW and you will meet people in colonial garb. They are the historical character interpreters. They are not there to be living decorations. Each person has taken on the role of an 18th-century citizen, researched it, and then brought that person to life. These interpreters are knowledgeable about many facets of life in the 1700s and are interested in engaging you in conversation. They can be anyone from a blacksmith, an enslaved man or woman, or a tavern maid, to Thomas Jefferson or Martha Washington. And it's not just adults who serve in this role. Children also serve as historical interpreters through CW's Junior Interpreter program. Aside from the experience it provides the children who participate—and it is a highly competitive program to join—they are often very successful in connecting with the young children who visit the area. Lest you think it's just fun and games, know that these Junior Interpreters are given thorough training in communication skills, 18th-century manners, interpretation techniques, and history, as well as training in 1700s education methods, chores, speaking, and costume-wearing. CW has found these Junior Interpreters are talented at not only engaging the many children who visit the Historic Area, but their parents as well. The Junior Interpreters are most often present during vacation seasons, school breaks, and weekends. The adult interpreters are always there.

Another way to approach creating a plan of action is that you could focus your visit around a specific theme. This allows you to choose exactly the type of experience you want at any particular moment. Some of my "themes" are:

- Heart: Interact with the dedicated staff and learn from them; Explore the barns and fields and just watch the animals.
- Causes: Participate in programs that explore the issues behind rebellion, slavery, and American Indian life.
- Gardening: Stroll through the vegetable, floral, and decorative gardens and enjoy the sensory abundance of sight, smell, and touch.
- Rest and Indulgence: Keep a light schedule for touring and instead savor the lovely hotels, taverns, spa, and a great dinner at the Fat Canary restaurant.

- Revisit past experiences: Stop by the Raleigh Tavern and enjoy the gingerbread cookies; sit in the Orlando Jones garden, or visit all the secluded spots throughout the Historic Area that I find relaxing and special.
- Geeky/Historical: Sign up to shoot the muskets; Take part in behind-the-scenes programs and tours; Participate in hands-on trade experiences; Visit the library and research some new aspect of history for my writing or just for my own interest; Discover some new restoration and conservation project that is going on and find out what they are learning; Revel in observing the multitude of accurate details that make CW what it is.
- Play the Tourist: Go on carriage rides; Take the ghost tour; Do the things that a first-time visitor would do and see what new things I notice that I missed before.
- Culture: Visit the art museums; Participate in art programs; Spend time with my camera or oil paints, capturing the beauty of CW; Indulge in classical music.

Finally, here's a list of just a few other CW activities available to choose from:
- Rent period clothes (You can rent them at the Visitor Center)
- Rent bikes
- Lawn bowling
- Miniature golf
- Eat in a tavern
- Golf at one of three Williamsburg golf courses
- Hike the nature trails in the area
- Participate in a one-hour horseback trail ride (offsite)
- Games, such as volleyball, table tennis and shuffleboard
- Pools & a playground

Whatever you decide to do or wherever you choose to start, it is helpful—especially for the first-time visitor—to obtain a CW map at the Visitor Center's Information Desk. If you can get familiar with the main street and basic town layout, it will be easier to navigate your visit.

Now, you've obtained your program guide, purchased your tickets, and are ready to embark on your adventure. And you've formed your plan for the important things like: Which place should you visit first? When should you have lunch? Where should you meet up?

That leaves just one more "basic needs" question to deal with, and an important one at that. For me, wherever I visit, one of the first things I determine is: Where are the bathrooms? After my many years of visiting CW, I know where all their facilities are. So, I now use my "superpower" for the benefit of others, pointing out the facilities for people frantically searching, especially those with young children in tow.

That CW map from the Information Desk is also a handy way to avoid frantic searchers because it lists all the restroom locations throughout the Historic Area and also indicates which ones are handicap-accessible and which ones are family restrooms. The CW app for your smart phone can also show this information too. Either resource is handy to have at the ready.

The Taverns also have restrooms—though I don't know if they are only for the use of their dining patrons—but bear in mind that some of them may be upstairs or downstairs, which could be a problem for accessibility.

Here's a quick list of some of the bathroom locations:
- The Visitor Center
- At the Capitol end of Duke of Gloucester Street, between the Capitol and the Christiana Campbell's Tavern bus stop

- Around the corner from Duke of Gloucester Street, on Botetourt Street, right where people can get on and off their carriage rides
- Behind the Magazine, near the bus stop
- Right at the bus stop for the Merchants Square Ticket Office
- Across the street from the Palace

Also, consider asking at the Visitor Center which facilities are best for handicap-accessibility and for families. Here is a list of some wheelchair-accessible restrooms:

- Colonial Williamsburg Regional Visitor Center
- Williamsburg Lodge
- Merchants Square Ticket Office
- The Art Museums of Colonial Williamsburg
- Bassett Hall Reception Center
- Adjacent to the Magazine on Francis Street between the Capitol and Waller Street
- On Botetourt Street between Duke of Gloucester Street and Nicholson Street
- On the Palace grounds
- The King's Arms Purdie Kitchen has a ramp and an ADA-accessible restroom
- Shields Tavern has a ramp and an ADA-accessible restroom
- Chowning's Tavern has a ramp and an ADA-accessible restroom

So now you're ready to get moving. If you're departing the CW Visitor Center by bus, head down to the ground floor level of the Visitor Center to catch the next one. The buses are great, use environmentally-friendly fuel, and most if not all have places to secure visitors in wheelchairs. The buses can "kneel" and even have ramps that can be extended for easier boarding.

During the peak tourist season, they run every five-to-ten minutes, so you won't have to wait very long. The only exception to this is trying to catch the bus at the Merchant Square stop at five p.m. Try to catch the bus *anywhere* but there at that time of day. It's just the combination of bad luck, time of day, crowds, and geography. It is the very last stop before the bus heads back to the Visitor Center. There are exhausted shoppers, overwrought kids, and *lots* of hungry people waiting to board. While CW does run extra buses at that time of day to alleviate the larger crowds, I just prefer to avoid them completely. I will often walk back toward a different stop to catch the bus there, instead.

Depending on the time of year or even the time of day, bus routes may vary. Over the years, they've had many variations of how to run their routes, so before leaving the Visitor Center, check on how they are currently operating. And however they operate during the day, the routes might change at night. Often there is an attendant right at the Visitor Center bus stop so you can ask them what the current schedule is.

A helpful hint to make bus riding even more pleasant, and efficient. Since the bus driver will ask that all riders exit by the back side-door, try to get the seat across from the back side-door exit. You'll be one of the first people off the bus, and won't have any hassles waiting for others to push by you. I would be lying if I said that every person who gets on the bus is polite, waits their turn, or doesn't hog the handicap-accessible seats. On occasion, I have seen people cut ahead of those in wheelchairs or using canes. I am not above snarling at someone when I see that. But most of the time, and considering the crowds that ride those buses every day, most people are pleasant and polite. Many will chat and ask for information about what to do next from other riders.

Armed with this information, you'll be on your way to a wonderful adventure in history. Just one last thing—try to remember to greet and thank the bus drivers. Most are really very nice and helpful, and not all visitors treat them very well.

CHAPTER THIRTY

···

TAVERN SMORGASBORD

There are a number of taverns in CW and they have a variety of uses. Some—like Wetherburn's Tavern near the Capitol, and the Raleigh Tavern right across the street—offer tours, concerts, plays, or programs. Two—the Market Square Tavern and the Brick House Tavern—are operated as hotels. And in spite of their colonial appearance, you *will* get your own room, complete with heat or air-conditioning, *and* an indoor bathroom! Four operate as restaurants—The King's Arms, Shields, Christiana Campbell's, and Chowning's. Lastly, there are a number of taverns or "ordinaries," as they were sometimes called, that are privately owned and not open to the public.

Regarding dining at the taverns, all except Chowning's require dinner reservations. Lunch at any of those that offer it will not need reservations. This would include Chowning's, King's Arms, and Shields, though the latter two have a varying lunch schedule as to who is open on which day. So, it is best to check ahead before you go. Each has varying degrees of handicap-accessibility and again, except for Chowning's, dinner schedules rotate at the various taverns and require reservations. It's best to plan ahead and to ask for recommendations to meet any special needs. Also, the taverns offer gluten-free selections.

One last thing to note. On a recent trip to CW in February, which is a time when a lot of the activities and buildings are closed due to staff training and facilities repairs, Chowning's was the only tavern open for lunch and dinner. The others were scheduled to reopen on March 1 or later. So, if traveling in winter, especially January or February, it's best to check ahead on what is available to avoid the disappointment I felt when I realized I would not be able to visit either the King's Arms Tavern or the Raleigh Tavern Bakeshop.

Here are some additional bits of information for the specific taverns.

The King's Arms Tavern

I've already shared a lot about this one so I'll keep it brief. The King's Arms Tavern, near the Capitol, has a more refined atmosphere than the others. They serve lunch and dinner and also have an outdoor garden for lunch behind the building. The main part of the restaurant does not have an ADA-accessible restroom; however, the Purdie Kitchen, which is part of the complex and is attached to the King's Arms, does have these facilities. So, when checking in with the hostess, be sure to specify if that is a need.

Shields Tavern

A few doors down from the King's Arms is Shields Tavern. Some of the dining areas are very similar to the decor of King's Arms, with the whitewashed walls, wooden floors, and simple but elegant table settings. The main difference between the two is that the King's Arms offers menu choices that would have been offered to the most elite in Williamsburg society. Shields' 18th-century patrons had a slightly more frugal budget and they try to reflect that in today's entrees. They include things such as Salmagundi, Ginger Sac Stewed Chicken, Grilled Vegetable Trencher, and

Ale-Potted Beef. For the complete descriptions of these dinners just go to the CW website and check out the menus listed under the various taverns.

In addition to colonial favorites, Shields also offers modern day options like their "All-American," all-beef, quarter-pound hot dogs, chopped beefsteak sandwiches, and Carolina-style barbecue. My absolute favorite place to sit in that tavern is down in the basement, especially on hot days. It is cool down there, dark, and more intimate. And at five p.m., their dinner theater takes place there. It's an audience-participatory event—meaning it's designed to put you into the action of a topic from the 1700s. The show's acts take place between the courses of the three-course meal. A recent example is a play about the life of a "jolly pyrate" (pirate).

Christiana Campbell's Tavern
Campbell's tavern specializes primarily in seafood and offers such dishes as the Waterman's Supper, Seafood Fricassee, Pan-Seared Codfish, and Shrimp Randolph. In a nod to non-seafood diners, they also offer Molly's Macaroni and a Hickory-Grilled Rib-Eye. Whatever you order, do have the sweet potato muffins. They are to die for.

Chowning's Tavern
The fourth tavern operated by CW as a restaurant is Chowning's. Situated further west on Duke of Gloucester Street, it is near Market Square and the Magazine. This is the working-man's tavern, the kind I think of more as a "tankards-and-slabs" kind of place—that is, tankards of ale and slabs of meats, cheeses, and breads to fill your insides. It was recently "re-interpreted," which resulted in three changes.

First, as mentioned above, it is the only tavern open for lunch and dinner that does not require reservations. Second, it's been reinvented as an 18th-century alehouse, which in itself is great. Alehouses, as the name implies, focused on serving beer and ales, and brewing them. So, while the King's Arms might serve primarily wine and cider with perhaps some ales, an alehouse primarily focused on the brews. Best of all in my book is the redesigned interior. The people who run CW have always had a willingness to look deeper into the past and correct any historical inaccuracies. Chowning's, for years, had dark-paneled walls, including around the fireplace. It was decorated in a fashion people "thought" was correct for colonial times. However, newer technology, including the equipment to view microscopic sections of paint chips, revealed that the interior colors were actually much lighter. The dark tones had resulted from the effects on pigments of time, age, and exposure. Armed with more accurate information, CW designers redid the interior of the tavern and restored it to that of an alehouse. Yet it has kept that earthy quality in terms of its clientele.

The third change is the updated menu that's in keeping with the alehouse approach. The choices are solid fare like: Roasted Corn Chowder with Ham Dust, Beef or Turkey Trenchers, Shepherd's Pye, Chowning's Pasty and Brunswick Stew, the last of which was delicious and hit the spot after a long morning of tours and walking. Drinks include historical offerings such as Josiah's Spiced Punch, or Chowning's Flip—described in the menu as "Art in the Age Root Liqueur, Dark Rum, Cinnamon Syrup, and Egg Whites." I don't necessarily understand what "Art in the Age Root Liqueur" means, but I'll often try something odd like that just to be adventurous. There are also many new creations and, of course, a wide range of ales and wines.

There is an arbor garden area behind the building. They offer music and tavern fare on Friday nights, as well as special nights where you can sample a variety of beers and talk to special guests from the local breweries. These events are the only things at Chowning's that may require advance reservations.

The other thing they offer is entertainment. From 5 p.m. on, every evening, they have something called Gambols—colonial drinks with games and music. The earlier part of the evening is family-oriented whereas later it shifts more to adult mode. Also, some Friday nights in the back garden they have live entertainment. So, if you like your nights a little louder and more casual than the other taverns, check out Chowning's.

Other Taverns

As mentioned, Wetherburn's Tavern is located close to the Capitol building at the east end of Duke of Gloucester Street and offers guided tours. Since Wetherburn's is one of the original buildings in CW, it has quite a history. The site has been restored and is interpreted using the decades' worth of research data they collected during the extensive archaeological excavations there.

The Raleigh Tavern, with its history steeped in everything from political intrigue and revolution, to dances, concerts, and slave auctions, continues that theme today. Located close to the Capitol on Duke of Gloucester Street, it offers onsite tours, after-hours plays, concerts, and interactive events. And of course, it has an amazing bakeshop in back, with all kinds of goodies to eat including delicious fresh-baked gingerbread cookies.

The Brick House and the Market Square Taverns are used as part of the Colonial houses lodging. In addition, scattered across the Historic Area are a number of homes that may have served as taverns or ordinaries. They are identified by the metal plaques on either the right or left corners of the building. Most of these houses are privately owned so they are not available to tour. Nevertheless, they give an indication of what the buildings were used for in the past, and how extensive the number of such places were. A few examples are Hartwell Perry's Tavern on the west end of Duke of Gloucester Street across from Bruton Parish Church; the Edinburgh Castle Tavern at the east end of Duke of Gloucester Street near the Capitol and Charlton's Coffeehouse; and the Red Lion on Duke of Gloucester Street near Chowning's Tavern.

CHAPTER THIRTY-ONE

....

FOOD AND SHELTER

I realize not everyone may find tavern fare to their liking, their budget, or their time constraints. Sometimes you just want modern food or familiar comforts. CW can offer that as well.

First, there are some options right at the Visitor Center. The cafe at the Visitor Center offers quick items all day, from hot meals to sandwiches, fruits, and snacks. Huzzah's Eatery, located behind the nearby Woodlands Hotel, is available for supper and has all modern fare including burgers and pizza.

Scattered throughout the Historic Area are a number of choices as well. If you get hungry while at the Art Museum you can stop in at their cafe, open from 11:00—4:00, and get a quick bite. Soups, salads, sandwiches, beverages, and snacks round out the options. The Williamsburg Lodge has a restaurant, Traditions, that serves breakfast and lunch, as well as a Friday-night seafood buffet. They also have the Sweet Tea & Barley pub with outdoor and bar seating for later in the day. The Williamsburg Inn has casual as well as fine dining options in the form of their five-star restaurant— The Regency Room—a more relaxed option in the Terrace Room, and the Gold Course Grill, and Green Course Clubhouse Grill for lunches and dinners. Throughout CW there are stands with drinks, cookies, fruit, and other snacks available for purchase.

Also, beverages and sandwiches, along with cookies and other snacks are available at the Raleigh Tavern Bakeshop.

For a different approach, on South England Street, there is an option that combines food with education—the Taste Studio. It's a full-service demonstration kitchen where you will not only get a good meal in an intimate setting, but you'll learn how the CW chefs work their magic to create it.

Merchants Square has a wide variety of options. There are a number of shops with family-friendly offerings within the square or nearby blocks: Stephanos Pizza and Subs; burgers, sandwiches, and great local brews at DoG Street Pub; sandwiches at the Barnes and Noble Cafe; and my #1 favorite, The Cheese Shop, which is right next to the Fat Canary restaurant. At the Cheese Shop, not only can you can get fresh bread, huge sandwiches big enough to share, and soup, but they also specialize in fresh cheeses. To walk through their aisles is to feel like you are in a European cheese cave.

In addition, they also have a wide range of salads, yogurts, desserts—pretty much anything you might want for lunch—and at reasonable prices. It's an informal "market" atmosphere with some indoor seating and tables on the patio outside.

Their wine cellar downstairs is fantastic and has a large selection of domestic and foreign wines, including a large number of "Highly Recommended" ones at http://www.winespectator.com/. I happen to like a particular crisp white wine, Gruner Veltliner. More specifically, I like a certain brand: Loimer Lois. I cannot find it easily; in fact I usually can only find it online. But The Cheese Shop carries it in their wine cellar.

On nearby streets there are breakfast places, cafes, seafood restaurants, bistros, and bakeries. You can find everything from fine cuisine to cinnamon sticky buns. Here's just a few of the places currently in the vicinity: Aromas Specialty Coffees, Bakery & Cafe; Blackbird Bakery; Blue Talon Bistro; Berret's Seafood; and the Trellis. There's even a Baskin-Robbins. A quick Google search will reveal the scrumptious details for each.

And if you are heading off the CW grounds, the town of Williamsburg has a large number of restaurants, ranging from pancake houses to fine dining. There are several shopping areas and factory outlets, with a variety of restaurants, pubs, and fast food. Just search online for Williamsburg restaurants to make your choices.

As to "shelter," during the years that we've been going to CW, we spent many of those lodging in offsite hotels. There are several, some close to CW, some closer to factory outlets. There are also campgrounds. Where you stay will depend partly on what activities you want to focus on while you're there, as well as your budget. My suggestion is to start by doing a web search for hotels in the area. Also, consider contacting hotel chains you like to stay at to get the latest info, availability, and prices. Summers are *busy*, and so is Thanksgiving and the entire month of December. Advanced planning is a must at those times.

While offsite lodging can provide some great deals, before you write off CW hotels as too expensive, consider that they also offer package deals, including admission tickets to CW and other locations (such as Busch Gardens, Water Country, Jamestown, and Yorktown) and reduced room rates at certain times of the year. Not only that, but being right on site, especially if your stay is a short one, you can get right to the action without any time lost commuting back and forth to a hotel. There are military, senior, and AAA discounts as well. I want to mention three places onsite at CW that we have stayed at and loved.

First, of course, are the Colonial Houses, which give a special touch to your stay. And no need to worry about modern-day conveniences like air-conditioning and plumbing. CW has made an art of running electricity, air-conditioning, heat, and modern plumbing into the historic homes, without really being obvious. Well, yes, the bathroom is obvious, but the introduction of our modern conveniences in these places has been done with a great degree of subtlety.

If this is an experience you would love, check out this link: http://www.colonialwilliamsburg.com/stay/colonial-houses/

At the bottom of that page they also note options for those who might require special assistance/handicap-accessible accommodations.

There is also the newly renovated Williamsburg Inn. I have not stayed there yet, but it has an aura of refinement and elegance.

As an adult, my family and I have stayed at the Woodlands, a hotel right on the grounds of the Visitor Center. It has the usual assortment of doubles, kings, and suites that will accommodate various-sized groups, with mini-refrigerators and microwaves in the rooms. They also have a free continental breakfast, including waffle-makers so you and your children can make fresh waffles (and as many as you want). For supper, Huzzah's Eatery featuring current-day cuisine and family favorites, is right next to the hotel.

The nice thing about staying at the Woodlands is that you can park your car and essentially forget about it. The Visitor Center is right next door and from there you can pick up the shuttle bus or walk down into the Historic Area. Who needs to drive when you're right there? It's nice not to have to face the daily battle of looking for a parking space in the visitor lot if you don't get there early. We always found it worth the price for the convenience of location, the free parking, the food, and the room arrangements.

The other onsite place we have stayed at more recently is the Williamsburg Lodge, which was renovated and expanded in 2006. We'd never stayed there before, but as we got older, we thought it might be nice to see what is was like. The Lodge is in the center of the Historic Area and just around the corner from the Williamsburg Inn. It has a shuttle bus stop right there, a bar/ grille restaurant (Sweet Tea & Barley) right off the main lobby, a full restaurant (Traditions), room service, and lovely decor. You are greeted at the door and they can take your bags directly to your room. No struggling with suitcases and carts, and also no struggles with cars if you don't want that hassle. While you can park your car yourself in a nearby lot, you can also have the valet park it for you in a secure lot or garage. Again, that's the last you need to see of, or worry about, your car, unless you want to leave CW's grounds for something. This hotel's style is a bit more upscale and quieter than the Woodlands, quieter being something I appreciate. I'm not an old curmudgeon, just tired, and when I go to CW now, I like a quiet place to retreat to.

Our room was spacious, had a soft couch to relax on as well as extra chairs and a desk. Little sensory details mean a lot now, especially simple things like the spicy smell of the body gel in the bathroom, something you can buy at the Spa. (I did...and I periodically order more via the website or phone when I start to run low at home.) There are very few things I really splurge on, but colognes, scented soaps, and oils, are things I find delightful and relaxing. So, the soap in the bathroom was appreciated. The other thing I am very much aware of these days is the comfort of a good bed. A sound night's sleep is high on my priority list, so a plush bed is my other indulgence. I wasn't disappointed.

Lodge guests are also given complimentary access to the Williamsburg Spa across the street. Suffice it to say here that you get free access to the indoor and outdoor swimming pools, exercise equipment, and locker rooms. And you're right near the golf courses, tennis courts, lawn bowling, and croquet grounds. I am a pool person, so having a heated indoor pool available for laps makes me happy.

Would I stay at the Lodge again? You bet! Between the lovely room, soap, comfortable bed, and the convenience of a restaurant *and* pub in the hotel, not to mention its perfect location right smack in the middle of the Historic Area, I couldn't ask for better accommodations. It's pricier than the Woodlands, but they do run specials and have discounts, so ask about those.

Traditions, their in-house restaurant, is available for breakfast and lunch as well as a Friday night seafood buffet. Frankly, my favorite meal there is the full buffet breakfast. They offer a continental breakfast on steroids (everything you can think of), *plus* hot breakfast items: eggs, bacon, sausage, fresh oatmeal, pancakes/ French toast ... With a breakfast like that, who needs to eat until supper? And by the way, as for Sweet Tea & Barley, think wood-paneled, comfortable chairs, fireplace, alehouse food, and jazz on a Friday evening (not to mention a fully stocked bar, including a good single-malt scotch selection). I could curl up in a corner chair and never leave.

CHAPTER THIRTY-TWO

....

EMOTIONAL HYPERLINKS

I am a sentimental person—one of those people who keeps ticket stubs, maps, snippets of a brochure, and photos (yes, even those black & white ones from our family's 1960s box cameras!). So, when it comes to CW trips, the things I've kept are more than just pieces of paper, they are slices of my lifetime. As I mentioned in the chapter about CW's mission statement, those bits with their scribbled notes on them are my own emotional hyperlinks. One look at them and I am immediately transported back to a specific time and place, and a specific memory or set of emotions.

While I realize not everyone shares this particular approach to life, for anyone who loves to keep mementos, here's a few tips on how I organize all those items so that I can easily access them and see the patterns of my life in them.

For many years, all I did was stuff the loose bits and pieces of paper from my CW trips into an ever-bulging, faded, purple file-folder. About the time I started writing this book, I recognized that that folder contained a wealth of information about my life and my trips that could be tapped. So, I dumped out everything onto the couch, and started sorting into various groups.

Finally, I had piles of:
- Admission tickets/badges
- Postcards and pamphlets
- Hotel key cards and valet parking tickets
- Artifacts and purchases
- RevQuest scarves, pencils, and booklets
- Weekly brochure or schedules listing all programs and activities

I bought some clear document binder pockets and stuck a label on each that had the date of the trip, and sometimes a few notes about the timing or reason for the visit. Now each trip had its own pocket into which I deposited any appropriate brochures, key cards, schedules and artifacts for that trip. I also reserved one pocket to hold all the admission badges I'd accumulated over the years.

Just by looking at the titles on each, I can see important phases of my life. First, aside from the obvious—year or month—there are life cycle notations, such as: "Childhood," "Teen" "On My Own," "Pregnant." Others denote holidays, such as "Thanksgiving." Some of the pockets are labeled with significant milestones: a new millennium, our son going off to college, our 25th wedding anniversary. And finally, there are the labels that denote "points of no return": "May, 2001—the last summer before 9/11;" July, 2006—the summer trip before my husband almost died. Just a few words of annotation can evoke such powerful emotions, as if the event was yesterday.

The pocket with the admission badges also speaks volumes. There are the obvious changes in the badges: a tan paper one from 1972 that the interpreters punched when you visited a particular building; another with an elastic band attached to it and the words "Colonial Williamsburg" across the ticket. Later ones are fancier, with credit-card type annual passes with our photos, held in plastic pockets. The photos add another layer of insight: the stages of my hair from brown to gray; the emotions of my son from happy childhood to middle school turmoil; my husband, always steady and smiling, even as his beard got grayer and hair got thinner. To look at the pictures is to have a flashback to specific moments and feelings.

By collecting and organizing a few key items from each trip, I now have at my fingertips the panorama of my entire life in those visits. Family history, world events, all of our journeys through emotions and life's stages, are preserved in a few key items. If these are the kinds of things you like to hang on to, if you want to be able to access your previous experiences and learn where you've been, and maybe where you're going, consider the concrete emotional hyperlinks. They are a godsend to me.

CHAPTER THIRTY-THREE

....

SOCIAL MEDIA, SHOPPING, AND SUCH

I t wouldn't be the 21st century without social media, and as far as shopping, well that's been around forever. So here's a few thoughts on both.

Social Media

For those who love their cellphones, don't forget social media. CW may be about history, but it uses the latest technology to connect you to it.

- Facebook: @ColonialWilliamsburg
- Twitter: @colonialwmsburg
- Instagram account: @colonialwmsburg
- YouTube: https://www.youtube.com/user/ColonialWilliamsburg

Shopping Onsite and Off

Onsite: Merchants Square has a wide range of shops. We love to wander through the shop that has Scottish products, as well as another with a variety of pewter jewelry and ornaments. There are clothing stores, an art gallery, College of William and Mary items, and The Craft House, which has all the CW reproductions. When I was younger, I could never afford anything down in Merchants

Square and I wasn't interested in dining or shopping. I still cannot afford a lot of things there, but it is always fun to stroll the area, sit on the benches, eat, and people watch. And there are sometimes concerts or special happenings there as well. Enjoy!

Offsite: Need an outing to indulge your shopping soul? In addition to all that is in Merchant Square and surrounding streets, you can also do a search on "Williamsburg shopping" and find a multitude of possibilities in the greater Williamsburg area.

There is a huge outlet mall not very far from CW, the Williamsburg Premium Outlets. As their website describes it, there are over 135 stores "including Ann Taylor, Banana Republic, J. Crew, Michael Kors, Nautica, and more. Conveniently located on Route 199 off of Richmond Road."

http://www.premiumoutlets.com/outlet/williamsburg

Finally, as mentioned in an earlier chapter, a quick web search on "things to do in Williamsburg" will yield a large number of attractions and activities in the greater area including Williamsburg, Jamestown, Yorktown, Newport News, and Norfolk. So be sure to check out the options.

CHAPTER THIRTY-FOUR

....

SANCTUARY

There comes that moment in all vacations where you just need
to stop for a while and rest. It's hot, people are annoying,
your feet hurt, or maybe someone in your group is having
a meltdown. I often find mid-afternoon to be the "witching hour"
for my own flagging energy and tolerance. So, when that happens,
I know that a few minutes in some gentle, tucked-away spot is all
I need to re-energize and soothe the spirit. Over the years, I have
identified a number of places around CW that are my sanctuaries,
and I have listed them below.

One absolute favorite is right in the middle of the Historic
Area on Duke of Gloucester Street. There, on the side of the Post
Office is a tree-shaded, ivy-lined set of stairs leading down behind
the building. At the bottom are the shops for the Bookbinder
and the Printer. Often there's just a few people there, but even
when there's more, most are going into the shops. I head past the
shops though, to the little wooden bridge over the small brook
that runs through the backyard. I could spend hours watching the
rivulets of water cascading over the pebbles in the shallow stream
bed. The sounds of the water burbling along just seems to screen
out people and allows me to instead hear the gentle chirps of a
cardinal in the tree overhead.

As an aside, if you don't feel like going down the stairs, you can still find benches to rest on just outside of the Post Office. It is one of those "hidden in plain sight" places, where you are in the middle of everything and can watch people go by, but they barely notice you. You may have to wait though, as lots of people seem to love those benches and they don't give them up quickly!

Another place, which I've spoken of earlier, is the ravine on the far right of the Magazine (when looking from Duke of Gloucester Street). During the day it is a green, lush, and peaceful place with benches nearby. It's a great spot to rest. I draw the line at dusk, however, when the lengthening shadows trigger my overactive imagination to see the ghosts of colonial spies plying their trade in its dark recesses. So, consider the ravine...at least during the day.

At the east end of town, down the hill behind Charlton's Coffeehouse, is a performance stage and set of benches shaded by large trees. Unless there is a program about to start, there's usually no one there, and it is just a quiet little pocket nestled at the bottom of the hill. The trees are a lot more massive than when I first came here fifty years ago and you can often catch some shade and a cool breeze—even in the heat of the summer. And maybe it's just the placebo effect, but you somehow feel a bit cooler just listening to the sounds of the small brook that winds its way through the dense bushes on the side. It is the perfect spot to relax and contemplate the Revolution.

Aside from having those wonderful gingerbread cookies, the Raleigh Tavern Bakeshop itself is a welcome respite during the day. Set behind the tavern, the place feels sheltered from some of the busyness, even if there are a number of people there with you. It is especially delightful in the mid-spring and fall seasons, when the trees are sporting either beautiful light spring greens or their vibrant autumn palette. And in the summer's heat, they seem to funnel cool breezes through the area. Add a cold ginger ale from the shop, and a shady bench to sit on and you're all set. In the winter, I love being *inside* the bakeshop. The warmth from the baking ovens provides an oasis from cold temperatures and frosty winds; and a hot cup of tea, cider, or coffee to warm your fingers and insides gives a sense of contentment and well-being.

It goes without saying that a colonial tavern lover like myself would find any and all of the CW taverns restorative, and they can be. However, there are certain spots that are better than others. As I mentioned in the earlier tavern chapter, there's no place quite like the basement of Shields Tavern on a hot, busy, summer's day. It is generally quieter than the upstairs. I am not sure why. At times, it can be just as full of people as the upstairs seating. But there is something about the fact that it's a little darker, and a fair bit cooler, that perhaps calms everyone down. As to the coolness, you can feel the temperature drop several degrees as you descend the stairs. Certainly, it's air-conditioned, but I think the basement itself is cooler and makes the air conditioning all the more effective. All in all, it's just a comfortable place. Just make sure you don't hit it at high noon.

Another tavern spot I like, especially in the early spring before the outside garden seating opens, is right behind the King's Arms Tavern. You can sit down at the tables there and just be with your thoughts. And speaking of gardens, which I did earlier in the book, CW abounds in them. Large or small, out in the open or tucked behind houses, either way, you can never go wrong visiting them. In addition, nestled in those hidden areas behind the houses are fascinating "detail-laden" backyard structures such as privies, wells, smokehouses, dairies, and office buildings. They offer a bit of quiet, and great photographic opportunities, too.

Even though this is not really a *quiet* spot, I love Anderson's Blacksmith Shop at all times of the year. Maybe it's the creativity of the place, and the admiration of the skill it takes to transform a bar of metal into a door handle or complex lock. Whatever it is, I can stand there and tune out the people and just absorb all the sensations. Creaking bellows and the smell of hot metal accents the red glow of coals. Measured beats of the hammer on soft iron have a hypnotic rhythm, as intricate shapes emerge from the amorphous red metal. I love the hiss of hot metal when plunged into the cold-water bucket, not to mention the accompanying billowing clouds of steam. My feet feel solid on the floor as the grit grinds beneath my shoes. And all around me is the rustic beauty of tools arranged on the walls and metal bars stockpiled in a corner. It is a simple place, not a fancy office. And though you may suffer the elements in the summer, in the cold of winter the heat of the forge penetrates your clothes and warms your face. Just like the bakeshop, I love it there because it is a place of hard work with one's hands, filled with the satisfaction of creation.

While anywhere in the Palace gardens is fine, my absolute favorite spot in the Palace compound is the storage basement under the building. The low-ceilinged stairs lead you to brick-lined arched storage vaults that are a cool refuge on hot days. The sense of enclosure, the reduced lighting, the quiet, and the coolness provide a lovely, soothing atmosphere. And as I walk through the subterranean chambers, I imagine what the vaults must have looked like during the Royal Governor's time, filled with jars of vegetables and fruits as well as casks of wines and madeira.

At the west end of Duke of Gloucester Street, there are a few spots I cherish. The first is the garden at the Taliaferro-Cole house. In the spring, brilliant tulips fill the beds, punctuated by patches of grass. Fruit trees and benches also adorn the area, which overlooks the rolling pasture below where the sheep placidly graze. In front of the Lumber House ticket office, there are also benches in the shade of the massive trees and you can watch the carriages come and go with their riders.

Down in Merchants Square, you can rest on a shaded bench outside the Williamsburg Craft House, or sip iced tea at an umbrella-shaded patio table outside of the College of William and Mary's Bookstore in the Barnes & Noble there. After five, these spots are also fun because there are sometimes bands or other events happening in the square, so you can sit and people-watch.

I should also mention that at least as of this moment, CW also has a couple of spots for special groups. At the east end of Duke of Gloucester Street, not far from the Raleigh Tavern, is the Liberty Lounge. It offers a place to relax for active-duty, veteran, or retired military members and their families. And for those who annually donate $100 or more to the CW Foundation, the St. George Tucker House at the other end of town offers a place to sit down, have some light refreshments, and participate in special programming.

Finally, just about any tree-shaded, ivy-lined walkway along the sides of buildings in the Historic Area seems to lead to a place of quiet where again, you can step out of the chaos for five minutes, and into your own momentary retreat. No doubt I've missed places, or my favorites won't be yours. But just have your eyes peeled because there's more than enough nooks and crannies scattered all over the Historic Area to offer you the peace you crave.

CHAPTER THIRTY-FIVE

....

FINAL WORDS

I want to take a moment to thank you for coming along with me on this "journey to CW." It has been a labor of love to share it. In the end, whether you go to CW or not, fall in love with it or not, I hope this book has at least gotten you to think about the places that are special to you, and why. My wish for you is that whether it's CW or somewhere else, may you be gifted with the chance to love a location so much that it feeds your soul. And maybe I hope, at least a little, that you *will* love CW. For me, I have many more trips left in me and *many* more things I want to do there. So now it is time to start planning my next trip!

RECOMMENDED READING

....

ARTICLES:

"A Look at the Archaeology Lab," Kelly Ladd-Kostro, http://makinghistorynow.com/2014/07/a-look-at-the-archaeology-lab/, July 1, 2014

"A Short History of Archaeology at Colonial Williamsburg," Meredith Poole, http://research.history.org/research/archaeology/history/index.cfm, 2014.

"Animating History: A Research Fellow Explores New Ways to Tell Our Story," Bill Sullivan, http://makinghistorynow.com/2016/08/animating-history-a-research-fellow-explores-new-ways-to-tell-our-story, August 24, 2016.

"Ivor Noël Hume," Wikipedia, https://en.wikipedia.org/wiki/Ivor_Noël_Hume, February 7, 2017.

"Ivor Noël Hume, Archaeologist of Colonial America, Dies at 89," Sam Roberts, https://www.nytimes.com/2017/02/19/us/ivor-noel-hume-dead-archaeologist-colonial-williamsburg.html, February 19, 2017.

"Ivor Noël Hume, Colonial Williamsburg Archaeologist and Pioneer of Historical Archaeology, Dies at 89," Michael Thompson, http://www.richmond.com/news/obituary/ivor-no-l-hume-colonial-williamsburg-archaeologist-and-pioneer-of/article_b30028dd-f2de-5db3-b792-3a9d8d842586.html, February 12, 2017.

"Our Online History Library is Now Yours For Free," Bill Sullivan, http://makinghistorynow.com/2016/08/our-online-history-library-is-now-yours-for-free/, August 16, 2016.

"Tiny Enormities: Pollen and Seeds Reveal Clues to Life in an 18th-Century Town," Gil Klein, http://www.history.org/foundation/magazine/spring16/tiny.cfm, Spring, 2016.

BOOKS:

General:

Colonial Williamsburg: A Pocket Guide, 1ˢᵗ edition. The Colonial
   Williamsburg Foundation: Williamsburg, VA, 2011. ISBN-13:
   978-0879352486.

Colonial Williamsburg: The Official Guide. The Colonial Williamsburg
   Foundation: Williamsburg, VA, 2014. ISBN-13: 978-0879352653.

Insiders' Guide to Williamsburg and Virginia's Historic Triangle, 17ᵗʰ edition. Sue Corbett, Globe Pequot: Guilford, CT, 2016. ISBN-13:
   978-1493018314.

The Revolution in Virginia, 1775-1783, Revised edition. John E. Selby,
   University of Virginia Press: Charlottesville, VA, 2007. ISBN-13:
   978-0879352332.

African American Topics:

The Art and Soul of African American Interpretation. Ywone D. Edwards-
   Ingram, The Colonial Williamsburg Foundation: Williamsburg, VA,
   2016. ISBN-13: 978-0879352806.

Foul Means: The Formation of a Slave Society in Virginia, 1660-1740, for the
   Omohundro Institute of Early American History and Culture, Williamsburg,
   Virginia. Anthony S. Parent Jr., The University of North Carolina
   Press: Chapel Hill, NC, 2003. ISBN-13: 978-0807854860.

From Calabar to Carter's Grove: The History of a Virginia Slave Community
   (Colonial Williamsburg Studies in Chesapeake History and Culture Series).
   Lorena S. Walsh, University of Virginia Press: Charlottesville,
   VA,1997. ISBN-13: 978-0813920405.

Slave Counterpoint: Black Culture in the Eighteenth-Century Chesapeake and
   Lowcountry (Published for the Omohundro Institute of Early American
   History and Culture, Williamsburg, Virginia). Philip D. Morgan, The
   University of North Carolina Press: Chapel Hill, NC, 1998. ISBN-13:
   978-0807847176.

Tobacco and Slaves: The Development of Southern Cultures in the Chesapeake,
   1680-1800 (Published for the Omohundro Institute of Early American

History and Culture, Williamsburg, Virginia). Allan Kulikoff, The University of North Carolina Press: Chapel Hill, NC, 1986. ISBN-13: 978-0807842249.

Animals in CW:
Link to the Past, Bridge to the Future: Colonial Williamsburg's Animals. John P. Hunter, The Colonial Williamsburg Foundation: Williamsburg, VA, 2005. ISBN-13: 978-0879351939

Archaeology:
Archaeology and Wetherburn's Tavern, Colonial Williamsburg Archaeological Series No. 3. Ivor Noël Hume, The Colonial Williamsburg Foundation: Williamsburg, VA, 1969. ISBN-13: 978-0910412087.

The Wells of Williamsburg, Colonial Williamsburg Archaeological Series No. 4. Ivor Noël Hume, The Colonial Williamsburg Foundation: Williamsburg, VA, 1969. ISBN-13: 978-0879350123.

Children's Books:
Colonial Williamsburg's Young Americans (6-book series). Joan Lowery Nixon, The Colonial Williamsburg Foundation: Williamsburg, VA. 2004:

Ann's Story: 1747	ISBN-13: 978-0879351984
Caesar's Story: 1759	ISBN-13: 978-0879351991
Nancy's Story: 1765	ISBN-13: 978-0879352257
Will's Story: 1771	ISBN-13: 978-0879352264
Maria's Story: 1773	ISBN-13: 978-0879352271
John's Story: 1775	ISBN-13: 978-0879352288

Hogsheads to Blockheads: The Kids Guide to Colonial Williamsburg's Historic Area. 1ˢᵗ edition. Barry Varela, The Colonial Williamsburg Foundation: Williamsburg, VA 2010. ISBN-13: 978-0879352455.

1776: A New Look at Revolutionary Williamsburg. K. M. Kostyal. The Colonial Williamsburg Foundation: Williamsburg, VA, and National Geographic Society, Washington, DC, 2009. ISBN-13: 978-1426305177.

Food:

The Colonial Williamsburg Tavern Cookbook. The Colonial Williamsburg Foundation: Williamsburg, VA, 2001. ISBN-13: 978-0609602867.

Recipes from the Raleigh Tavern Bake Shop. Mary Miley Theobald, The Colonial Williamsburg Foundation: Williamsburg, VA, 2006. ISBN-13: 978-0879351069.

The Williamsburg Art of Cookery. Helen Bullock, The Colonial Williamsburg Foundation: Williamsburg, VA, 1985. ISBN-13: 978-0910412308.

The Williamsburg Cookbook: Traditional and Contemporary Recipes Adapted from the Taverns and Inns of Colonial Williamsburg. Letha Booth, The Colonial Williamsburg Foundation: Williamsburg, VA, 1971. ISBN-13: 978-0910412919.

Gardening:

Flowers and Herbs of Early America. Lawrence D. Griffith, The Colonial Williamsburg Foundation: Williamsburg, VA, and Yale University Press, New Haven, CT, 2008. ISBN-13: 978-0300145366.

The Gardens of Colonial Williamsburg. M. Kent Brinkley and Gordon W. Chappell, The Colonial Williamsburg Foundation: Williamsburg, VA, 1996. ISBN-13: 978-0879351588

Plants of Colonial Williamsburg. Joan Parry Dutton, The Colonial Williamsburg Foundation: Williamsburg, VA, 1979. ISBN-13: 978-0879350420.

Vegetable Gardening the Colonial Williamsburg Way: 18th-Century Methods for Today's Organic Gardeners. Wesley Greene, The Colonial Williamsburg Foundation: Williamsburg, VA, and Rodale Books, New York, NY. 2012. ISBN-13: 978-1609611620

THE WEB:

CW Historical Website: http://www.history.org/

CW Blog: http://makinghistorynow.com/

AUTHOR BIO

D ebra Bailey is a freelance writer, nature artist, and science educator whose previous projects range from magazine articles and CliffsNotes, to dictionary and medical editing. In addition, Debra has over thirty years of experience in clinical and research laboratories, pharmaceutical AIDS research, and medical ethics. An unrepentant history geek, her favorite time periods are the American Revolution, World War II, the Middle Ages, and Ancient Greece, and her only regret is not getting to meet Apollo's Oracle at Delphi. She is currently at work on a middle-grade historical-fiction book—*The Reluctant Hero*—which is set in Williamsburg during the American Revolution. Originally from New England, she lives with her husband and soulmate, Ed, in Durham, NC. They have a son, Matt, whose patience in dealing with the antics of the college students he works with, and the beauty of his photographic creations, never ceases to amaze them.

CPSIA information can be obtained
at www.ICGtesting.com
Printed in the USA
LVOW12s1708270318
571328LV00003B/422/P